THE FIRST PARTITION OF POLAND

East Central European Studies
of Columbia University

HERBERT H. KAPLAN

THE FIRST PARTITION OF POLAND

COLUMBIA UNIVERSITY PRESS
NEW YORK AND LONDON 1962

FIRST PUBLISHED IN BOOK FORM 1962

LIBRARY OF CONGRESS CATALOG CARD NUMBER: 62-17550

EAST CENTRAL EUROPEAN STUDIES
OF COLUMBIA UNIVERSITY

The East Central European Studies, a companion series to the Studies of the Russian Institute, comprise scholarly books prepared under the auspices of the Program on East Central Europe of Columbia University or through other divisions of the University. The publication of these studies is designed to enlarge our understanding of an important region of the world, which, because of its relative inaccessibility in recent years as well as because of the linguistic problems it presents, has been somewhat neglected in serious academic study. The faculty of the Program on East Central Europe, without necessarily endorsing the conclusions reached by the authors, believe that these studies contribute substantially to knowledge of the area and should serve to stimulate further inquiry and research.

In Memory of

JACOB KAPLAN

FOREWORD

The Goettingen historian, A. H. L. Heeren, writing under the shattering impact of the French Revolution and the Napoleonic wars, saw in the first partition of Poland the beginnings of the catastrophic collapse of the European *Staatensystem:* "But what were the consequences to Poland, in comparison with those which threatened the political system of Europe? The potentates themselves had begun its subversion! . . . What dismemberment could be illegal, if this should be regarded as lawful?"

The eventual disappearance of the Polish state cast its shadow on into the nineteenth century and, indeed, up to our own day. One might argue that the presence or absence of Poland in the European political system has reflected, and determined, to a quite surprising degree both the articulation of that system and its moral climate.

Herbert Kaplan's study provides us, then, with a new appraisal of the origins and first stages of a major historical event. Making extensive use of the diplomatic sources and also of hitherto untapped archives within Poland, he has traced, with admirable dispassion, the exceedingly intricate interplay of international rivalry and suspicion and of domestic Polish controversy and confusion that led, in ways unforeseen and unanticipated by even the partitioners, to the drastic diminution of a once great state. It is a sad but illuminating narrative.

HENRY L. ROBERTS

Columbia University

[illegible]

[illegible]

[illegible]

[illegible]

[illegible]

PREFACE

"No prudent man," wrote Thomas Carlyle in his history of Frederick the Great, "would wish to write of the Polish Question." For Carlyle the question was "altogether dead and indifferent." Many men of letters have chosen to disregard his advice—for them the Polish question remained very much alive. But what has been written has not always added to our knowledge; sometimes, in fact, it has added to our confusion.

No major work has been published in any language on the first partition of Poland since Adolf Beer's pioneer effort *Die erste Theilung Polens* and *Documente* (Vienna, 1873). Although Beer's work was published a hundred years after the partition and for his time was a good synthesis from which I have greatly benefited, it does not satisfy the needs of present-day scholars. Beer included irrelevant material, and he did not use source materials in Polish and Russian. Thus, a work using these available source materials has been badly needed.

In narrating the events from 1762 to 1773 that led to and included the partition, I have attempted to show the interaction between European diplomacy and Poland's domestic history. No attempt has been made to describe the long-range effect of the partition on the powers not involved.

All dates used are adjusted to the New Style calendar. All proper names are spelled as in the native language (the Russian being transliterated), except a few for which there are other firmly established forms in English, for example, Stanislas Augustus Poniatowski, Warsaw, Dnieper, Dniester, Vistula. The expression "Polish-Lithuanian Commonwealth" comes nearer to the official term *Rzeczpospolita* than any other given to the specific land area. For purposes of brevity, "Poland" is sometimes substituted. When it is necessary to distinguish the two component parts of the Commonwealth, the terms "Crown" and "Grand Duchy" are used for Polish and Lithuanian territories respectively.

Many people have aided me in the writing of this book. I am particularly indebted to Henry L. Roberts of the Russian Institute of Columbia University for supervising much of my work and for reading the manuscript. I have benefited greatly from his criticism and from the kindness he has shown me.

I would like to acknowledge the help and criticism of the following people, who read either a portion of the manuscript, or all of it: Alexander Dallin, the late Walter L. Dorn, W. T. R. Fox, Oscar Halecki, and Ludwik Krzyzanowski, of Columbia University; J. Rogers Hollingsworth, Maurice Dupont Lee, Jr., and Raymond P. Stearns of the University of Illinois; Robert L. Haan of Queens College, New York; and Adam Bielnicki, Joe Breu, Richard Geiger, Ellen Jane Hollingsworth, Jacob B. Hoptner, Barbara Polan Kaplan, Margaret Ellen Sloas, and Lois Levine Wolfe. Especially to be thanked are Henry H. Wiggins, Diane L. Olsen, Eugenia Porter, and Mildred Pollock of Columbia University Press, and Willard A. Heaps, who compiled the index.

I would also like to thank many other people who have given me a great deal of assistance: Jesse D. Clarkson of Brooklyn College, New York; Dr. L. R. Lewitter of Christs College, Cambridge University; Peter Brock of Columbia University; Otakar Odlozilik of the University of Pennsylvania; Pierce Olsen; Yale Richmond; Elinor Schmitt; Arthur Wortzel; and members and associates of the Jagiellonian University, Kraków, Poland.

During the past few years I have been awarded several grants and fellowships which enabled me to do the research for and write this book. I gratefully acknowledge the American Council of Learned Societies, which partially subsidized publication; the Graduate Research Board of the University of Illinois; the Program on East Central Europe of Columbia University; and the United States National Student Association Exchange program, for a scholarship to Poland.

Finally, I would like to extend my gratitude to Louise E. Luke of the Russian Institute of Columbia University, who has been exceptionally generous with her time and expert advice throughout the preparation of the book.

HERBERT KAPLAN

August, 1962

CONTENTS

MAP

ABBREVIATIONS USED IN NOTES

ACz	Archiwum Czartoryskich (The Archive of the Czartoryskis)
AGS	Arkhiv gosudarstvennago soveta (The Archive of the State Council)
BC	Collyer, Adelaide d'Arcy (ed.). The Despatches and Correspondence of John, Second Earl of Buckinghamshire, Ambassador to the Court of Catherine II of Russia, 1762-1765
BJag	Biblioteka Jagiellońska (Jagiellonian Library)
BMAddMSS	British Museum, Additional Manuscripts
BPAN	Biblioteka Polskiej Akademii Nauk (The Library of the Polish Academy of Sciences)
Oeuvres	Oeuvres de Frédéric le Grand
PC	Politische Correspondenz Friedrichs des Grossen
PreusBer	Preussen, Berichte
PreusWeis	Preussen, Weisungen
PROSP	Public Record Office, State Papers
RIDA	Recueil des instructions données aux ambassadeurs et ministres de France depuis les traités de Westphalie, jusqu'à la révolution française
RussBer	Russland II, Berichte
RussWeis	Russland II, Weisungen
SAPMém	Mémoires du roi Stanislas-Auguste Poniatowski
Sb	Sbornik imperatorskago russkago istoricheskago obschestva (The Collection of the Imperial Russian Historical Society)
VA	Vienna Archives
VolLeg	Volumina Legum

THE FIRST PARTITION OF POLAND

Let me remind you of this before everything else. History is infinite. It is unfixable. We are always trying to state past reality in terms of certainty, but all that we are able to do is to render our own impression of it. No book can reproduce more than a part of that reality, even within the confines of its particular subject; and each book contains something else, which gets mixed up with historical truth in an almost untraceable manner—I mean the opinion, or the sentiment, or the philosophy of life, of the narrator; or, in other words, the personality of the historian. The admixture does not necessarily turn historical truth into falsehood, but it does transform it into something different from the simple truth.

PIETER GEYL, *Debates with Historians*
(New York, 1958), p. 9.

INTRODUCTION

After three separate acts of partition in the eighteenth century, the Polish-Lithuanian Commonwealth disappeared from the community of nations. Prussia, Russia, and Austria, collaborating to add Polish territory to their realms, partitioned Poland for the first time in 1773. To trace the beginning of the dissolution of the Commonwealth, however, one should go back at least to 1762.

In 1762-63 there was a drastic change in the European and colonial balance of power; Elizabeth of Russia died, and after the short reign of Peter III, Russia came under the rule of Catherine II; the end of the Seven Years War brought with it the diminished power of France and Austria; and Augustus III died, leaving vacant the Polish throne. Among European rulers questions of succession created a spirit of intrigue.

During the next decade Austria, Russia, and Prussia maintained a lively interest in Poland. Their quest for territory and their efforts to preserve the balance of power in East Central Europe jeopardized Poland's territorial integrity. The rulers of these three powers seriously considered the question whether to dismember Poland or to make her a vassal state of one of them.

The Polish-Lithuanian Commonwealth was a supranational, composite state, consisting of the Kingdom of Poland and the Grand Duchy of Lithuania. It had been united in 1386 through the marriage of the Queen of Poland to the Grand Duke of Lithuania. In 1569 the Union of Lublin reinforced this personal union by providing that the King of Poland and Grand Duke of Lithuania should always be elected in common and that the newly created Commonwealth should have a single Diet. Although the Commonwealth had a definite Polish and Catholic character, it included Lithuanians, Ruthenians or Ukrainians, Belorussians, Germans, Jews, followers of the Greek Orthodox church, and

Protestants. At times conflicts between these groups created excuses for neighboring states to interfere in Polish domestic affairs.

Geography has always been the bane of Poland. One vast plain open to invasion on all sides, she has had to resist the eastward expansion of the Germans and defend herself against the westward movement of the Muscovites. In the south, Poland and the Ottoman Empire disputed for many years over the borderlands, but with the growth of Russian power they found a common enemy. The difficulties that Poland had with Sweden, due partly to dynastic quarrels, religious differences, and rivalry over the Baltic area, began to lessen with the decline of Swedish power in the first half of the eighteenth century. Competition in the Baltic area continued, however, as Sweden was replaced by Prussia and Russia.

A new era in Saxon history opened in 1697 when, after a contested election, the Elector of Saxony, Frederick Augustus, became Augustus II, King of Poland. Saxony was now transformed from a mere German principality into a European power. Until the final collapse of Saxon hopes in 1764, her policy was determined by the desire to perpetuate the union of Saxony and Poland and to consolidate the combined state as a great power in the center of Europe.

Instead of turning his attention to Poland, which badly needed reform, Augustus II conspired with other powers in an aggressive war against Sweden in the hope of wresting vital Baltic possessions from her. The Great Northern War, which lasted twenty-one years, exhausted Saxon-Polish resources; and for a brief moment in 1720, Augustus even sought to partition the Polish land which he ruled. It was during this same period that intolerance toward religious minorities was intensified. Beginning with the Diet of 1717, the Catholics dominated the spiritual and civil affairs of the country.

When Augustus II died in 1733, various candidates were once again offered by both Poles and foreigners. A double election resulted, precipitating a war, which lasted for two years. In the end, Austria and Russia were victorious and succeeded in placing upon the Polish throne the eldest son of Augustus II.

Augustus III, the new King of Poland, was a patron of art and literature and a vigorous hunter; but he had little interest in, and less talent for, the art of government. He left the administration of his realms to his favorite ministers. From the time Heinrich Brühl succeeded to the office of chief minister in 1738, he exercised almost unlimited authority in the conduct of Saxon affairs until the death of Augustus III in 1763. Brühl's main objective was to secure, during the lifetime of Augustus, the Saxon succession to the Polish throne.

In order to accomplish this, Brühl sought the aid of foreign powers and relied heavily upon the most prominent families in the Commonwealth. Two families which competed for political and financial dominance over Poland were the Francophile Potockis and the pro-Russian Czartoryskis. From time to time Brühl found it expedient to ally himself with one or the other, as he could expect either French or Russian support to follow.

A few years prior to the outbreak of the Seven Years War the Czartoryskis had gained a virtual monopoly of power in the Commonwealth. The patriarch of the family, Michał, held the high office of Chancellor of Lithuania, while his younger brother, August, was Governor of Ruthenia. Through family ties and political alliances, some of the highest posts in the church, the military, and the civil authority were controlled by the Czartoryskis. It is no wonder that the immense wealth and power of the Czartoryskis had earned them the title of "The Family."

The Czartoryskis envisioned a radical reorganization of the army, finance, and the law courts of the Commonwealth. Most important they wanted the *Liberum Veto* (*nie pozwalam,* meaning "I forbid") to be restricted, if not abolished. The *Liberum Veto* was a constitutional privilege based on the assumption of the absolute political equality and freedom of all Polish citizens and on the principle that every measure introduced into the Polish Diet must be adopted without a single vote of opposition. The Polish nobility thought that unanimity was the prerequisite for full expression of political liberty and equality. A Deputy, by interposing his individual veto, could at any time block a measure and dissolve the Diet. The origin of this procedure in the National Diet may be traced to the sixteenth century, when it was agreed that the decision of the Deputies was not to depend upon the majority but must be unanimous. The many openings for bribery and intrigue which this practice offered not only continued the anarchy and lack of effective government in the Commonwealth but also gave opportunity to neighboring powers to interfere in the internal affairs of the state. Since the reforms proposed by the Czartoryskis aimed at the destruction of the freedoms of the *szlachta* (gentry), the Diet opposed their passage.

The Commonwealth's domestic problems were further complicated by the outbreak of the Seven Years War. Poland played no role except as a battlefield—a fate she had suffered many times before. The war continued in Europe and the colonies until each state became exhausted and sued for peace. In the year following the end of the war the Polish throne once again became vacant, and a struggle began for the succession. As in the past, foreign powers were interested in the election contest, and this time their interference led eventually to the dismemberment of the country.

Poland is constantly being plunged into internal discord and disorders which take up her whole attention; as long as she preserves her constitution she does not deserve to be considered among the European Powers.[1]

CHANCELLOR M. V. VORONTSOV TO PETER III

I

THE GREAT POWERS AND POLAND
MAY 5, 1762—OCTOBER 5, 1763

One of the events that hastened the end of the Seven Years War was the accession of Peter III to the throne of Russia on the death of his aunt, Empress Elizabeth. A Holsteiner and a Lutheran by birth, Peter did not take his conversion to Orthodoxy very seriously, nor did he fondly embrace Russian culture and traditions. He found his pleasure in mistresses, periodic drunks, and playing with wooden soldiers. From early manhood he worshiped Frederick II of Prussia, often dressing in a Prussian uniform and referring to Frederick as his master. As Emperor, one of his first acts was to effect a *rapprochement* between the Russian and Prussian courts.

The negotiations, begun early in 1762, led first to an armistice and then to a treaty (May 5)—characterized as "more like a declaration of love than one of alliance between two sovereigns."[2] Another treaty, concerned specifically with the Polish-Lithuanian Commonwealth, was concluded on June 19. Peter was, however, unable to execute this treaty because on July 9 he was overthrown by his wife, Catherine. Nevertheless, the provisions of the treaty are of vital importance since they outline policies which were in

[1] Quoted in N. D. Chechulin, *Vneshniaia politika Rossii v nachale tsarstvovaniia Ekateriny II,* p. 208.

[2] Duc de Broglie (ed.), *The King's Secret: Being the Secret Correspondence of Louis XV with His Diplomatic Agents from 1752 to 1774,* II, 9, and Geo. Fred. de Martens (ed.), *Recueil de traités de puissances et états de l'Europe,* I, 30-37. See also PC, XXI/13410-13637/189-392; BMAddMSS, 6809/24-102 and 35485/26; L. Häusser, "Zur Geschichte Friedrichs II und Peter III," *Forschungen zur deutschen Geschichte,* IV (Göttingen, 1864), 3-4.

substance followed by the two courts in three major areas: the future election of a king of Poland, the succession in the Duchy of Kurland, and the protection of the Dissidents.[3]

Poland was to continue to have free elections and was under no circumstances to become a hereditary realm. On Augustus's death, the two powers were to secure the throne for a suitable *Piast,* that is, a native-born Pole. Secondly, Peter's uncle, George of Holstein-Gottorp, would replace Charles Christian, Augustus's third son, as Duke of Kurland. Finally, the Dissidents (approximately 600,000 Greek Orthodox and 200,000 Protestants) living in the Commonwealth were to have their former liberties restored.

Since early in the eighteenth century the Duchy of Kurland, a fief of the Polish Crown, had been directly or indirectly under Russian influence. In 1710 Peter I's niece, Anna Ivanovna, married Frederick Wilhelm of the house of Kettler, the Duke of Kurland, but within one year she was widowed. Frederick Wilhelm's uncle, Ferdinand, succeeded as duke but resided most of the time in Gdańsk (Danzig). For all practical purposes Kurland was ruled by Peter Bestuzhev-Riumin, the Russian agent at the ducal court and Anna's lover. When Ferdinand died childless in 1737, Anna, now Empress of Russia, procured from Augustus the investiture of the Duchy for her favorite, Ernest Biron. Biron's rule lasted only three years, for with Anna's demise in 1740 he was exiled to eastern Russia. Henceforth, for almost two decades, Kurland was without a duke, and during that time Russia paid little attention to Kurland's affairs.

In 1758, Augustus obtained the permission of Empress Elizabeth of Russia to invest his son Charles Christian with the ducal throne. Within four years, however, Russia began to agitate for changes. Now, under the treaty of June 19, 1762, George of Holstein-Gottorp would replace Charles.

The Kurland issue did not end there. When Catherine took the throne, Ernest Biron once more was the choice of the Russian court. When the Russian ambassador's demands were ignored by

[3] Le Comte D'Angeberg [pseudonym of J. L. Chodźko] (ed.), *Recueil des traités, conventions et actes diplomatiques concernant la Pologne 1762-1862,* pp. 1-2.

Augustus and negotiations came to a standstill, Catherine proceeded to expedite matters by sending 15,000 Russian troops into Kurland. Biron was installed as duke at Mittau on January 21, 1763, and Charles Christian was forced to leave the city. The remonstrances of the Polish Senate Council, which met in Warsaw during March, had no effect upon the Russian court. By the spring of 1763, Kurland, for all practical purposes, had become a Russian protectorate, thus giving Russia greater access to the Baltic area. The following year, after the demise of Augustus and the ascendancy of the Czartoryskis to a dominant position in the Commonwealth, the Convocation and Coronation Diets enacted into law Biron's investiture.[4]

Another problem, more complex in its origin and crucial in its effect on the forthcoming partition, was that of the Dissidents. Since the inception of the Commonwealth, the Polish statesmen, in their search for national unity, were concerned with the major problem of religion. If we choose to evaluate the results of their endeavors from the latter part of the sixteenth century to the latter part of the seventeenth and use as a yardstick the presence of religious freedom as well as, in comparison to most other European states, the absence of religious wars, then we must accord them a large measure of success.

At the beginning of this period the principle of religious freedom in the Commonwealth for the Dissidents was accepted by the Confederation of Warsaw (1573) and subsequently was sworn to by every elected king. However, a departure from this policy took place toward the end of the seventeenth century. Significantly, an intolerant attitude which pervaded the minds and habits of the provincial populace also found its way into legislative acts and administrative ordinances. At times this intolerant attitude was translated into acts of persecution.

[4] See Ernest Seraphim, *Geschichte Liv-. Est-und Kurlands,* II, 605-26; Claude de Rulhière, *Histoire de l'anarchie de Pologne,* I, 252-55, II, 1, 8, 30-48; B. Bilbassoff, *Geschichte Katerina II,* II, Part I, 380-416; Wroughton to Buckinghamshire, BC, I, 197, II, 3-35, *passim;* Chechulin, pp. 126-46; Sergei Mikhailovich Solov'ëv, *Istoriia Rossii s drevneishikh vremën,* XXV, 1416-19, 1424-26, 1491-96; SAPMém, I, 389, 418-30, 440, 442-43; BJag, 101/VII/1-65, and BJag, 111/25-30; ACz, 1983/1009, and ACz, 820/190-233; and BPAN, 304/102, and BPAN, 647/90-93.

SWEDEN
GOTLAND
ÖLAND
BORNHOLM
Baltic Sea
LIVONIA
Riga
Dźwina R.
To Polish Livonia
KURLAND
Mittau
Dynaburg
ŻMUDŹ
Wiłkomierz
Kowno
WILN
Wilno
Troki
TROKI
LIT
Grodno
Niemen R.
Nowogródek
Nieśwież
NOWOG
Słonim
Niemen R.
EAST PRUSSIA
Gdańsk
Oliwa
Malbork
Elbląg
WARMIA
Marienwerder
Grudziądz
Wisła R.
PRUSSIA
Fordon
Bydgoszcz
Chełmno
Noteć R.
Drezdenko
Toruń
Inowrocław
Gniezno
Poznań
Brześć-Kujawski
Płock
Gostyń
Narew R.
Białystok
Bug R.
Drohiczyn
WARSZAWA
BRZEŚĆ-LIT
Brześć-Litewski
Pińsk
BRANDENBURG
Obra R.
Warta R.
Kalisz
Łęczyca
Rawa
Sieradz
Wieluń
Piotrków
Biała
Radom
Kozienice
Zwoleń
Parczew
Wieprz R.
Lublin
(Land of Chełm)
Chełm
Włodzimierz
Łuck
Oder R.
Częstochowa
Sandomierz
Siewierz
Bełz
Wisła
Oświęcim
Kraków
Zator
Bochnia
Wieliczka
Nowy Sącz
Przemyśl
Lwów
Sanok
Tarnopol
Zbrucz R.
Nowy Targ
Czorsztyn
Spisz
Halicz
HABSBURG DOMINIONS
K
O
R
O
1
2
3
4
5
6
7
8
9
10
11
12
13
14
15
16
17
18
19
20
18
0
100
200 miles
V. GRAY

THE POLISH-LITHUANIAN COMMONWEALTH
Boundary of Poland, 1771
Province boundaries
Boundary between Litwa (Lithuania) and Korona (Crown)
FIRST PARTITION 1773
To Prussia
To Russia
To Austria
PROVINCES OF KORONA
1 MALBORK
2 POMORZE
3 POZNAN
4 GNIEZNO
5 INOWROCŁAW
6 CHEŁMNO
7 BRZEŚĆ-KUJAWSKI
8 PŁOCK
9 MAZOWSZE
10 PODLASIE
11 KALISZ
12 SIERADZ
13 ŁĘCZYCA
14 RAWA
15 KRAKÓW
16 SANDOMIERZ
17 LUBLIN
18 RUŚ and ZIEMIA CHEŁMSKA
19 BEŁZ
20 WOŁYŃ
21 KIEV
22 PODOLE
23 BRACŁAW
NORWAY AND DENMARK
SWEDEN
Baltic Sea
RUSSIA
PRUSSIA
POLAND
THE EMPIRE
FRANCE
HABSBURG DOMINIONS
ITALIAN STATES
OTTOMAN EMPIRE
Black Sea
200 miles
POLISH LIVONIA
POŁOCK
Połock
Uła
WITEBSK
Witebsk
Dniepr R.
Smolensk
Orsza
Mścisław
Mohilew
MŚCISŁAW
Druć R.
Rohaczew
Mińsk
MIŃSK
Słuck
NOWOGRÓDEK
BRZEŚĆ LITEWSKI
LITWA
RUSSIA
Kiev
21
Żytomierz
UKRAINA
Nowy Konstantynów
Winnica
Bar
22
Kamieniec Podolski
Bracław
23
Chocim
Bałta
Dniestr R.
Dniepr R.
OTTOMAN EMPIRE

By 1717 the political power of the Dissidents was nonexistent, and the subsequent Diets of 1733 and 1736 reaffirmed this position. The Dissidents were excluded from the Chamber of Deputies, the Senate, public office, and the courts. In the sphere of religious activity they fared no better. Laws and administrative ordinance prevented the Dissidents from rehabilitating their old churches or building new ones. Public worship and religious procession could be performed only by obtaining the permission of unsympathetic officials. The forced conversion of members of the Greek Orthodox church to Uniat was a commonplace. Church synods were restricted and sometimes prohibited. If the ecclesiastical estates were not brought to ruin by marauding mobs, provincial governments saw fit to tax them into bankruptcy. The care of the young was hampered with the closing of schools and the restrictions placed upon the children of mixed marriages.

It was only natural, therefore, that in reaction to the treatment accorded them, the Dissidents would protest not only to the legal officials of the Commonwealth, but also to their coreligionists abroad. Not uncommon, too, were the protests made to the Polish king by the rulers of Brandenburg-Prussia and Russia, separately or in concert, on behalf of their coreligionists in the Commonwealth. From their side, these rulers were motivated by either an enlightened, humane interest, or special foreign policy interest, or both.

One of the earliest responses to Dissident appeals was made by Russia in 1674 when her Resident in Warsaw was instructed to watch over the Greek Orthodox community in the Commonwealth. Several years later official sanction was given to the Greek Orthodox protest. Article IX of the Treaty of "Perpetual Peace" (1686) between Poland and Russia required the King of Poland not to oppress or allow to be oppressed any person professing the Greek Orthodox religion. Furthermore, such a person was not to be compelled to adopt the Roman Catholic faith or the Uniat rite. Nonetheless oppression and forced conversion continued, and the Russian protests were fruitless.

When protest did not succeed, action was often taken on the spot. Peter I sometimes would aid his coreligionists with funds, clothing for a monastic community, or by rehabilitating a Greek Orthodox church. During the years 1704-9, when armies clashed in the Northern War, it was not uncommon for Russian troops in Lithuania and the eastern provinces of the Commonwealth to loot and even reconvert Uniat churches and monasteries to Greek Orthodox. In similar manner, when Charles XII overran Poland, he provided for complete freedom of worship for Protestants. But these efforts were of short duration. When reconquest was made by Augustus II, Polish law ordered those Protestant churches built during 1704-9 to be destroyed and inflicted punishment on those who still continued to worship in the ruins.

As the tide of discrimination mounted and the Commonwealth was overtaken by waves of fanaticism, especially during the "Dark Age" period (1717-33), the "victims of persecution" redoubled their cries for salvation. When all political power was taken from the Dissidents in 1717-18, consternation struck their hearts because they believed this to be only the beginning of a greater peril. Both Greek Orthodox and Protestant called upon Peter I to intervene on their behalf. Peter's reaction was a strong protest for Dissident reform, but as before it fell upon deaf ears.

The movement for international intervention did not subside. At the end of 1722 it seemed that all Reformed Europe would enter into the Polish Dissident question. Frederick William of Brandenburg-Prussia took the lead in calling for a meeting of the representatives of Great Britain, Sweden, the Netherlands, and Russia. But the meeting never took place because of Russia's refusal to participate. Peter had too many pressing problems to be concerned with the Dissidents at that time, said the official Russian reply. Be that as it may, Peter's distrust of Frederick William was, perhaps, the real reason for the Tsar's lack of cooperation. This was not the first time that Frederick William had tried to inveigle him into a joint policy in Polish affairs. Peter suspected, and rightly so, that this meeting would provide an avenue for Prussian intervention in Poland—something Peter did not want. Peter had a privileged position in directing Polish affairs, and he guarded it jealously.

Although Prussia made repeated attempts to have Russia join

her in a *démarche* on Polish affairs, it was not until 1730, after Peter had passed from the scene and the oppression of the Dissidents worsened, that these two states were finally able to join forces to defend their coreligionists in the Commonwealth. In the Russo-Prussian alliance of 1730 both states pledged to protect the Dissidents and to secure for them the enjoyment of their former privileges in both spiritual and secular matters. This declaration was substantially repeated in every Russo-Prussian treaty since that time, including that of 1762.

However, for more than a generation no direct action was taken on this matter. This fact may be readily understood if we accept the principle that the Dissident question was in itself neither the most important issue involved nor an issue important enough to demand Russia's and Prussia's forceful intervention when mere written protest proved insufficient to settle the problem. Because Poland played an important role in eastern Europe, neither Russia nor Prussia could dispense with the support of the Polish nobility, which opposed any significant change in the Roman Catholic or Uniat position in the Commonwealth. The Dissident question could be used as a pretext for intervention in Polish affairs but never as a fundamental political policy.

Thus, by the time Stanislas Augustus Poniatowski became King of Poland, the Dissident problem had already complicated Poland's relations with her neighbors for some time. But more important is the fact that, had the course of events related to the Dissident question during the early years of his reign taken a different turn, the Polish-Lithuanian Commonwealth might have averted dismemberment in 1773.[5]

After seizing power in Russia, Catherine began her reign by withdrawing from the Seven Years War, but she still wanted to maintain friendly relations with Prussia as part of the projected

[5] See L. R. Lewitter, "Peter the Great and the Polish Dissenters," *The Slavonic and East European Review*, XXXIII, No. 80, 75-101; L. R. Lewitter, "Poland Under the Saxon Kings," *The New Cambridge Modern History*, VII, 365-90; Władysław Konopczyński, "Early Saxon Period, 1697-1733," *The Cambridge History of Poland*, II, 1-24; G. Rhode, *Brandenburg-Preussen und die Protestanten in Polen 1640-1740: Ein Jahrhundert preussischer Schutzpolitik für unterdrückte Minderheit;* F. Martens, *Recueil des traités conclus par la Russie avec les puissances étrangères*, V, 290-91, 327-28, 351-52, 407-8; and BPAN, 645/38-61.

"Northern System," which was initiated by Nikita Panin, her chief adviser in foreign affairs. Under this system Russia was to undertake the formation of a coalition among the northern states of Prussia, Sweden, Denmark, Saxony, Great Britain, and Poland, against Austria, France, and Spain in the south.[6] To implement the "Northern System" and at the same time to promote her particular interest in Poland, Catherine confirmed the appointment of Count Herman Charles Keyserling as Russian ambassador to the Polish court,[7] and handed him secret instructions. In them, Catherine disclosed that she favored Ernest Biron as Charles's replacement in Kurland and that Keyserling was to support Biron's claim. She instructed Keyserling to make strong representations on behalf of the Greek Orthodox inhabitants of the Commonwealth. And he was to inquire among the Polish gentry who would be their choice as King of Poland in the event of Augustus's death.[8]

Before Keyserling left St. Petersburg, Catherine had declared her intentions for the forthcoming election in a letter to her former lover, the young Stanislas Poniatowski, a member of the powerful pro-Russian Czartoryski family.

> I am sending at once Count Keyserling as ambassador to Poland to declare you king after the death of the present monarch and, in the event of his not proving successful so far as you are concerned, I want it to be Prince Adam [Czartoryski].
>
> All minds are still in a state of ferment. I beg you not to come here now, for fear of increasing it.[9]

It was no wonder that when Keyserling arrived in Warsaw in December 1762 he was "courted to an inconceivable degree."[10]

Keyserling quickly ascertained from the Czartoryskis that there was no love lost between them and the reigning Saxon court, especially since the last Polish Diet.[11] In their present struggle, the

[6] K. Rahbek Schmidt, "Wie ist Panins Plan zu einem Nordischen System enstaden?" *Zeitschrift für Slawistik,* II (Berlin, 1957), No. 3, 406-22.

[7] Keyserling had actually been appointed during Peter's reign, but Catherine did not choose to change the appointment. Chechulin, p. 209, and Solov'ëv, XXV, 1413.

[8] Sb, XLVIII/63/59-66.

[9] SAPMém, I, 376 (Aug. 13, 1762), and Dominique Maroger (ed.), *Memoirs of Catherine the Great,* p. 341. See also SAPMém, I, 387 (Aug. 20, 1762).

[10] Wroughton to Grenville, Dec. 4, 1762, PROSP, 88/86 and ACz, 1983/969.

[11] The Polish Diet had convened on October 4 but was broken within a few

Czartoryskis again sought Russian support, which they had in the past often received, and to this end presented Keyserling with two "Memoranda" requesting the formation of a Russian-financed "confederation" against the Saxon court.[12]

Confederations—a characteristic medieval constitutional device —were very much in vogue in Poland in the late fourteenth and fifteenth centuries, then disappeared for a time, but recurred frequently after 1572. Confederations, voluntary armed associations of individuals formed for the purpose of putting through specified projects, were of three kinds: (a) those formed during an interregnum to prevent disorders and hold the realm together; (b) those formed during the lifetime of a king for the purpose of assisting him in some great emergency; and (c) those formed in opposition to the king.

Keyserling could not grant these requests and forwarded the "Memoranda" to Catherine. She replied that the Czartoryskis as well as the Commonwealth could count on her support and friendship, for her principal desire was to lift the Commonwealth out of its present confused state. But before anything could be done she wanted to know the amount of money and troops that would be needed, whether the confederation would be directed solely against the King or merely against his recent abuses, and who would lead the confederation.[13]

The Czartoryskis explained that the confederation would be directed against the abuses, not the King. They requested that Russian troops be placed in Smolensk and Kiev, and that the Czartoryskis be sent 50,000 ducats to meet expenses. Within the next three months the Czartoryskis expected to gather their own corps of armed partisans.[14] But before Catherine had an oppor-

days, primarily owing to the Czartoryski protest against the seating of the son of Heinrich Brühl in the Chamber of Deputies. Although there was a legal basis for this protest, it was made because the Czartoryskis wanted to embarrass the court party. See ACz, 597/909-20, and ACz, 599/289-307; and SAPMém, I, 399-418.

[12] "Promemoria," Dec. 14, 1762, and "Mémoire," Dec. 15, 1762, in Henryk Schmitt, *Dzieje panowania Stanisława Augusta Poniatowskiego,* I, "Dokumenta," 321-22, 323-25, respectively.

[13] *Ibid.,* pp. 326-27, and SAPMém, I, 467-68 (Jan. 23, 1763).

[14] "Promemoria" was handed to Keyserling on Feb. 12, 1763. Schmitt, I. "Dokumenta," 327-29, and SAPMém, I, 440.

tunity to act upon this latest request, all the European courts were thrown into a state of agitation over the news that Augustus had become seriously ill and might die.[15]

The views of Great Britain, France, Austria, and Prussia toward the succession were mixed. Great Britain's primary objective was above all else to establish a close friendship and a commercial treaty with Russia. British commerce with Russia had proven profitable to both countries; moreover, English statesmen wanted Russia as a counterpoise to France. In August 1762, when peace seemed imminent, the Earl of Buckinghamshire was sent as ambassador to St. Petersburg to negotiate a commercial and political alliance with Russia.[16]

At the turn of the year Catherine asked Buckinghamshire to solicit his government's opinion on the succession question because she desired "to act in concert and in confidence with the King of Great Britain."[17] The British implied that their support of Russia in Poland would be forthcoming, "but whilst the King remains totally unacquainted with the intention of her Imperial Majesty in relation thereto . . . it is not possible to give a direct and particular answer to the question proposed."[18]

Whatever information George III may have been seeking from Catherine, he was certainly not lacking it from his Resident in Warsaw, Wroughton. Wroughton correctly informed Halifax of the British Northern Department: "I think the view of the Empress of Russia is to place either Poniatowski or Prince Adam on the throne." The first, Wroughton explained, was a young man of great talents but of no great independent wealth and was somewhat disliked because of his "haughty behaviour." Prince Adam was in no way inferior to him in talents, but "greatly in ap-

[15] Szymon Askenazy, *Die letzte polnische Königswahl,* p. 26, and E. Reimann, *Neuere Geschichte des preussischen Staates,* I, 50.

[16] Bute to Keith, May 26, 1762, BMAddMSS, 35485/15-16; Grenville to Keith, July 14 and August 4, 1762, *ibid.,* pp. 81, 92-93, respectively; BC, I, 3-5, 53-54; William Edward Hartpole Lecky, *A History of England in the Eighteenth Century* (new ed., New York, 1893), VI, 76; and David Bayne Horn, *British Public Opinion and the First Partition of Poland,* p. 3.

[17] Buckinghamshire to Halifax, December 28, 1762, BC, I, 117. See also Buckinghamshire to Halifax, January 20, 1763, *ibid.,* p. 207.

[18] Halifax to Buckinghamshire, February 11, 1763, *ibid.,* p. 221. See also Halifax to Buckinghamshire, March 1, 1763, *ibid.,* II, 10-11.

plication," because "pleasure, not business [was] his pursuit." Prince Adam had told Wroughton "that if the Crown was offered him, he would leave the country, and refuse it." Russia's intention in placing one of these two on the throne would be to "pursue her own interest, which is to preserve the Republican Government and a division in the Country; a foreign Prince of capacity and resolution might establish a despotism, the natural step from anarchy which is the situation now." Prussia, in Wroughton's opinion, would also be opposed to a strong government for Poland. As for France, she would oppose the election of any candidate except a member of the Saxon house; however, "the opposition they could make would be of no consequence, the Saxon Family is quite lost here in my opinion."[19] Wroughton was instructed to "cultivate the strictest friendship" with Keyserling, but he was not to "enter into full and perfect concert" until more particular knowledge of Catherine's sentiment was possessed by the British government.[20]

When Buckinghamshire pressed Catherine to explain her intentions in Poland, she said that she could not offer further information, especially in the choice of a candidate, because the least suspicion of her intentions would make his election impossible. Catherine assured Buckinghamshire that all she desired and thought necessary at that time was that the British government join her in keeping a French candidate from obtaining the throne of Poland.[21] By this, Catherine did not clarify her position, she merely played upon Great Britain's traditional policy of preventing the success of any French venture.

France had always been more interested than had Great Britain in the affairs of Poland, regarding her as "one of the pivots of French policy in Eastern Europe, as a confederate that might be used either to take the Hapsburgs in the rear or to checkmate Brandenburg-Prussia and Russia."[22] But the eighteenth century had witnessed a change in the position of Poland

[19] PROSP, 88/87 and ACz, 1983/973, 975 (Feb. 2, 1763).
[20] Halifax to Buckinghamshire, April 5, 1763, BC, II, 18.
[21] Buckinghamshire to Halifax, April 15, 1763, *ibid.*, p. 21. See also Solov'ëv, XXV, 1529-34.
[22] Robert Howard Lord. *The Second Partition of Poland*, p. 38.

in French diplomacy. Although Poland, like Sweden, no longer had any great value as an ally, France still desired to maintain her influence at Warsaw. A primary object of French policy was to keep Russia out of European affairs and prevent her from thwarting Louis XV's aims "in case of an election in Poland," because for France "Poland [was] the chief object of the secret correspondence."[23] The attention French diplomatists gave to Poland and Russia should, however, be considered part of a larger plan, a "System of the South," as Choiseul, Louis's chief minister, termed it. In justifying his administration from 1757 to 1770, Choiseul wrote to Louis:

> We formed the formidable plan of the alliance of the South which Your Majesty adopted during the war and we strove to prevent the union of the North which the enemies of France conceived because they had been frightened by the alliance of the Midi. . . . The southern alliance being solidly established for France, it was necessary to keep the peace, to prevent one favorable to England from being formed in the North, for there is no moral possibility that Europe, divided by two great systems of alliances, can remain long in peace.[24]

Early in 1763 Catherine sent Prince Dmitrii A. Golitsyn to Versailles in the hope that he might be able to persuade the French court to act jointly with Russia in the choice of a candidate for the Polish throne. Choiseul, believing Catherine's real intention was to compromise the French and expose their inability to act independently, refused Golitsyn's request.[25] But the ineptness of French policy on the Polish succession derived not from its lack of "independent" action but rather from the absence of "unified" action. At the time of Golitsyn's visit the Versailles court was debating whether, in the event of a vacancy on the Polish throne,

[23] Louis XV to Breteuil (n.d., c. mid-August 1762), in Broglie, II, 20-25. During the Seven Years War there developed a strange pattern of French diplomacy: on the one hand, official, conducted by Choiseul, Louis's chief minister, and, on the other, secret, carried on by the King himself through his own agents. Often the policy conducted by the two was completely contradictory. This deceitful habit led to a whole system of secret diplomacy called "The King's Secret" or "The Secret Correspondence."

[24] Quoted in John Fraser Ramsey, "Anglo-French Relations, 1763-1770: A Study of Choiseul's Foreign Policy," *University of California Publications in History,* XVII, No. 3 (1939), 147.

[25] See Broglie, II, 65-66, and Solov'ëv, XXV, 1517-20.

France should interfere directly in the election, thereby reasserting her former influence in Poland, or abstain.

Choiseul had for some time declared his opposition to France's traditional policy. In his view, the condition of Poland was abject and anarchic. Continued French involvement in Polish affairs could only mean immense expenditure with no results. Choiseul recommended that Poland be abandoned to her natural fate, that France not interfere in the Polish succession. He had no faith that Poland could be reformed and no fear of her dismemberment. Each of Poland's enemies had everything to fear from the others aggrandizing themselves at Poland's expense. Even if Poland's neighbors jointly agreed to dismember her, France still had nothing to fear, because within a short time the despoilers would fall into disagreement among themselves and the balance of power in eastern Europe would be readjusted.[26]

Louis did not agree with his chief minister. Prompted by his personal relationship with the Saxon house (the Dauphiness, Maria Josepha, was Augustus's daughter), his hatred of Prussia, and his dislike for Russia, he chose to help Poland. This would be diplomatic, not military, aid, and Louis did not inform his foreign office of his plans. He chose to work through his secret agents. Hennin, the French chargé at Warsaw, was instructed to become more active in Poland's domestic affairs, to ingratiate himself with all parties and factions so that when the propitious moment arrived, Louis "might declare himself for whoever is most in accord with his interests."[27]

A visit by Stanislas Poniatowski to Hennin heightened the confusion of French policy. He asked Hennin to communicate to Versailles the following: "In case of an election, if the votes were divided, and if the larger number were in favor of the candidate whom the Czartoryski family should put forward, with the support of Russia, would His Most Christian Majesty order the French party . . . to join ours to turn the scale?" Poniatowski added: "It being well understood that . . . we should pledge ourselves to do

[26] Francis X. Lambert, "The Foreign Policy of the Duke de Choiseul, 1763-1770" (unpublished Ph.D. dissertation, Department of History, Harvard University, 1952), pp. 314 ff.

[27] Broglie to Tercier, May 23, 1763, and Tercier to Hennin, Sept. 18, 1763, RIDA, V, 238-41.

the same thing for the candidate whom France should support." He gave his word that he would seek to "unite Poland closely to France, for the advantage of the two nations and the peace of Europe."[28]

To follow the policy outlined by Poniatowski, Louis would have had to turn away from the pleas of the Dauphiness and announce his abandonment of the Saxon house. As we shall see later, Louis thought the solution to the problem was to support both the Saxon line and the candidate of the Czartoryski family.

Austria had hardly as much difficulty as France in deciding its Polish policy. Frederick II of Prussia, viewing the political situation of Europe after the peace of Hubertusburg, pointed to the principle then underlying Austrian policy: "All [Europe's] kingdoms were exhausted to almost the same degree. . . . The Empress-Queen would not have concluded the peace of Hubertusburg, if her own resources had not been entirely used up. . . . The want of specie influenced political views, and each power wanted to maintain the peace, that it might gain time to recover its strength."[29]

The conclusion of the war left Maria Theresa sick in spirit and deeply humiliated. The war had been fought in vain; Austria had not regained Silesia. Kaunitz, one of the chief architects of Austrian foreign policy, knew, as did Maria Theresa, that Austria was not capable of conducting a war in the near future with any prospect of success and would therefore shy away from any issue which would involve the country in such a predicament. Thus, when Golitsyn arrived in Vienna in April 1763 (duplicating his mission to France), he was told that the Austrian court did not anticipate any difficulty over the succession to a throne which was not yet vacant. Austria declared her traditional policy on the subject: The freedoms, liberties, and the territory of the Commonwealth must be secured. When asked, Kaunitz stated his preference for a Saxon successor to the throne.[30]

[28] Hennin to Tercier, Sept. 20, 1763, in Broglie, II, 199-201, and RIDA, V, 243-44.

[29] Oeuvres, VI, 9-10.

[30] See Alfred Ritter von Arneth, *Geschichte Maria Theresia,* VIII, 26, 29, 47; Solov'ëv, XXV, 1515-16; and Saul K. Padover, "Prince Kaunitz and the First Partition of Poland" (unpublished Ph.D. dissertation, Department of History, University of Chicago, 1932), pp. 14-21, *passim.*

Like the Austrians, Frederick wanted a period of tranquillity in Europe at the end of the Seven Years War. Frederick's policy during the decade that followed was motivated by his desire to maintain the position Prussia had won among the powers and by his fear of being drawn into another war, in which he might lose all he had gained. To implement a defensive foreign policy he sought an imposing alliance that would ensure him against attack. He could not, of course, arrange such an alliance with Austria, and, although he did not fear France as a potential enemy, neither did he respect her as a worthwhile ally. The distrust between Frederick and the British ministry of the time precluded the possibility of an alliance in that direction.

But Russia was a different matter. He had feared the Russia of Zorndorf and Kunersdorf, which might have crushed Prussia had it not been for the timely death of Empress Elizabeth and the accession of the friendly Peter. Now, with the advent of Catherine, the surest way to gain a Russian alliance would be to support her policy in Poland and her candidate for the Polish throne.[31]

An alliance with Russia would also serve to further Frederick's own aims concerning Poland. Frederick had for some time coveted Polish territory, particularly Polish Prussia. The long-range scheme of Prussian expansion as articulated by Frederick's *Political Testament of 1752,* required the conquest of first Saxony and then Polish Prussia. With the latter acquisition, Prussia would obtain the valuable German-populated city of Gdańsk and further protection against possible attack from Russia.

However, this conquest would be best effected by means of peaceful diplomatic intrigue rather than through force of arms. Since Poland was an elective monarchy constantly troubled by factions on the death of her kings, the best opportunity to influence Polish affairs would be during an interregnum. Frederick quoted, as an example of the method he intended to use in Poland, what Victor Amadeus of Savoy had told Charles Emanuel: "My

[31] See Chester V. Easum, *Prince Henry of Prussia, Brother of Frederick the Great,* p. 249; Albert Sorel, *The Eastern Question in the Eighteenth Century,* pp. 12-13; and Frederick to Catherine, July 18, and Frederick to Goltz, July 23, 1762, PC, XXII/13868, 13898/42-43, 67, respectively.

son, it is necessary to eat the Milanese like an artichoke, leaf by leaf . . . . That is how it is necessary to profit and gain . . . sometimes a city, sometimes a district, until all is eaten."[32]

When the news of Augustus's illness reached him, Frederick wrote Catherine a letter, inaugurating the exchange of ideas that was to culminate in a treaty in 1764. Frederick was fearful that if Augustus should die unexpectedly foreign intrigues over the succession might rekindle the fires of war which had been so recently extinguished. He was opposed to any Habsburg succeeding to the Polish throne and reaffirmed one of the principles of the abortive treaty of June 19, 1762: A *Piast* should be the next king of Poland.[33]

Catherine was in complete accord with Frederick's proposal, but she needed several guarantees. First, although she would oppose any Austrian candidate, she wanted Frederick's assurance that he would oppose any French candidate. Second, she explained that she too preferred a *Piast,* but someone young and not in the pay of any other power. Finally, she wanted Frederick to oppose any movement of Saxon troops that might threaten to enter Poland after Augustus's death.[34] Frederick acceded to her wishes, and, since Catherine had not officially recognized the treaties of May and June 1762, he urged that a treaty be concluded between the two courts.[35] This request fitted exactly into Russian plans for a "Northern System."

Catherine did not disclose to Frederick that she had already chosen a candidate for the Polish throne. Prompted by the news of Augustus's failing health, Catherine in mid-February had called a meeting of her Council to discuss the question of the successor. The majority of the Council understood quite well that Augustus's oldest son could not be Russia's choice, as he would probably be under the influence of France and Austria. The

[32] Frederick II, *Die politischen Testamente Friedrichs des Grossen* (ed. by G. B. Volz), pp. 61-64.

[33] Frederick to Benoit, Feb. 12, 1763, PC, XXII/14442/519-20; Frederick to Catherine, Feb. 15, 1763, *ibid.*, 14449/524-25, and Sb, XX/7/158-60.

[34] Catherine to Frederick, March 4, 1763, PC, XXIII/14560/4-5 and Sb, XX/9/161-63.

[35] Frederick to Catherine, April 5, 1763, PC, XXIII/14560/5-6. See also Mitchell to Halifax, June 14, 1763, BMAddMSS, 6809/223.

Council agreed with Catherine that either Stanislas Poniatowski or Adam Czartoryski would be Russia's candidate. Moreover, Russia would station some 30,000 troops on the Russo-Polish border and keep another 50,000 in readiness.[36] On April 3 Catherine wrote to Keyserling that by May there would be some 30,000 troops in Smolensk and about 44,000 men assembled on the borders of Kurland. She was also sending 50,000 ducats and would send more later.[37]

With this renewed evidence of Russia's support, the Czartoryskis continued their plans for the confederation. On May 20 they sent another "Promemoria" to Catherine, this time elaborating a plan for the simultaneous invasion of Poland by Russian troops and the formation of a confederation in the Commonwealth by "The Family." At the end of July, the "Promemoria" stated, the Lithuanian provinces would begin to confederate simultaneously with the arrival of 4,000–5,000 Russian troops from Smolensk. This example would be followed by the Crown provinces, which would be assisted by 10,000–12,000 Russian troops from Kiev. The two confederations would then unite into one general confederation for the entire Commonwealth under the protection of the Russian Empress and under the direction of Keyserling. In this manner all the demands of Catherine that Keyserling had earlier announced would be satisfied, and the confederation would facilitate the speedy election of a new king according to Catherine's wishes. The Czartoryskis also requested an additional 200,000 ducats for expenses.[38]

With considerable hesitancy Catherine, who hoped to influence the elections of the Wilno (Vilna) Tribunal (the highest judicial body in the Grand Duchy) in favor of the Czartoryskis, decided to demonstrate Russian power in Poland. In June, General Soltykov, who was already in Kurland with three infantry regiments and a cavalry unit, was ordered to march through Poland toward Kiev.[39] Catherine did not intend this action to precipitate a confederation because, for several important reasons, she had

[36] Sb, XLVIII/341-56/298-313.

[37] Catherine to Keyserling, in Schmitt, I, "Dokumenta," 335.

[38] *Ibid.*, pp. 338-43, and SAPMém, I, 440.

[39] See Keyserling to Soltykov, June 1763, in Schmitt, I, "Dokumenta," pp. 348-49, and Catherine to Keyserling, July 25, 1763, Sb, XLVIII/572, 573/546-49, 549-50.

changed her mind. About the time that Soltykov was to march, Catherine wrote to Keyserling:

I see that our friends are very excited and are preparing for a confederation, but I do not see to what purpose a confederation leads during the lifetime of the King of Poland. I speak to you the real truth: My coffers are empty and will remain empty as long as I am unable to bring my finances into order, but that at the moment is impossible. My army is not able to advance in a campaign this year. I charge you to restrain your friends, and chiefly that they are not to arm themselves or ask too much.[40]

But it was already too late to restrain "The Family." As soon as they heard of Soltykov's preparations, they began to marshal their forces for the forming of a confederation. Confusion reigned in Warsaw and in the near-by provinces. Since Massalski, the Grand Hetman (the commanding general) of Lithuania, was in the camp of "The Family," no opposition would be made by the regimental commander of Lithuania to Soltykov's entry. As Soltykov approached the Lithuanian frontier in the third week of July, the fever of "The Family" increased, but his approach also evoked protests from the pro-Saxon magnates who had traditionally been anti-Czartoryski and anti-Russian.[41]

During the days that followed, several meetings were held between the pro-Saxon magnates and Keyserling, to whom they complained about the invasion of the Commonwealth by Russian troops. One such meeting is reported to have taken place with General Andrzej Mokronowski. Keyserling tried in vain to explain to him that the march was only a routine military transfer of troops from one point to another and that Russia was a nation friendly to Poland—a supporter of Polish constitutional reform. To this Mokronowski declared that "Poland, whatever need she had of reform and protection, would never consent to receive her laws from a foreign power; to employ force there would be to begin a war which would interest more than one power in her quarrel."[42]

Keyserling, perceiving that a civil war might break out if Rus-

[40] Sb, XLVIII/572, 573/546-49, 549-50 (July, 25, 1763).
[41] See Schmitt, I, 140-42, and SAPMém, I, 455. See also Mitchell to Halifax, Sept. 3, 1763, BMAddMSS, 6809/236.
[42] Quoted in Rulhière, II, 83.

sian troops continued their march through Poland, promised Mokronowski that he would send word to halt their movement.[43] On August 12 a courier left Warsaw for St. Petersburg with instructions to explain to Catherine the present situation in Poland. Keyserling also sent word to Soltykov to halt his movement.[44]

By the middle of September the disturbances caused by the entry of Russian troops and the marshaling of the forces of the Czartoryskis for a confederation had subsided. "The Family" gave up its quest for a confederation during the lifetime of Augustus, Russian troops retired from Lithuania, and conditions returned to normal.[45]

The quietude that September brought to Poland was shattered on October 5, when Augustus III, ruler of two states, Saxony and the Polish-Lithuanian Commonwealth, died.

[43] *Ibid.* Stanislas Poniatowski wrote to Keyserling on August 11 that Joachim Potocki had marshaled troops and had already marched. Potocki had asked Stanislas Poniatowski to request Keyserling to remove Soltykov. SAPMém, I, 456-57.

[44] See Prince Charles to Ant. Zabiełło, August 25, 1763, ACz, 2375/85-86. See also Burnet to Weston, August 27, 1763, BMAddMSS, 6809/233. Already, on August 6, Catherine had written to Keyserling that "the family" had "evil intentions" and that they were acting as though "they already had my positive command to form a conferedation. . . . The present entry into Poland of my four regiments can cause trouble again. . . . I ask you to call off the sojourn of my regiments in the country, as much as you possibly can." SAPMém, I, 444-45.

[45] See Buckinghamshire to Halifax, Sept. 23, 1763, BC, II, 72. There has been considerable speculation as to the confederation's purpose. Although none of the "Memoranda" submitted to Catherine ever contained a statement that the Czartoryskis wished to dethrone Augustus, several critics seem to be of that opinion. Among them are Askenazy (p. 11) and Schmitt (I, 149). Most interesting of all is Wroughton's letter to Halifax of June 28, 1763 (PROSP, 88/87 and ACz, 1983/1007): "Their present scheme is not to do any harm to the King, but to redress the grievances of the Government, and to restore it to better order. When the fire is raised, can they say where the flame will end?" For a review of this problem see Jerzy Michalski, "Plan Czartoryskich naprawy Rzeczypospolitej," *Kwartalnik Historyczny,* LXIII, Nos. 4-5 (1956), 29-43.

And now the King of Poland has died like a fool! I confess to you that I do not like these people who do everything at the wrong time. I hope, however, that this election will pass off without resulting in any new troubles. I have a domestic grief—my poor dog is about to die. I console myself with the thought that if death does not spare crowned heads, poor Alcimène could expect no better fate.[1]

FREDERICK II TO PRINCE HENRY

II

THE INTERREGNUM
OCTOBER 5, 1763—MAY 7, 1764

Frederick Christian was Augustus's eldest son and his successor as Elector of Saxony, but he also desired to be the King of Poland. However, he was neither so naive nor so passive as to allow destiny to take its course. His father and his grandfather had succeeded to the Polish throne not by firm resolve alone—the intervention of the Great Powers had made Saxon dreams a reality. Therefore, immediately after the death of his father, Frederick Christian solicited the aid of the powerful and the influential.[2]

The replies he received were mixed and not reassuring. Catherine extended her condolences but withheld her blessings; she expressed her desire to see a free and open election.[3] Kajetan Sołtyk, the Bishop of Kraków (Cracow), one of the most powerful clerics in Poland, stated that if the nation accepted Frederick Christian he would do the same.[4] King Frederick of Prussia appreciated the confidence Saxony had placed in him but explained that he could not influence the election in the favor of the Saxon

[1] Oeuvres, XXVI, 288 (Oct. 9, 1763).

[2] ACz, 1693/272-74; BC, II, 80; Adolf Beer, *Die erste Theilung Polens,* II, 324-25; Oeuvres, XXIV, 47-48; PC, XXIII/14763/141-43; Sb, XX/17/174-76, XXII/75, 77/134, 136; BJag, 101/VII/111-12; BMAddMSS, 6809/248; and C. W. Böttiger, *Geschichte des Kurstaates und Konigreiches Sachsen,* II, 347-48.

[3] BJag, 101/VII/141-42; Sb, XXII/76-78/135-37, LI/727/52-55; and BC, II, 92.

[4] BJag, 101/VII/112-13.

house.[5] King George III's reply reflected his continuing negotiation with the court of Russia for an alliance and his concern for the position that France would take in the election. He was satisfied that British interests in the Baltic area were not in jeopardy.

All my views are directed towards an object so just and so wholesome and I would draw the reproach of having begun the troubles that I search carefully to prevent, if I showed myself in advance too intendent to support the pretensions of any rival, so much more that my Realms are uniquely interested in the affairs of Poland only in connection with my allies.[6]

Although more encouragement came from the southern courts, there was no basis for hope that their support would be firm or constant. Soon after Augustus died, Kaunitz announced Austria's policy in a circular note to his ambassadors: "We desire that the Polish crown should go to the Saxon Elector, that the dismemberment of the Polish Republic should be avoided, and that any intrigues of the Berlin and St. Petersburg courts should be opposed."[7] This policy was, however, soon compromised by the activities of Russia. After hearing of Augustus's death, Catherine wrote to Maria Theresa that her intention was "to allow freedom in the choice of a new king provided that foreign intrigues do not interfere and do not force me to take a side contrary to my feeling. . . . I will not be opposed to the choice of a *Piast.*" Catherine explained that the troops recently stationed on the Russian frontiers should not be considered a threat to peace.[8] Sensing the impending danger, Maria Theresa decided to modify her former position. She now explained to Catherine that, although

[5] PC, XXIII/14764/143-44, and Oeuvres, XXIV, 48 ff. See also BMAddMSS, 6809/248.

[6] King George III to Elector of Saxony, Oct. 25, 1763, in L. G. Wickham Legg (ed.), *British Diplomatic Instructions 1689-1789,* VII, Part IV, 91-92n; and BC, II, 90-91. The British ambassador to France reported that "His Most Christian Majesty had determined to take no active part in the affair of the Polish election." See Halifax to Hertford, Oct. 18 and Nov. 8, 1763, in Legg, VII, Part IV, 91, and Sandwich to Buckinghamshire, Oct. 28, 1763, BC, II, 93. Sandwich informed Buckinghamshire that "when a vacancy should happen in the Crown of Poland his Majesty has no other part than to assure the Empress of his very sincere inclination to promote as far as might depend upon his influence what might be most agreeable to that Princess." BC, II, 86 (Oct. 18, 1763).

[7] Kaunitz to Starhemberg, Oct. 10, 1763, quoted in Alfred Ritter von Arneth, *Geschichte Maria Theresia,* VII, 507. See also Beer, I, 120; and Mitchell to Sandwich, Oct. 29, 1763, BMAddMSS, 6809/249.

[8] Beer, *Dokumente,* p. 80 (Oct. 17, 1763).

she preferred the successor in the Saxon line, she would concur with Catherine in the choice of a *Piast* if the Saxon candidate were not elected.[9]

The French policy was as contradictory and confusing as ever. Louis's insatiable appetite to create another "secret" engaged France in a policy which could not end in anything but failure. The foreign office, at first given no information concerning Hennin's interview with Poniatowski, instructed its envoy, Paulmy, to leave Dresden and go to Warsaw, which would be the center of political activity until after the next election. Paulmy was to declare France's preference for the continuance of the Saxon line on the Polish throne and to reaffirm the two essential points of Louis's policy: complete freedom of election and the maintenance of Poland's territorial integrity and independence.[10]

On October 25 Tercier, who directed Louis's secret correspondence, wrote to Hennin that, although no decision could yet be made on Poniatowski's request, he was to continue cultivating Poniatowski. Under no circumstances was Hennin to write the foreign office of this matter.[11] But in November, Louis again changed his mind—Hennin was given permission to inform the foreign office of Poniatowski's proposals. The foreign office was now faced with an impossible situation. Paulmy had surely been won over by the Saxon court and would probably reveal the secret negotiations to them if he were informed. It was decided that a special agent should be sent to Poland to enter into discreet discussions with the Czartoryskis in order to come to an arrangement on the election. The officer chosen for this task was General Monet, a former tutor to one of the young Czartoryskis.[12] When Monet arrived in Warsaw, however, he disregarded his instruc-

[9] *Ibid.*, pp. 80-82 (Nov. 9, 1763). See also Sergei Mikhailovich Solov'ëv, *Istoriia Rossii s drevneishikh vremën*, XXV, 1516-17, and Saul K. Padover, "Prince Kaunitz and the First Partition of Poland" (unpublished Ph.D. dissertation, Department of History, University of Chicago, 1932), p. 22.

[10] Duc de Broglie (ed.), *The King's Secret: Being the Secret Correpondence of Louis XV with His Diplomatic Agents from 1752 to 1774*, II, 205-06 (Oct. 20, 1763).

[11] *Ibid.*, p. 204. On November 4 Comte de Broglie wrote Tercier: "If we are not to act we should then keep on good terms with all the candidates, and reserve ourselves for turning the scale at the last moment We should oppose no one, not even the Czartoryskis." *Ibid.*, p. 198.

[12] RIDA, V, 243-44; Broglie, II, 207-08; and Francis X. Lambert, "The Foreign Policy of the Duke de Choiseul, 1763-1770," (unpublished Ph.D. dissertation, Department of History, Harvard University, 1952), pp. 328-29.

tions to speak with discretion and openly resumed his friendship with the Czartoryskis. This new thread in the tangled skein only caused greater confusion in Warsaw.[13]

On the morning of October 17, when news arrived in the Russian capital of Augustus's demise, Catherine called a meeting of her advisory Council. As before, the Council voted to support a *Piast* for the throne. It was also decided that Russian troops were to be ready to move at a moment's notice. At the conclusion of the conference, Chernyshev, vice president of the War College, submitted a secret memorandum. Chernyshev advocated that Russia now occupy and annex Commonwealth territory in order to round out Russia's frontiers and provide her with greater security. In general, Chernyshev wanted Russia to acquire Polish Livonia and large portions of Połock (Polotsk), Witebsk (Vitebsk), and Mścislaw. The Council was of the opinion that Chernyshev's plan went beyond what actually could be attained at the moment. It was, therefore, not accepted as a plan for immediate action; but it was not forgotten.[14]

As a means of conveying new instructions to Keyserling and at the same time affording him assistance (since he had recently become ill), Prince Repnin, Panin's son-in-law, was to be sent to Warsaw. He carried Catherine's endorsement of Stanislas Poniatowski as her choice for the Polish throne. There were several reasons for choosing Poniatowski over his cousin, Adam Czartoryski, including the important fact that Adam did not want the crown and had made this well known in Warsaw.[15] Catherine again made explicit her desires that the realm should not be hereditary, that the *Liberum Veto* should not be abolished, and that the standing army should not be increased. The Russian ambassadors were to make it known that all opposition to Poniatowski's election

[13] Broglie, II, 210-12. See also Wroughton to Sandwich, Dec. 14 and 17, 1763, PROSP, 88/87 and ACz, 1983/1059, 1061, and 1063, respectively.

[14] See Sb, LI/662, 663, 748/5-8, 9-11, 92-101, respectively and Solov'ëv, XXV, 1501-3.

[15] Poniatowski told Wroughton that "Prince Adam had frequently declared his resolution of refusing the Crown; if it should even be voluntarily offered him, and particularly not to run after it; that he had often said to M. Keyserling, that his extreme levity and detestation of all manner of application were too well known . . . not to believe him sincere in the declaration." Wroughton to Sandwich, Oct. 15, 1763, PROSP, 88/87 and ACz, 1983/1023, 1025.

would be suppressed: Polish Livonia would be occupied and incorporated into the Russian Empire if Russian troops had to be sent into Poland. Poniatowski, when King, was to establish a commission that would secure the rights of the Dissidents.[16]

To allay suspicious minds which feared that her intention was to dismember the Commonwealth, Catherine, in a circular note to the European courts, stated:

If ever malice, in concert with lie, has been able to invent an absolutely false rumor, it is assuredly the one that has been spread to the public—that We have resolved to support the election of a *Piast* only so that, by his help and connivance, We could then easily invade several provinces of the Realm of Poland and of the Grand Duchy of Lithuania, dismember them, and appropriate them forthwith to Ourselves and Our Empire. . . . At the same time We will make it known to all that We would wish that at the future election of Her King, [Poland] place on the throne a *Piast* born in Poland, of a father and mother of Polish nobility.[17]

The news of Augustus's death reached Warsaw on October 9, and two days later the Primate, Władysław Łubieński, arrived from Gniezno to arrange for the election. In this sickly man of sixty years was vested, as Interrex, the highest legal authority during the interregnum.[18] On November 12 the Primate, on the advice

[16] Le Comte D'Angeberg [pseudonym of J. L. Chodźko] (ed.), *Recueil des traités, conventions et actes diplomatiques concernant la Pologne 1762-1862*, pp. 5-11, and Sb, LI/748/92-101 (Nov. 17, 1763). Keyserling and Repnin had also been authorized to use over 100,000 rubles to secure votes for the Russian candidate. The election, however, was to cost Russia over eight times that amount. See Buckinghamshire to Sandwich, Sept. 28, 1764, BC, II, 232, and Alexandr Kraushar, *Książe Repnin i Polska w pierwszym czteroleciu panowania Stanisława Augusta (1764-1768)*, I, 65.

[17] Karol Lutostański (ed.), *Les Partages de la Pologne et la lutte pour l'indépendance*, p. 4 (Dec. 26, 1763). Frederick's declaration of January 22, 1764, contained a similar message (*ibid.*, pp. 5-6). Frederick had already, on November 25, 1763, enjoined his subjects in the provinces neighboring on the Polish frontier not to interfere with or disturb the Poles during the interregnum (D'Angeberg, p. 13). See also BJag, 101/VII/146; BC, II, 106-8, 131; ACz, 1983/1055, 1061; and BMAddMSS, 6809/243-57 and 6810/2.

[18] Henryk Schmitt, *Dzieje panowania Stanisława Augusta Poniatowskiego*, I, 170-71, and Richard Roepell, "Das Interregnum: Wahl und Kronung von Stanislaw August Poniatowski: 5 Oktober 1763 bis 7 Dezember 1764," *Zeitschrift der Historischen Gesellschaft für die Provinz Posen*, VI (1891), 255. Upon his arrival, Keyserling began his intrigues in the attempt to win over the Primate, and other members of "The Family." Although Łubieński denied that he accepted a bribe ("Keyserling offered me 80,000 rubles for my expense. I refused it, however, because I could not allow the election to be corrupted"), there is evidence to the contrary.

of the Senate Council, which had met on November 7, issued a proclamation announcing the time and place of the Dietines (the provincial assemblies, which elected Deputies to the National Diet) and the Convocation Diet. With few exceptions the Dietines were to meet on February 6, 1764, to elect representatives to the Convocation Diet, which would meet on May 7. No limit was placed on the future deliberations of the Convocation Diet, but the Senators and Deputies were requested to arrive earlier than the date appointed to prevent delays.[19]

But before the Dietines convened the Saxon house suffered a serious setback which made its chances of gaining the Polish throne very slim indeed. On December 17 Frederick Christian died.[20] His son, Frederick Augustus, was merely a boy of thirteen and, consequently, was not allowed to rule. The administration of the Saxon state fell upon his wife, Maria Antonia, and his oldest brother, Prince Xavier, who now became the Saxon candidate for the throne of Poland.[21]

Neither France nor Austria, the only states previously willing to aid the Saxon house, gave Prince Xavier serious support. They displayed a general inability to find common ground with other European states—or they lacked the courage—to defend Poland against a ruinous Russo-Prussian policy.

Austria had at first declared her support of Xavier. But in January 1764, when her ambassador at St. Petersburg informed

Before Keyserling died on September 30, 1764, he had managed to dispose of 85,566 ducats in the form of bribes, gifts, or expenses for military operations. Significant among those listed on the tally sheet found in Keyserling's cash box were: 3,000 ducats to August Czartoryski; 4,000 to Michał Czartoryski; 300 to Michał Ogiński; 1,200 to Stanislas Poniatowski; and 17,000 out of a designated 80,000 to Łubieński. See Szymon Askenazy, *Die letzte polnische Königswahl,* p. 39n; Kraushar, I, 65; E. Reimann, *Neuere Geschichte des preussischen Staates,* I, 93; and Solov'ëv, XXV, 1505.

[19] ACz, 820/240-60, and ACz, 878/7-14.

[20] ACz, 2375/89.

[21] See Böttiger, II, 375-80. About three weeks after Augustus's death, Heinrich Brühl resigned his office, and on October 28 he died. See Robert L. Koehl, "Heinrich Brühl: A Saxon Politician of the Eighteenth Century," *Journal of Central European Affairs,* XIV (Jan. 1954), 328; Aldàr von Boroviczeny, *Graf von Brühl: Der Medici, Richelieu und Rothschild, seiner Zeit,* p. 505; Otto Edward Schmidt, *Minister Graf Brühl und Karl Heinrich von Heincken: Briefe und Akten. Charakteristiken und Darstellungen zur Sachsischen Geschichte (1733-1763),* p. 316. See Mitchell to Sandwich, Dec. 31, 1763, BMAddMSS, 6809/257.

Kaunitz that Russian troops were prepared to enter Poland, Kaunitz knew that it would mean risking war to venture further Austrian support for a candidate not favored by Russia. But in the hope that a united stand by France, Turkey, and Austria might dissuade Russia, Kaunitz sought to convince the Porte and France to oppose the Russian party in Poland.[22]

The hostility of Russia and Prussia toward the Saxon house and the apathy of the Porte were too much for the French court to overcome. But, the King of France promised, if Maria Theresa were to use her military forces and if the King of Spain were to contribute half the cost of influencing the Election Diet, he himself would not refuse to complete the sum.[23] Soon afterwards, however, Louis wrote to Tercier:

> Spain declines to give any assistance and Vienna also; consequently we, like they, can give nothing to the Prince of Saxony but a recommendation. With these replies, Prince Xavier will not offer himself, although he is still advised to do so, but he will certainly not be elected. . . . No foreign prince will succeed this time, so we must turn to the Piasts.[24]

France now decided to follow a policy of neutrality by not supporting any candidate.[25]

Turkey explained its policy in a "Memorial" delivered in March to the foreign ministers at its court. The Porte wanted to see a native-born Pole become king and would not tolerate any foreigner taking the throne. Above all, the Porte wanted to maintain Polish peace and freedom.[26]

When Kaunitz learned that France was halfhearted in her support of the Saxon candidate, he withdrew Austrian support. With the full support of France and the possibility of support from the Porte, he might have opposed Catherine's aims—fearful as he was of entangling Austria in a war with Prussia and Russia—but

[22] See Beer, I, 135-36.
[23] Broglie, II, 215-16.
[24] *Ibid.*, p. 217.
[25] See Lambert, p. 334, and Lutostański, p. 8.
[26] William Tooke, *The Life of Catherine II, Empress of Russia,* Vol. II, Appendix II. See also Yorke to Buckinghamshire, Dec. 6, 1763; Buckinghamshire to Sandwich, Feb. 14, 1764; and Grenville to Buckinghamshire, March 10, 1764; all in BC, II, 111, 142, 152-53, respectively.

alone he did not dare.[27] The pessimistic pragmatism of his statesmanship was expressed in his reported conversation with Girard, the French chargé at Vienna:

What is the use of tying our own hands? Either the Poles, in spite of your assurances, will be afraid, and will follow the impulse which Russia will give them, and then all is at an end, or else there will be a double election, and the two parties will fight. Then Russia will send in her troops, and their superiority will crush the opposing party, unless other Powers go to war for it. Now as none of them will do so, all will be at an end.[28]

Since no money or troops could be expected from any foreign power, Prince Xavier understood that he could not compete for the Polish crown.[29]

As the date of the Dietine convocations approached, propaganda in the form of letters from leading magnates to the provinces played a significant role in determining the results. In general, the letters called for reform in the country. But actually the only organized and planned effort toward reform came from the side of "The Family." Most important to them was the strengthening of the central government, to give more power to the Diet and the King and to reduce the influence of the intractable conservatism exhibited by the provinces. They hoped to subordinate the hetmans and Treasurers, who had virtual control over the military and finances, to a commission appointed by the King and responsible to the Diet. Implicit in this was the hope that the Diet could be persuaded to abolish the *Liberum Veto* in most important state matters.[30]

When the written word or the preeminence of a noble family failed to persuade a Dietine to follow a certain view, bribes, sabre rattling, and sometimes bloodshed "captured" a Dietine for one group or the other. The two groups that contended for the support of the Dietines were those of the Grand Hetman of the Crown,

[27] See Beer, I, 144; Solov'ëv, XXVI, 64-65; Stormont to Buckinghamshire, Dec. 7, 1763, BC, II, 114; and D'Angeberg, pp. 16-17.

[28] Broglie, II, 218-19 (March 6, 1764).

[29] See Beer, I, 137-38; and Wroughton to Sandwich, March 7, 1764, PROSP, 88/88 and ACz, 1984/25.

[30] See Schmitt, I, 206-7, and Jerzy Michalski, "Plan Czartoryskich naprawy Rzeczypospolitej," *Kwartalnik Historyczny*, LXIII, Nos. 4-5 (1956), 29-43, and "Propaganda konserwatywna w walce z reformą w początkach panowania Stanisława Augusta," *Przegląd Historyczny*, XLVI (1952), 536-62.

Jan Klemens Branicki, and "The Family." Although the former comprised many of the leading families of the Commonwealth, the Radziwiłłs, the Potockis, and several leading bishops, it was wanting in money and foreign support. The only major force it could exert was through the Crown army, which the Branicki commanded. Often he would send Crown troops to the provinces to "influence" a Dietine election.

To aid "The Family" in consolidating their increasingly dominant position, Catherine offered a body of 3,000 Russian troops which would encamp near Warsaw and act as a check on the forces belonging to the Grand Hetman. The Czartoryskis immediately accepted the offer and were told that by the end of April, Prince Dashkov would arrive with his forces.[31] By the end of March reports had reached Warsaw that Prince Volkonskii had already been ordered to take command of the 36,000 Russian troops stationed on the border, that Prince Dashkov was approaching Riga and was awaiting orders from Keyserling, and that an advance body of 500 troops had entered Lithuania.[32]

This news struck fear into the hearts of all in the Grand Hetman's party, and they immediately began protesting the violation of Polish sovereignty. They petitioned the Primate until he was virtually forced to call a meeting of the Senators present in Warsaw. At this Senate Council (held on April 10), Branicki demanded that the Russian ambassadors show cause for the invasion of the Commonwealth by Russian troops and that the Primate send letters to foreign courts explaining the breach of the laws of the Commonwealth, with a request for mediation. The Primate agreed only to the former point and merely as a matter of form, because the delegation that was appointed to speak to the Russian ambassadors was composed of members of "The Family."[33]

[31] M. Czartoryski to M. Ogiński, March 6, 1764, ACz, 2289/17-18, and Wroughton to Sandwich, March 10, 1764, PROSP, 88/88 and ACz, 1984/37-38. See also BJag, 111/39-42.

[32] Wroughton to Sandwich, March 24, 1764, PROSP, 88/88 and ACz, 1984/39-40.

[33] See Wroughton to Sandwich, April 14, 1764, PROSP, 88/88 and ACz, 1984/69-71, Schmitt, I, 220-21; and N. D. Chechulin, *Vneshniaia politika Rossi v nachale tsarstvovaniia Ekateriny II*, p. 252. On April 9 the foreign ministers at the court of St. Petersburg were informed that the reason for the invasion of the Commonwealth was the acts of violence committed by the Grand Hetman's party. Solov'ëv, XXVI, 65.

As the days passed, the situation of the Hetman's group grew worse. Even while they were deliberating on their future course of action, news arrived that Warsaw was being surrounded by Russian troops and Dashkov's forces were deep into Lithuania.[34] With firm resolve but little support, the Hetman's party petitioned the courts of Vienna, the Porte, and Versailles for intervention. The answer to these pleas was that a handful of nobles did not represent the Commonwealth.[35]

But even before these replies were received, news had arrived in Warsaw that on April 16, under the protection of Russian troops and with the support of the powerful Massalski family, a confederation led by Michał Brzostowski had been formed in Lithuania. Its manifesto proclaimed that the reason for its existence was to protect the motherland against the abuses of the Hetman's party.[36]

Little more remained to be done to make the election a foregone conclusion. The Saxon house had been defeated on the diplomatic field, and it seemed likely that if the Hetman attempted any military offensive his forces would be crushed by the sheer weight of Russian and "Family" numbers. The course pursued by the Russian court, ably assisted by the Prussian court, had thus far been successful. To crown their already evident success and to ensure their position for the future, the two courts officially allied themselves on April 11. This alliance was what Frederick had wanted since the closing days of the Seven Years War. The death of Augustus provided a greater opportunity for its realization. Even a month before Augustus died, Frederick had written to Catherine: "You will make a king without war, Madame. But the alliances that these people might conclude should be opposed in order to prevent measures that would impede execution of Your designs."[37] For the Russian court, the alliance served a two-

[34] See Wroughton to Sandwich, April 14, 1764, PROSP, 88/88 and ACz, 1984/72.

[35] D'Angeberg, pp. 18-19; Arneth, VIII, 51; Beer, I, 149, 152-53; Lambert, pp. 335 ff.; and Wroughton to Sandwich, April 14, 1764, PROSP, 88/88 and ACz, 1984/72.

[36] VolLeg, VII, 56-63. In March the Massalski family requested permission from Russia to form a confederation. Russia gave her blessings and also promised her military support. Chechulin, pp. 251-52.

[37] Frederick to Catherine, Sept. 8, 1763, PC, XXIII/14719/114. See also BMAdd-MSS, 6810/3-24, *passim*.

fold purpose. First, it provided for an immediate agreement on the election with one of the strongest powers of Europe, and, second, it was the first major step toward the conclusion of the "Northern System."

In the event that either country should be attacked, the other would send 10,000 troops and 2,000 cavalry, but if Prussia became engaged in a war in Prussian Rhineland territories, or Russia in Turkey or Persia, an annual subsidy could be substituted for military aid.[38] The alliance was to last for eight years and could be renewed.[39] As in the treaties concluded in years past, an article provided for the protection of the Dissidents in the Commonwealth. When the favorable moment occurred, they were to have their property and their former civil and religious rights restored to them. Since Russian troops had already marched to the Polish frontier, Prussia was to make a similar movement of troops. In the event of disturbances in Poland or of foreign intervention, the two contracting parties were to invade Poland. However, a force of 20,000 Prussian troops would enter Poland only when troops of a foreign power other than Russia had entered Poland. Regarding the election, the two powers agreed on Stanislas Poniatowski and arranged that their respective ministers at Warsaw work together to place him on the throne.[40]

It remained only for the Polish National Diet to put into law what had already been decided.

[38] Article III, Geo. Fred. de Martens (ed.), *Recueil de traités de puissances et états de l'Europe*, I, 225-26.

[39] Article XIII, *ibid.*, p. 228.

[40] Lutostański, pp. 8-13.

In all our history there is no example of an election as quiet and as perfectly unanimous.[1]

PONIATOWSKI TO MADAME GEOFFRIN

III

THE MAKING OF A KING
MAY 7, 1764—DECEMBER 20, 1764

"The approach of our Diet put the whole town [Warsaw] in motion, every measure was taken, every argument made use of to gain friends to each party."[2] Large numbers of soldiers, whose brightly colored uniforms indicated their loyalties to political group and family, gathered in the streets and courtyards and loitered in the hallways of the Diet chambers. Russian troops, under the leadership of Keyserling and Repnin, alone numbered 8,000, and their presence made known to all that Russian interests in the coming election were real.[3]

The Convocation Diet was by definition the calling together of all the estates of the Commonwealth during an interregnum for the purpose of deciding the term and form of the Election Diet. The Convocation Diet was, from its first session, a general confederation of the estates and bore such a name lawfully. Because it was a confederation, decisions were taken by plurality vote and could not be overturned by the *Liberum Veto*. The sessions (in the eighteenth century) lasted from two to six weeks.[4]

[1] Charles de Mouy (ed.), *Correspondance inédite du Roi Stanislas-Auguste Poniatowski et de Madame Geoffrin (1764-1777)*, p. 101 (Sept. 9, 1764).

[2] Wroughton to Sandwich, May 9, 1764, PROSP, 88/88 and ACz, 1984/81.

[3] See A. Kitowicz, *Pamiętniki Ks. A. Kitowicza do panowania Augusta III i Stanisława Augusta*, I, 93. It is estimated that there were about 14,500 Russian troops on Polish soil at the end of May 1764. See Szymon Askenazy, *Die letzte polnische Königswahl*, pp. 101-2, and Adolf Beer, *Die erste Theilung Polens*, I, 161.

[4] "In the time of the Jagiellonians the convocation diet was not known, and immediately after the declaration of an interregnum the time of the election diet was announced. When, however, political life had begun to develop on a large scale with the union of the Crown, Lithuania, and Ruthenia, a convocation of estates was held at Warsaw in January 1573, after the death of Zygmunt August, in order to

In accordance with custom, mass was held at St. John's Cathedral early on the morning of May 7, prior to the opening of the first session of the Diet. When the Deputies and Senators returned, they arranged themselves in the Chamber of Deputies and awaited the arrival of Adam Małachowski, the former Marshal of the Diet of 1762, who would hold the Marshal's post until a new one was elected. After several minutes Małachowski appeared in the Chamber. Just as he was about to invoke the assembly formally, General Andrzej Mokronowski, ardent adherent of the Grand Hetman's party and Deputy from Bielsko, cried "No!" To all present, this "no" meant a declaration against the Diet's continuing.

Quick anger flashed through the assembly, and several members drew their sabres. Only because the Poniatowskis and Czartoryskis quickly surrounded Mokronowski was bloodshed avoided. Małachowski, not knowing what to do, left the Marshal's post to God (as it was expressed) and pushed his way out of the Chamber along with Mokronowski and a few others of the Hetman's group.[5] The Diet proceeded with its business in spite of Mokronowski's declaration and immediately elected Adam Czartoryski as its Marshal.[6]

Later in the day a formal declaration of protest, signed by twenty-two Senators and forty-five Deputies, was delivered to the Diet explicitly stating the case of the Grand Hetman's party. First, the Diet was not to be held in the presence of foreign troops. Second, the Senators had not invited the Russians, and the Russians had not explained the occasion for their arrival. Third, the Russians had committed an act of violence by supporting the establishment in Lithuania of a pernicious confederation which was at present disturbing public order. Finally, all good patriots who loved justice were invited to unite for the support of liberty.[7]

---

decide the time and form of the election. From this necessary temporary understanding arose the convocation diet, which henceforth became custom and law and had a duration of two weeks. Several months after the convocation the election diet followed." (Zygmunt Gloger, *Encyklopedia staropolska illustrowana,* II, Part IV, 207.) See also VolLeg, VII, 7.

[5] BPAN, 1082/747-51. See also Wroughton to Sandwich, May 9, 1764, PROSP, 88/88 and ACz, 1984/82.

[6] BPAN, 1082/751-53.

[7] BPAN, 1082/747-51, 753-58. See also PROSP, 88/88 and ACz, 1984/101-8.

The very fact that the Grand Hetman's party had dared to oppose the opening of the Diet led to a tightening of security measures in Warsaw. A body of guards under the command of General Kazimierz Poniatowski was placed around the castle in which the Diet was held as well as about the houses of the most important nobles. During the night the Grand Hetman's group left Warsaw. By late afternoon of May 8, Warsaw was completely in the hands of "The Family" and Russian troops.[8]

On May 10 the Primate proposed the agenda for the Diet to deliberate: provisions for internal and external security, the preservation of the present position of the Catholic faith in the country, the kind of person that should be elected king of Poland, the *Pacta Conventa,*[9] internal improvements, judicial and financial reform, and the security of the deliberations of the Diet.[10]

During the next two days the deliberations were disorderly. The only general opposition to the proceedings came from Bishop Sołtyk of Kraków, who had previously chosen to be neutral in the hope that he could effect a *rapprochement* between the two groups. He submitted a manifesto, which was supported by Bishops Adam Krasiński of Kamieniec and Józef Załuski of Kiev and by members of his own family who held official positions in the Commonwealth, opposing any deliberation while foreign troops were on the soil of the Commonwealth. After its presentation, this group left the Diet.[11]

The manifesto did not ruffle the nerves of those assembled, and business continued as before. When news arrived on May 12 that the Grand Hetman's party had gathered at his estate at Piaseczno and it was rumored that a military demonstration would be attempted, the Primate demanded that Branicki be stripped of his title. Subsequently, the Diet removed Branicki from his office as Grand Hetman. August Czartoryski was then elected Regimentary General of all Crown forces in the hope that this would

[8] See Wroughton to Sandwich, May 9, 1764, PROSP, 88/88 and ACz, 1984/82-85.

[9] The *Pacta Conventa* were laws of state and in essence a bilateral contract between ruler and society. The contract defined the mutual obligations of the two. It came into practice in 1573 during the reign of Henri de Valois and had to be issued anew after every royal election.

[10] BPAN, 1082/758-84.

[11] *Ibid.*, pp. 784-94 (May 11, 1764).

effectively remove all military power from Branicki.[12] On May 16 August Czartoryski was formally given the command of the Crown army. At the same session the Crown and Grand Duchy Confederations were formally united.[13]

The Dissident question was discussed during the following two days. The moderating influence of the Primate kept the more severe bills from reaching the floor, as he warned repeatedly that foreign powers would not approve of a change in the existing laws. He submitted a bill, subsequently enacted into law, which merely reaffirmed the existing position of the Dissidents in the Commonwealth.[14]

Measures were enacted in June to provide for a general customs toll for the country, including the province of Prussia, and the establishment of Financial Commissions for the Crown and the Grand Duchy of Lithuania. It was the purpose of the general customs toll to regulate on a national basis the imports and exports of the country and to provide for a better system of collection as well as an increase in national revenue. Its enactment was a break with tradition, since for centuries the Prussian province had had special privileges regarding commercial affairs. Moreover, it was certain to bring a sharp reproach from Prussia, whose trade would be seriously affected by this new imposition.[15]

The establishment of the Commissions of Finance was an even greater departure from tradition, for it effectively, by administrative means, avoided the pitfall of the *Liberum Veto* and paved the way for a sound economic policy for the Commonwealth. The Commissions' range of competence was very wide indeed. They had the power and the responsibility to discuss and decide on Treasury incomes, to establish new instruction books for the collection of taxes, to obtain receipts on all payments, to

[12] *Ibid.*, pp. 794-810, and VolLeg, VII, 10-11.

[13] BPAN, 1082/810-47; BJag, 101/VII/186-87; and VolLeg, VII, 72. This same day, news reached Warsaw that a corps of 8,000 to 10,000 Russian troops was to enter the Commonwealth from Kiev to prevent any military opposition that might arrive in that area. At the same time 6,000 troops were destined for Wilno and had already entered Lithuania. See Wroughton to Sandwich, May 16, 1764, PROSP, 88/88 and ACz, 1984/96-97.

[14] BPAN, 1082/847-56, and VolLeg, VII, 7-8.

[15] BPAN, 1082/909-30, and VolLeg, VII, 22-23, 78-79 (enacted on June 5, 1764).

unify weights and measures, to appoint the only roads which might be used by merchants, to summon merchants for inquiries and discussions, to have their own body of soldiers, and to arbitrate all commercial and financial disputes that might arise. But, since each Commission was responsible to the Diet, it would have to submit a report of its activities. Moreover, if a Commission chose to introduce a new project not already provided for by the laws of the land, it had to have the approval of the Diet. Each Commission would be composed of Senators and Deputies (for the Crown, four Senators and twelve Deputies; for the Grand Duchy, two Senators and seven Deputies) elected by majority vote of the Diet. The Commissioners would have immunity from judicial proceedings during their term of office. They would not have the vote in the Diet on financial measures nor in the Commission when a personal matter was being discussed. Each Commission would be presided over by the Treasurer or, in the event of his absence, the senior Senator. The Commissions would have regular meetings during the week.[16]

Several days later a Commission of the Army for the Crown was established. In effect it subordinated the power of the hetmans to itself, and the hetmans could no longer take independent action. Similar to the Commission of Finance, it was composed of Senators and Deputies (four and twelve, respectively) and was responsible to the Diet. Its president would be the Grand Hetman, or, in the event of his absence, the Field Hetman or a senior Senator. Its principal responsibilities and powers were the regulation of the Crown army, the establishment of military tribunals, and the reception of all military embassies from foreign courts.[17]

Another break with tradition surrounded the decisions concerning the Coronation. After the Election Diet, which would begin meeting on August 27 on the Wola field outside Warsaw, the Coronation would take place in Warsaw instead of Kraków. Preparations were set in motion for transferring the crown jewels from Kraków to Warsaw for the occasion.[18]

While the Diet had successfully secured the nation from the abuses of future hetmans, the influence and power of the former

[16] BPAN, 1082/909-30, and VolLeg, VII, 18-22, 75-8.
[17] VolLeg, VII, 29-30.
[18] BPAN, 1082/856-63, 984-85, and VolLeg, VII, 9, 52-53.

Grand Hetman, Branicki, and his adherents were waning. On May 10 meetings had taken place at Piaseczno and Kozienice to determine what action Branicki's party would take. Within a few days, the leaders of the party dispersed because they could not agree among themselves. The idea of forming a confederation was in the end abandoned when no agreement could be reached on the choice of a marshal. There was a general belief that such a venture would result in failure, as they had insufficient forces and funds. Any military opposition from Branicki's party would henceforth be sporadic, retaliatory, and disorganized.[19]

On May 13 August Czartoryski issued an ordinance announcing to all military detachments of the Crown that he was now their commander and requesting that representatives be sent to Warsaw to obtain further instructions.[20] Furthermore, he ordered Crown and Russian troops to march on the forces of Branicki's party, which then numbered about 9,000. It was hoped that no bloodshed would result, since it was thought that most of the troops with Branicki would defect once they saw the superiority of the opposing force. Skirmishes did occur and losses resulted on both sides. The standoff continued during the month of June until finally, after repeated losses and defections (Bishop Sołtyk and Franciszek Potocki, Governor of Kiev, withdrew their forces), Branicki's party succumbed to "The Family" and the Russians. Branicki had to seek refuge in Hungary, while Karol Radziwiłł, the Governor of Wilno, fled to the Porte.[21]

Before the Grand Hetman's party had met defeat, they had made a last desperate effort to keep Poland from falling to Russian domination. General Andrzej Mokronowski was sent with all possible haste to Berlin to offer the Polish crown to Prince Henry of Prussia, Frederick's brother. It is difficult to see what they expected

[19] See Henryk Schmitt, *Dzieje panowania Stanislawa Augusta Poniatowskiego,* I, 241-51; Beer, I, 162-63; and Kazimierz Rudnicki, *Biskup Kajetan Sołtyk, 1715-1788,* pp. 67-70.

[20] BJag, 101/VII/172-73. See also Wrougton to Sandwich, May 16, 1764, PROSP, 88/88 and ACz 1984/95-97.

[21] See Wroughton to Sandwich, May 19, 23, and 26 and June 6, 23, 27, and 30, 1764, PROSP, 88/88 and ACz, 1984/109-10, 111, 114-16, 117, 133-35, 137-39, 151-53, respectively; Wroughton to Buckinghamshire, May 30, 1764, and Panin to Buckinghamshire, June 29, 1764, BC, II, 185-86, 201, respectively; Le Comte D'Angeberg [pseudonym of J. L. Chodźko] (ed.), *Receuil des traités, conventions et actes diplomatiques concernant la Pologne 1762-1862,* pp. 26-27; and Askenazy, pp. 102-4.

from such a proposal. Although the Prince had every personal qualification for the position and merited the honor, Austria would never have agreed to it, especially during the lifetime of Frederick. Moreover, Frederick himself would rather have denied Henry that doubtful distinction than forfeit the friendship of Russia. Frederick desired a long peace and would naturally not choose to offend the two empresses simultaneously. A Polish king disposed to Russo-Prussian policy would serve the same purpose as a Prussian on the throne. Frederick even branded as "false" a report from Warsaw that the Polish throne had been offered Henry. His main desire was to suppress the movement for Henry's candidacy, and in this he was successful.[22]

General Mokronowski, under the pseudonym of Captain von Kersky, a dealer in Polish horses, arrived in Berlin on July 24. The next day he was granted an interview with Frederick at Potsdam. But Frederick quickly dismissed Mokronowski stating that Prince Henry "would not want to turn Catholic."[23] Frederick told Mokronowski to accept the inevitable. "One fragment of the Republic cannot impose laws on the most numerous party of the nation," he said. "The intentions of the allied powers are not to make any attempts against the liberties of the Realm, but on the contrary to assure them."[24]

Believing he had put Mokronowski and his associates "back on the right track," Frederick informed St. Petersburg of Mokronowski's visit but omitted all reference to the suggestion that his brother be a candidate for the Polish throne or that he intervene in Polish affairs as a mediator. However, he instructed Count Solms, his minister at St. Petersburg, to suggest to the Russians the advisability of treating Branicki's party with all possible moderation, for fear that some ill-intentioned outsiders should find a pretext for intervention.[25]

Frederick's apprehensions exceeded reality. Not only had the

[22] See Chester V. Easum, *Prince Henry of Prussia, Brother of Frederick the Great,* pp. 250-52, and G. B. Volz, "Prinz Heinrich von Preussen und die preussische Politik vor der ersten Teilung Polens," *Forschungen zur brandenburgischen und preussischen Geschichte,* XVIII (1905), 188-201.

[23] Easum, p. 251, and Claude de Rulhière, *Histoire de l'anarchie de Pologne,* II, 232-33.

[24] See Frédéric Smitt, *Frédéric II, Catherine, et la partage de Pologne,* pp. 93-95, and Easum, pp. 251-52.

[25] PC, XXIII/15177/447-48 (July 26, 1764).

two prominent courts of the south already refused to aid Branicki, but they had broken off diplomatic relations with the Commonwealth by withdrawing their ambassadors from Warsaw.[26] The Porte reaffirmed its opposition to a foreign prince on the Polish throne.[27] Although Great Britain was disappointed in its hopes of obtaining the desired alliance with Russia during the early part of 1764, it still hoped to succeed and continued supporting Russian policy in Poland. Great Britain was, however, opposed to the abrogation of "the constitution of Poland, or [to anything] tending to the dismemberment of any part of the Republick."[28]

The formality of the election itself was the only thing that stood in the way of the total success of Russo-Prussian policy. On August 27 the Election Diet began on the Wola field, which was surrounded by Russian troops as well as by those of "The Family." The order of business went smoothly and without interruption.[29] On September 6 the voting took place, and the candidate of Russia and Prussia was elected unanimously. The following day Stanislas Augustus Poniatowski was proclaimed King of the Polish-Lithuanian Commonwealth.[30] One week later, the King accepted the *Pacta Conventa* and on November 25 was ceremoniously crowned by the Primate at St. John's.[31]

[26] See Duc de Broglie (ed.), *The King's Secret: Being the Secret Correspondence of Louis XV with His Diplomatic Agents from 1752 to 1774,* II, 224-27; Wroughton to Sandwich, May 12, and 26 and June 9, 1764, PROSP, 88/88 and ACz, 1984/91, 113-14, 119-27, respectively; Alfred Ritter von Arneth, *Geschichte Maria Theresia,* VIII, 546-49; Beer, I, 155-56; and E. Reimann, *Neuere Geschichte des preussischen Staates,* I, 100n.

[27] See Wroughton to Sandwich, May 26, 1764, PROSP, 88/88 and ACz, 1984/113.

[28] Sandwich to Wroughton, June 19, 1764, PROSP, 88/88 and ACz, 1984/131. The Anglo-Russian alliance did not materialize because Great Britain refused to supply funds for Catherine's ventures in Poland. See BC, II, 74-140, *passim,* and Appendix Note A, pp. 291-92. For a good summary of British policy toward Poland, see W. F. Reddaway, "Great Britain and Poland, 1762-72," *The Cambridge Historical Journal,* IV, No. 3 (1934), 223-62.

[29] ACz, 869/1-8; VolLeg, VII, 94-97; and BJag, 5117/34-39. See also SAPMém, I, 482-83.

[30] ACz, 869/8-10, 19-421, and VolLeg, VII, 96, 103-5. See also BJag, 101/VII/217-18.

[31] ACz, 869/11-15; VolLeg, VII, 105-6; BPAN, 1082/581-97; and SAPMém, I, 516-18. On September 30 Keyserling died and was succeeded by Repnin. See Sergei Mikhailovich Solov'ëv, *Istoriia Rossii s drevneishikh vremën,* XXVI, 52. Shortly after the election all the major European powers, except France and Austria, accorded Stanislas Augustus Poniatowski recognition as king. See Beer, I, 175-76; Frederick to Poniatowski, Sept. 10, 1764, PC, XXIII/15239/488; Francis X. Lambert, "The Foreign Policy of the Duke de Choiseul, 1763-1770," (unpublished Ph.D. dissertation, Department of History, Harvard University, 1952), pp. 339-40.

The *Pacta Conventa* that Stanislas Poniatowski accepted included the following principles: the King would not choose a successor during his lifetime; his children would not pretend to the throne; his wife must be a Catholic and was not to take part in the affairs of state; he was to treat everyone equally, not giving preference to members of his own family, and at all times to execute the due process of law in all litigations; he was not to receive money for appointments and all vacancies were to be filled according to ancient law; he was to execute the laws of the land; he was to attempt to redeem those territories lost by the Commonwealth in years gone by; he was not to conduct an offensive war without the permission of the Commonwealth; the King was to recognize Ernest Biron as Duke of Kurland; he was to establish a cadet school and support it with his private funds. And most important:

In the States of the Commonwealth, there are found many dissidents of the *Christian religion.* Therefore, we promise to *these dissidents peace in the Christian religion,* assured *by all the laws of the Roman Catholic church and the rite of the Uniats,* according to the description of the Constitutions of 1717, 1733, and 1736.[32]

On December 3 the Coronation Diet opened in Warsaw as the last formal step to conclude the interregnum. Jacek Małachowski, Deputy from Sieradz and *starosta* of Piotrków, was elected Marshal.[33] The following day, Andrzej Zamojski, Governor of Inowrocław was elected Chancellor of the Crown, Andrzej Młodziejowski as Vice Chancellor of the Crown, and Antoni Przezdziecki as Vice Chancellor of Lithuania. All were strong adherents of "The Family."[34] During the next week the acts of the Convocation Diet were reaffirmed.[35]

On December 12 discussions were held on a bill to establish a Commission of the Army for the Grand Duchy of Lithuania similar to that established for the Crown. As was to be expected, con-

[32] VolLeg, VII, 97-102. Ironically, the *Pacta Conventa* also included this: "We shall not invite a foreign army into the State of the Crown and the Grand Duchy of Lithuania." See *ibid.*, p. 99.

[33] BPAN, 1082/596-605.

[34] *Ibid.*, pp. 605-23.

[35] *Ibid.*, pp. 623-60, and VolLeg, VII, 138-86, *passim*. See also BJag, 101/VII/208-17; and ACz, 2471/1-3.

siderable opposition came from the Grand Hetman of Lithuania, Massalski, and his adherents, but the bill was enacted over their opposition.[36] Similarly, over the opposition of the Deputies and Senators from the Prussian province, the general customs toll was enacted by the Diet on December 17.[37]

As was not uncommon in Diet proceedings, the last session proved to be the longest and at times the most heated. Beginning in the morning of December 20, the session lasted until two o'clock the following morning. Proposal after proposal was submitted and agreed upon. Most attention and speech-making were devoted to the Dissident problem, when the Primate announced that Repnin had asked for an amelioration of the Dissidents' position in the Commonwealth. In spite of this request the Diet chose only to reaffirm the position it had taken at the Convocation Diet. Moreover, the act of unification of both confederations was upheld, and the General Confederation of the Commonwealth, in an uncommon procedure, was not dissolved. This legally prohibited the *Liberum Veto* from being introduced in the national Diet and effectively removed the most destructive element in Polish parliamentary procedure.[38]

Undoubtedly, the national Diets had taken a heroic step toward strengthening the Commonwealth beyond all previous expectations. Nonetheless, the true test of the reform program would be in its permanence. The crucial question was whether Poland's neighbors were willing to allow her to be strong and independent. The previous hundred years of the Commonwealth's history had shown that the trend was decidedly the other way.

[36] BPAN, 1082/660-86; VolLeg, VII, 170; and ACz, 1684/275-78. See also Wroughton to Sandwich, Dec. 15, 1764, PROSP, 88/89 and ACz, 1984/195-96.

[37] BPAN, 1082/703-10. See also Wroughton to Sandwich, December 19, 1764, PROSP, 88/89 and ACz, 1984/197-98.

[38] BPAN, 1082/713-22, and VolLeg, VII, 154-59. See also ACz, 754/203-4; Sandwich to Wroughton, Nov. 23, and Wroughton to Sandwich, Nov. 24, Dec. 15, 19, and 22, 1764, PROSP, 88/89 and ACz, 1984/187-88, 191-94, 195-96, 197-99, 201-2, respectively; Rudnicki, pp. 86-88; N. D. Chechulin, *Vneshniaia politika Rossii v nachale tsarstvovaniia Ekateriny II,* p. 260; and Solov'ëv, XXVI, 56-57.

The election of Stanislas Poniatowski brought peace; but there were signs that the enemies of the new government had still not settled down—and meanwhile, the Dissident question loomed like a storm cloud.[1]

IV

THE INDIAN SUMMER OF POLISH POLITICS DECEMBER 21, 1764—OCTOBER 5, 1766

The dramatic events of the year 1764, during which Poland had nearly been torn asunder by domestic quarrel and foreign intervention, culminated in the coronation of Stanislas Augustus Poniatowski. For the next year and a half there was relative peace in the Commonwealth, and only three developments during that period had a direct bearing on the partition. These were the growing estrangement between the King and the Czartoryskis, the solution of the Polish-Prussian customs toll controversy, and the continuing debate over the Dissident question. Of the three, the last is the most important, but no significant decision was made until the Diet of 1766.

Born into a wealthy and powerful family, Stanislas Augustus had grown up in an atmosphere of aristocratic and intellectual sophistication. His father Stanislas, the Castellan of Kraków, had already made his mark in Polish society. With his marriage to Konstantina Czartoryska, the Castellan gained admittance to one of Poland's most influential and wealthy families, and as long as the Czartoryskis remained high in the hierarchy of Polish society so would the Poniatowski family.

Stanislas Augustus received a thorough education. At sixteen he began his travels in Europe, and five years later he was making a favorable impression on those who frequented the salons of Paris. Broglie has an amusing comment on Stanislas Augustus during this period: "He excelled in the triple talent of the French courtier, in capturing women, conducting himself with éclat in

[1] Sergei Mikhailovich Solov'ëv, *Istoriia Rossii s drevneishikh vremën*, XXVI, 132.

the affairs of honour and contracting debts without paying them. . . . On all occasions he was ready with quotations from Voltaire."[2]

After a brief sojourn in England, where he met the Prince of Wales, the future George III, and was impressed by the English system of government, Stanislas Augustus returned to Poland to embark upon his political career. As a step in this direction, his father obtained for him the position of *Stolnik* (Steward) of Lithuania, which gave him "standing" but did not necessitate his presence in the Commonwealth. Thus, he willingly accepted the invitation of Charles Hanbury Williams, the new British ambassador to Russia, to become his secretary, and both left for St. Petersburg in 1755. There, this tall, handsome, witty, and well-bred Polish nobleman was quick to ingratiate himself with the Russian nobility. He won the friendship of the Grand Duchess Catherine, with whom he had a passionate love affair. The Polish court recognized his true ability and made him its ambassador to Russia the following year. As his love affair deepened, he became more involved in court intrigue. His complicity in an attempt to overthrow Empress Elizabeth in 1758 forced him to leave St. Petersburg.

On his return to Warsaw, he entered domestic politics and won a seat in the Chamber of Deputies. As an heir to the political power of the Czartoryskis, Stanislas Augustus captured the attention of elder statesmen and impressed them as a person of considerable ability and ambition. When the time came for choosing probable successors to the throne, it was only natural that his name would be placed high on the list, especially since he had continued his romantic correspondence with Catherine, who was now Empress.

Until his coronation, Stanislas Augustus worked hand in hand with his uncles, August and Michał Czartoryski, not only because he needed their experienced judgment, but also because agreement and cooperation with them was the only way he could attain the Polish crown. After the Coronation Diet, however, Stanislas Augustus developed that feeling of importance and desire for independence so common among young and ambitious rulers.

[2] Duc de Broglie (ed.), *The King's Secret: Being the Secret Correspondence of Louis XV with His Diplomatic Agents from 1752 to 1774*, I, 241.

He minimized the support of his uncles and emphasized his own popularity. He chose no longer to rely solely on their advice but sought that of men closer to him in opinion and age. Moreover, he irritated his uncles by employing the services of persons who in the past had been opponents of theirs.

Stanislas Augustus wanted to reform the government. The aid of Russia for this purpose appeared indispensable to him. He was prepared, therefore, to yield in the most humiliating manner to Catherine, but he did not believe that it would be necessary. After all, was it not Catherine who had chosen her former lover to wear the Polish crown? Had not Catherine often declared her good wishes for the Commonwealth and announced that she would defend it against any evil? To be sure, Russian troops had invaded Poland, causing damage to property and life, but this had been to secure his election and was therefore justified. Stanislas Augustus was convinced that he could command the destiny of Poland. He firmly believed he would never be faced with the necessity of choosing between a particular reform measure and the preservation of his crown.

For two years Stanislas Augustus labored under this naive belief. When finally he did see clearly the true intentions of Russian policy in Poland, Stanislas Augustus chose to keep his crown, even though it did not command the obedience or respect of his people. Whatever support he might have been able to muster was already seriously undermined by his estrangement from his uncles.

From their side, the Czartoryskis had legitimate reason for their disappointment. They naturally expected to dominate court policy, since it was their party that had been decisive in the election. They did not enjoy having their position undermined at court, and when their opinion was not accepted they vigorously opposed the policy of the King.

This estrangement prevented the Polish court from presenting a unified and decisive policy when unity and decision were vital to complete the reform program and to thwart the designs of Russia. Petty jealousies and their desires for self-aggrandizement blinded both the King and the Czartoryskis to their real duties.[3]

[3] For background on the life of Stanislas Augustus and court activity during the

From the beginning, the establishment of the Polish customs toll infuriated Frederick, but all his demands and threats were to no avail. Finally, Frederick made good his threats by establishing a toll house and fort below Marienwerder on the Vistula. Polish goods being carried on the Vistula to and from Gdańsk had to pass Marienwerder. In this strategic position it was easy for the Prussians to compel vessels carrying Polish goods to pay an extra duty on their cargoes, ranging from 10 percent on grain to 15 percent on other goods. The Polish vessels were forcibly subjected to search and were threatened with bombardment if Prussian commands were not heeded. When an attempt was made to stay close to the Polish side of the river and thereby avoid detection, Prussian ships would take the Polish vessel in tow and exact the required toll.

This Prussian policy led to several complaints by the Polish court and groups of merchants in Gdańsk, but they did not halt Frederick's activities. Finally, Great Britain and Russia intervened, settling the matter through mediation to the disadvantage of Poland. Frederick, in the summer of 1765, dismantled his customs house when he was promised by the Polish court that it would abolish the general customs toll at the next Diet.[4]

The opposition to Dissident reform demonstrated by the Diets of 1764—opposition from persons indebted to Russia for their political existence—had greatly disappointed the court of St. Petersburg. On February 12, 1765, Panin, Catherine's chief minister, informed Repnin that "We are unable nor do we wish to consider the Polish affair absolutely finished. For the present it will not be possible to improve the condition of the Dissidents."

---

first year of his reign see SAPMém, Vol. I, especially pp. 532-33; *Pamiętniki Stanisława Augusta Poniatowskiego; Die Memoiren des letzten Königs von Polen Stanislaw August Poniatowski,* Vol. I; Otto Forst-Battaglia, *Stanislaw August Poniatowski und der Ausgang des alten Polenstaates;* R. Nisbet Bain, *The Last King of Poland and His Contemporaries;* David Bayne Horn, *Sir Charles Hanbury Williams & European Diplomacy (1747-58);* Henryk Schmitt *Dzieje panowania Stanisława Augusta Poniatowskiego,* II, 11-42; and Solms to Frederick, Jan. 21, 1766, PC, XXV/15912/33-35.

[4] See PC, XXIV, XXV *passim;* Solov'ëv, XXVI, 137-42; W. F. Reddaway, "Great Britain and Poland, 1762-72." *The Cambridge Historical Journal,* IV (1934), 239; Szymon Askenazy, *Dantzig & Poland,* pp. 33-34; Schmitt, II, 17-20; ACz, 3081/47-60, *passim;* BJag, 73/107-52; and PROSP, 88/91, 92, *passim.*

Panin blamed the Czartoryskis for the failure of Dissident reform. Repnin was instructed to urge the Czartoryskis to reconsider their position, but, in the event that this was hopeless, Repnin was to turn the King against his uncles.[5]

To present the Dissident case, Catherine sent to Warsaw the Greek Orthodox Bishop of Belorussia, Jerzy Koniski, asking Stanislas Augustus to afford him protection and listen to his petition. On July 27, 1765, Koniski submitted a list of grievances and recommendations for the alleviation of the alleged injuries to the Greek Orthodox community living in the Commonwealth. Although the respective positions of the Greek and Uniat churches were regulated by the Treaty of 1686, Koniski submitted a document containing a list of about two hundred Greek Orthodox churches and monasteries that were supposed to have been forcibly taken by the Uniats since 1687. Koniski, on behalf of the Greek Orthodox community, wanted the Polish Diet to pass a law containing the following points: the restoration to the Greek Orthodox people of all their ancient privileges and freedoms; the restoration of their churches and monasteries; the right of the Greek Orthodox clergy to be judged by their own diocesan courts (although cases involving their estates would be tried by the royal courts); repeal of taxes for investitures; complete freedom of religious ceremonies; the right of children of Greek Orthodox parents not to be forcibly converted and, for those who had been, the privilege of choosing what religion they wished without being called heretics or schismatics if they chose to return to Greek Orthodoxy; the right of children of mixed marriages to follow the religious persuasion of their parents, according to sex (a girl taking the mother's religion; a boy, the father's); the return to the Greek Orthodox Seminary of Mohilev of all its ancient privileges; and, finally, but most important, the opening of all public offices, high and low, to all members of the Greek Orthodox *szlachta*.[6]

Stanislas Augustus recommended that Koniski's petition be submitted to a religious synod, but not until the grievances had

[5] Quoted in Solov'ëv, XXVI, 132-33, and Sb, LVII/1151/179-81.

[6] ACz, 754/223-43. See also M. C. Łubieńska, *Sprawa dysydencka 1764-1766,* pp. 6-13, 48-53, 153-60; Tadeusz Korzon, *Wewnętrzne dzieje Polski za Stanisława Augusta (1764-1794),* I, 177-80; Solov'ëv, XXVI, 53-54, 142; and ACz, 3081/81.

been investigated.[7] He was relatively favorable to Dissident reform, even though his uncles considered the idea politically inopportune, since it would lead to endless domestic disturbances. The King was tolerant, but he would not allow the Dissidents complete freedom of public religious observances nor grant them total exemption from the jurisdiction of Catholic courts. Most of all, the privilege of political equality with the Catholics was out of the question.[8]

This halfway position of the King did not, of course, please Catherine. Early in October Repnin received instructions to keep trying to free the King from the influence of his uncles, whom the Russian court believed to be the major obstacle to rehabilitating the Dissidents. Catherine wanted the next Diet to satisfy all the demands of the Dissidents. She also wanted an alliance concluded between the two countries by which Russia would guarantee the Polish "constitution."[9]

The stubbornness of the Czartoryskis in regard to Dissident reform created a great deal of speculation at the Russian court as to the proficiency of Repnin in executing policy. The court decided that Otto von Saldern, a career diplomat on a mission to Berlin, should stop over in Warsaw to help, as well as to observe, Repnin. He arrived in Warsaw the first week of April 1766.[10]

Saldern consulted with the King and his uncles, all of whom promised that they would attempt a reconciliation and abandon their opposition to a complete program of Dissident reform. But if the Czartoryskis withdrew their opposition, it was probably because they were convinced that the rest of the country would not. In any event, they promised merely to withdraw their opposition, not to support the Dissidents. As for the King—in his desire to placate all factions Stanislas Augustus was easily swayed and, pressed by Saldern, was persuaded, for the time at least, to follow the

[7] Łubieńska, pp. 53-54.

[8] *Ibid.*, pp. 62, 64; Schmitt, II, 27; and Alexandr Kraushar, *Książe Repnin i Polska w pierwszym czteroleciu panowania Stanisława Augusta (1764-1768)*, I, 82.

[9] See Panin to Repnin, Sept. 16, 1765, Sb, LVII/1235/340-43, and Kazimierz Rudnicki, *Biskup Kajetan Sołtyk, 1715-1788*, pp. 100-1.

[10] See Kraushar, I, 97; Schmitt, II, 33-37; Solov'ëv, XXVI, 419-22; and Wroughton to Grafton, March 5 and April 9, 1766, PROSP, 88/92 and ACz, 1984/208-9. See also Frederick to Solms, Feb. 6, 1766, PC, XXV/15912/35-36; Frederick to Benoit, March 12 and April 30, 1766, PC, XXV/15952, 16018/59-60, respectively.

bidding of Russia. Thus, Saldren was able to report that the Russian court should not expect any opposition to Dissident reform. He suggested that the Empress delay her demands for Dissident reform until the Diet convened later that year. But to ensure the success of Russian intentions at the Diet, Saldern recommended that Russian troops should surround Warsaw when it opened.[11]

In a Universal published on July 3, Stanislas Augustus scheduled the opening of the Diet for October 6 and the convening of the Dietines beginning August 25. The agenda for the Diet was divided into three categories: financial, military, and judicial. The Universal contained no statement concerning Dissident reform.[12]

Immediately after the publication of the Universal a heated contest began in the provinces among the various groups hoping to gain a majority of the Deputies at the Diet. Although there were no distinct lines of demarcation, three groups were discernible: the King's, the Czartoryskis', and another, which might be labeled "traditionalist." Politically, the latter stood for the overthrow of the reform laws passed during the interregnum—that is, the Commissions of Finance and the Army, and the General Confederation. The Catholic faith would be defended: the "traditionalists" would be uncompromising in their opposition to Dissident reform. In general, they were completely opposed to the King and the Czartoryskis, but on several political issues an alliance was possible with the court of St. Petersburg.[13]

Among the "traditionalists" one person stood out above all others in ability, courage, and sincerity—Bishop Sołtyk. He began writing letters and pamphlets to his parishioners urging that they vote for Deputies who would not give the Dissidents the slightest satisfaction. In one of his polemical writings he stated:

> Because . . . the Dissidents have the intention of exerting themselves in order that at the next Diet they may obtain for themselves the ex-

[11] See Kraushar, I, 97-99; Schmitt, II, 37; and Rudnicki, pp. 105-6. See also "Unterredung(s) . . ." PC, XXV/16045, 16424, 16425/ 112, 350-55, 355-64, respectively.

[12] See Schmitt, II, 40-41, 365; Rudnicki, pp. 107-8; and Kraushar, I, 116. See also Solms to Frederick, Aug. 5, 1766, PC, XXV/16194/200.

[13] See Schmitt, II, 41-45; Kraushar, I, 95-116; and Adolf Beer, *Die erste Theilung Polens,* I, 194-95. See also BPAN, 314/43-44, 57-58.

tension of tolerance, we call upon God . . . that He thwart and put to shame their endeavors, that He not allow them to encroach upon the bosom of the predominant religion, and that He prevent the possibility of ghastly war of which we have had ghastly examples in past times whenever the Dissidents usurped by force and made themselves equal in all things with the Catholics.[14]

Whereas Sołtyk became the leading exponent on matters of religion, others in his group campaigned on other issues. For example, a popular pamphlet of the time, *Considerations of a Good Patriot,* which was attributed to the Massalski family, demanded that the Hetmans be restored to their former rights, that no unauthorized person should be present at the meetings of the Senate Council, and that the General Confederation be dissolved because it was unnecessary and harmful to the country.[15] Letters and pamphlets of this type flooded the country, creating excitement and tension in the provincial assemblies and parishes. A vigorous anticourt and anti-Dissident movement grew rapidly, convincing Wroughton, the British Resident, that only force would accomplish the aims of Russia and Prussia.[16]

Repnin, hoping that he might stem the tide of the anti-Dissident movement, attempted to bargain with Sołtyk. On Repnin's suggestion, Wessel, Treasurer of the Crown, wrote to Sołtyk, who was in Kraków, asking him to send a trusted messenger to Warsaw because he had important information which he could not put on paper. Six days later (July 29) a priest arrived in Warsaw from Kraków and attended a late evening meeting at Wessel's residence. Repnin was there. The Russian ambassador wasted no time in coming to the point. He told Sołtyk's messenger that Sołtyk had but two roads open to him, one rewarding, the other disastrous. If he yielded on the Dissident question, he would obtain the favor of the Empress. If he refused and chose to continue his present irritating and inflammatory activities, he would suffer the pain of the Empress's displeasure, which would put him in immediate danger. Repnin warned that Russian troops might invade

[14] Quoted in Rudnicki, p. 108 (July 8, 1766). See also BPAN, 314/57-58.

[15] See Schmitt, II, 45, and BPAN, 314/43-44.

[16] BJag, 101/VII/272-74; BPAN, 314/41-42, 56; Wroughton to Conway, July 23, 1766, PROSP, 88/92; and Schmitt, II, 51.

the Bishop's estates, sequester them, and arrest the Bishop himself.[17]

But threats could not weaken Sołtyk's determination. They would, as he wrote to Wessel on August 1, only increase his zeal.[18] At the same time he wrote to the King describing the meeting that had taken place in Warsaw. He was appalled that bishops were being subjected to threats. He closed his letter by reminding the King of his royal oath to defend the faith.[19] As for himself, he wrote Jerzy Mniszech, Crown Marshal for the Court, "Not only am I completely prepared to sustain the loss of my estates, my fortune, but I am also ready to give my life for the faith."[20]

Sołtyk was prepared, but so was Catherine. This was the greatest obstacle to face her since the election, and she was bent on victory. Once committed to Dissident reform in Poland, Catherine, as Empress of Orthodox Russia, could not retreat—it was a matter of pride as well as policy.

During the summer Catherine had requested and received from other non-Catholic courts their pledges of support for the Dissidents in Poland. Frederick agreed to declare himself on behalf of the Dissidents, but his recommendation would not be as strong as the Russian declaration. He advised Catherine to be careful, because, as he intimated, the Catholics could exert a force greater than she could imagine. He feared that the Poles would involve Austria in their troubles and that this would inflame all Europe.[21] Frederick was equally fearful of the possibility of Poland going completely into the Russian camp. He wrote his Min-

[17] BJag, 101/VII/255; ACz, 1701/147-48; and BPAN, 314/53-54.

[18] BJag, 101/VII/255-58, and ACz, 1701/150-51.

[19] BJag, 101/VII/256-57; ACz, 1701/148-50; and BPAN, 314/53, 55.

[20] Quoted in Rudnicki, p. 111 (Aug. 1, 1766). See also BJag, 101/VII/263-69.

[21] See Wroughton to Conway, Aug. 27, 1766, PROSP, 88/92; Macartney to Conway, Aug. 30, 1766, PROSP, 91/79; Panin to Pushkin, Aug. 21, 1766, Sb, XXVII/1386/63-64/468-69; Solms to Frederick, July 8, 1766, PC, XXV/16150/172-73; Frederick to Solms, July 24, Aug. 25, Sept. 6, 10, 13, and 15, 1766, PC, XXV/16150, 16194, 16210, 16213, 16223, 16226/173, 200, 211, 213, 221, 223 respectively; and Frederick to Benoit, Aug. 17, Sept. 13, and Oct. 1, 1766, PC, XXV/16184, 16222, 16260/193-94, 220-21, 245 respectively. Conway wrote to Wroughton on August 27 that "the King wishes very much to secure to [the Dissidents] the free and uninterrupted exercise of the reformed religion, as well as the recovery of the privileges they formerly enjoyed, it is his pleasure, that you should join with the Russian and Prussian ministers in any representations that it may be thought advisable to make in their favour at the ensuing Dyet." PROSP, 88/92.

ister of State, Hertzberg: "And does it not clearly follow that the Empress of Russia in acting despotically in Poland, and in supporting the Dissidents intends for them to form an independent party in Poland which will obey all her wishes?"[22]

At the same time, Catherine sent Colonels Kar and Igelstrom to Warsaw to help Repnin and provide him with new instructions. Catherine now wanted the Polish court informed that she was taking under her protection all the non-Catholic Christians of the Commonwealth and would not rest until they were accorded equality with the Catholics in all things.[23]

Early in September reports trickled into Warsaw that indicated a victory for the forces of the "traditionalists." The Dietines returned Deputies who would stand fast on the religious question.[24] Repnin threatened Stanislas Augustus by saying that Russia was prepared to send in 40,000 more troops if the Dissident demands were not satisfied by the Diet.[25]

On October 1 Repnin sent Igelstrom to tell the King that he was sending troops to the estates of Sołtyk, but would delay the order if he could have the King's promise to use all his power to obtain the satisfaction of Catherine's demands for the Dissidents. When the King brought this proposition before his council, his ministers stated that they could not agree to such blackmail.[26]

There was no arguing with Repnin, who was merely carrying out instructions. On the eve of the opening session of the Diet, Stanislas Augustus, in a desperate attempt to avert disaster for the Commonwealth, wrote Catherine:

> The principles of universal benevolence have undoubtedly guided your magnanimous soul in wishing a happier fate for the Polish Dissenters, and through the same an amelioration in this Kingdom; but the degree of advantage which should be accorded to the Dissenters must be determined with great justice, to produce in fact this good

[22] PC, XXV/16195/201 (Aug. 25, 1766).

[23] See Schmitt, II, 54.

[24] See Wroughton to Conway, Sept. 3, 1766, PROSP, 88/92, and Kraushar, I, 127-28.

[25] Panin had already informed Macartney that "fifty thousand can do anything in Poland and [he] declared to me a few days since he would [rather] sacrifice double that number and overthrow everything than fail." See Macartney to Goodrike, Aug. 15, 1766, ACz, 2251/111-12. See also Panin to Repnin, Sept. 6, 1766, Sb, LXVII/1393/94-97; and Schmitt, II, 55.

[26] ACz, 653/505.

for Poland, which Your Imperial Majesty wishes to procure for her. The nature of a free state such as ours is incompatible even with the most limited admission to the legislature of those who do not profess the dominant religion. . . .

Your ambassador . . . tells us that Your armies are going to exercise all the power of the sword, if the Diet does not admit the Dissenters to the legislature. . . .

I believe I have clearly explained to Your Imperial Majesty why we regard all that exceeds mere tolerance as an essential evil, to which from conviction we cannot give our consent, and it is impossible for me . . . to believe that You could ever desire to force anyone to do himself an injury. . . . No, once more I have faith; You will not cause the troops You have here to act in a hostile manner, because the Nation will not admit a Dissenter to the legislature and judicature. You are too just and too humane for this.

When You recommend me to the choice of this Nation, You surely did not wish me to become the object of her malediction; neither could You have reckoned upon converting my person into a target to be aimed at by Your arms. I conjure You, nevertheless, to observe that if all that Prince Repnin announced to me is verified, there remains no middle course for me: I must either expose myself to Your blows, or betray my Nation and my duty. You would not have wished me to be King, were I capable of the latter. The thunder is in Your hands; but will You hurl it at the innocent head of him who for so long a time has been so tenderly and sincerely attached to You?[27]

[27] SAPMém, I, 537-39, and Sb, XXII/276/528-32.

He said that the Empress opposed everything that tended to the establishment of a good Government here, therefore, he could never be in cordial friendship with her.[1]

STANISLAS AUGUSTUS TO WROUGHTON

V

THE DIET OF 1766
OCTOBER 6—NOVEMBER 29

Because the General Confederation was still in existence, all the decisions of the Diet would be decided by plurality vote, and thus the Diet could not be broken by the *Liberum Veto*. The first few days of the Diet passed in formalities. The Deputies elected Celestyn Czaplic, Chamberlain of Łuck and Deputy from Kiev, as their Marshal.[2]

Immediately after the session of October 11 was opened Sołtyk delivered a polemic against the Dissidents and their supporters. Sołtyk was heroic—he depicted himself standing before the gates of the Senate, the Deputies, and the Tribunals as a defender against the encroachments of the Dissidents. He was self-sacrificing—if he were to see stones being prepared for the building of a Dissident church, he would place his head under the first one. He was desperate—if no one would help him, he would act alone. Since he was a bishop, it was his duty to defend the Church against any encroachment. Likewise, as a Senator of the Commonwealth, he was responsible for defending the Church in the Diet. To his mind, unity of religion was truly advantageous to every royal government, but many religions, each with vested power and prerogatives, were infinitely harmful. Dissidents, who chose to disturb the peace of the land and who requested foreign powers to aid their cause, should be punished. The only religion was the Roman Catholic faith, and it must be defended with all vigor.

[1] Wroughton to Conway, Oct. 29, 1766, PROSP, 88/92, and ACz, 1984/222.
[2] ACz, 1691/5-7, and ACz, 1692/4-7.

He then submitted a proposal entitled "Security of the Faith."

Desiring to secure as most fundamental our Holy Roman Catholic faith, for centuries dominant in our Kingdom, we promise and establish as eternal law, that no citizen, being of any status or condition, will, at the present or at the future Diets, under any title or pretense, on account of the Dissidents, venture to propose a constringent to the Roman Catholic religion, under the penalty of confiscation of his estates. We reaffirm all the ancient laws regarding this problem.[3]

As he finished reading the last few words, scores of Senators and Deputies rose and exclaimed, "Agreed! Agreed!" They demanded that the proposal be signed immediately and entered in the statute books.

Stanislas Augustus took the floor and praised Sołtyk for his diligent adherence to his duties as a bishop and a Senator. He was proud, he told the Diet, to be the King of a nation that was willing to make sacrifices on behalf of the ancient faith. Calling upon God to be his witness, he stated that he, too, was willing to give his life for the faith. However, he reminded the Deputies, the formalities of Diet procedure made it impossible to accept Sołtyk's proposal that day. Action on it would have to await the conclusion of financial, military, and judicial affairs.

As if there had been no interruption, Sołtyk resumed talking in the same tone and with equal vigor. Since it was a time of peace, he began, there was no need to have Russian troops stationed in the country; everyone knew they were there only to force upon the nation the demands of the Dissidents. He concluded that there was no purpose in keeping the General Confederation since it had long outlived its usefulness.[4] Without allowing discussion of Sołtyk's speech, the Crown immediately introduced a series of financial matters, which were to be considered by the Diet during the next few days.[5]

After a week and a half had passed, the patience of Sołtyk and his staunch adherents began to wear thin. On October 22 a pro-

[3] ACz, 1691/7-11 and ACz, 1692/7-9. See also Wroughton to Conway, Oct. 15, 1766, PROSP, 88/92, and ACz, 1984/215.

[4] ACz, 1691/11-15, and ACz, 1692/10. The Grand Marshal of the Crown, Bieliński, had died a few days before, and Stanisław Lubomirski, the Keeper of the Crown, had been elevated to his position.

[5] ACz, 1691/15, and ACz, 1692/10.

posal for the removal of the general customs toll was submitted. It never entered the discussion stage, however, because the Archbishop of Lwów (Lvov), Sierakowski, declared that since everyone had agreed to Sołtyk's proposal, it should be signed. In response to the statement that only the Crown could call for the reading of projects, Sołtyk only grumbled. Then he and his supporters began shouting that they would not permit any other bill to be read or enacted unless the "Security of the Faith" was enacted into law. The responses to this declaration made it clear that nothing would be accomplished that day.

The Crown attempted to return the Diet to its agenda and ordered that the toll proposal be read. At this point, the Bishop of Kiev, Załuski, jumped up, tore the proposal from the hands of the secretary of the Diet, and began to shove him. Deputies and Senators entered into an exchange of angry words. Just as the clamor began to subside and Załuski was about to take his seat, Poniński, Deputy from Poznań (Posen), cursed him in Latin, and the uproar began anew.

During the tumult, the Crown asked for a vote on the toll bill, which had not been read. Sierakowski cried that he and his compatriots would boycott any such vote if Sołtyk's proposal were not signed immediately. This outburst brought applause from the gallery. Sierakowski was reproached by several Deputies for his disgraceful performance, but the Bishop of Łuck took up Sierakowski's cause by shouting that there would be no vote until Sołtyk's proposal was accepted. Others wanted to speak, but this was impossible; as soon as they took the floor, Załuski shouted over their voices.

The King tried to bring order to the assembly. He began speaking, but it was difficult to hear him. He declared that the proposal on religion would be put on the agenda but in its proper place. The Crown repeated its demand that a vote be taken on the toll bill. Finally, it was carried by plurality, signed, and the session was adjourned.[6]

On October 31 the Senators and Deputies were informed that Repnin was to be given a public audience with the Diet.[7] It was

[6] ACz, 1691/24-28; ACz, 1692/19-22; and VolLeg, VII, 192.
[7] ACz, 1691/50-54, and ACz, 1692/32-33.

common knowledge that Repnin would state Russia's demand that the Dissidents enjoy equal rights, political as well as religious, with the Catholics of the Commonwealth. He was given a red-carpet welcome on the morning of November 4. His speech, which contained all the amenities of parliamentary courtesy, was delivered in Russian and was promptly translated into Latin by the secretary of the Diet. Repnin then submitted the Declaration of his court.[8]

The Declaration[9] was both the clearest expression up to this time of Catherine's demands concerning the Dissidents and a firm warning that she would not tolerate hesitancy or opposition from anyone in the Commonwealth. Although it was unmistakably intended as a lever to pry into the domestic affairs of the Commonwealth, the Declaration did reflect Enlightened philosophy.

On November 10 Benoit, the Prussian Resident, was given a public audience which had the same purpose as Repnin's audience. Although not as lengthy or detailed as the Russian one, the Prussian Declaration also pleaded the Dissident cause.[10]

In an attempt to balance the influence of the Declarations of those courts seeking Dissident reform, the Papal Nuncio addressed the Diet on November 12 and declared that the Diet should under no circumstances allow the Dissidents more privileges than they already had.[11] Before the close of this session, Zamojski announced that on the preceding day Repnin and Benoit had submitted another Declaration, which would be printed together with the Papal Nuncio's and distributed in a few days.[12]

These latest Declarations of the courts of Russia and Prussia concerned a problem of as much importance as that of Dissident reform. During the turbulent months of 1764 the most important consideration of both courts had been the election of the candidate to the throne, and only casual attention had been paid to several

[8] ACz, 1691/54-55, and ACz, 1692/33-34.

[9] See Appendix of this book for the Declaration.

[10] ACz, 1691/55-98; ACz, 1692/35-47; and ACz, 1693/XV-XVI. Great Britain and Denmark also submitted Declarations to the same effect. See ACz, 1693/XVII-XIX. See also Wroughton to Conway, Nov. 1, 1766, PROSP, 88/92, and Frederick to Solms, Nov. 6 and 7, 1766, PC, XXV/16332/291-93.

[11] ACz, 1691/99-108, and ACz, 1692/47-49.

[12] *Ibid.*

of the laws that the Diets had enacted. The two courts had not even objected to the extension of the General Confederation, which effectively provided for greater unity in the country and at the Diet since the *Liberum Veto* was no longer applicable. But the relations between the Polish court and Russia and Prussia had not continued along the most amicable lines. Prussia was annoyed at the establishment of the general customs toll. Both Russia and Prussia were irritated by the cool attitude of the Polish court toward executing Dissident reform.

Nor was this all. There was every indication that the Polish court again intended to reform and strengthen the Commonwealth without asking the advice of Russia and Prussia. Russia and Prussia feared an increase in the taxes and an increase in the army of the Commonwealth. Their Declarations sought to put an end to such tendencies before they might be incorporated into law. The Declarations specifically called for the removal of the plurality vote in matters "which relate to the establishment of taxes and the augmenting of the army. *Unity* depends on *unanimity*. [In this principle] lies the value of the *Liberum Veto*."[13]

This representation, like the one concerning the Dissidents, placed the King in a difficult position. Since his election, Stanislas Augustus had endeavored to deliver the country from her abject condition, but he found himself increasingly without support. He had broken with his uncles and divided "The Family." The split was widened when the Massalskis, disappointed with the law establishing the Commission of the Army for Lithuania, withdrew their support from "The Family." Furthermore, court opposition, centering about the "traditionalists," was being revitalized under the able leadership of Sołtyk, who not only was steadfast on the religious question but also strove for the abolition of the laws of 1764 and for the abolition of the General Confederation. Finally, by his desire for a compromise on the religious question, Stanislas Augustus angered both Sołtyk and Repnin (although for different reasons), and, by his refusal to give up the laws of 1764, he drove the two men closer together.

Stanislas Augustus made his feelings known to Wroughton:

[13] ACz, 1693/XXI-XXVII.

[The King said that] He saw himself upon the brink of the most serious danger, but that he was determined to suffer all, rather than betray his country or act like a dishonest man; that her Imperial Majesty had never pretended to more than procuring [for the Dissidents] the full exercise of their religion, and that he had laboured for many months past on that plan. [He said] that this sudden and violent resolution of the Empress to put them on a level with his other subjects convinced him that Religion was only a pretext, and that She and the King of Prussia, repenting of having placed a man on the Throne that worked for the elevation of his country, were taking measures to overset what they themselves had done; that he waited the event with utmost tranquillity, conscious of having ever acted on the principles of justice and patriotism.[14]

On November 21 Zamojski announced to the Diet that the previous night the Russian and Prussian ministers had demanded that an answer be given to their Declarations concerning the Dissidents and on the Constitution of 1764.[15] On the following day Stanislas Augustus asked Sołtyk to report to the Diet the recommendation of the bishops who had, in council, been deliberating the religious question. Sołtyk began with a plea to God, calling on Him to condemn him if he permitted the Dissidents their former liberties. He declared that he would not be defending the Church if he allowed a heretic to enter the Diet. The bishops had found no foundation to the Dissidents' claims. On Monday, November 24, the bishops, Sołtyk asserted, would present a formal proposal on the Dissident question.[16]

The secretary of the Diet then read a proposal entitled "The Security of the Free Vote." It provided that under no circumstances could the Commissions of Finance and the Army increase the taxes or augment the army without the unanimous consent of the Diet. Oddly enough, there was no discussion of this proposal, and it was carried by a majority.[17]

The King was very much affected by the decision of the Diet. On the following day he told Wroughton that "it was the death's wound for the Republick, and that neither his Crown nor his life was of any value to him." When Wroughton asked him to en-

[14] Wroughton to Conway, Oct. 29, 1766, PROSP, 88/92 and ACz, 1984/221-22.
[15] ACz, 1691/109-35, and ACz, 1692/49-58.
[16] ACz, 1691/139 ff., and ACz, 1692/59 ff.
[17] ACz, 1691/139-54; ACz, 1692/59-63; and VolLeg, VII, 200-4.

deavor to regain the friendship and confidence of Catherine, Stanislas Augustus replied that "there was no way left but sacrificing his conscience, and betraying his Country in the affair of Religion, which he would never think of."[18] The test of his resolution was not far off.

On November 24 Czaplic opened the session of the Diet and asked that the Council of Bishops' proposal on faith be submitted. Zamojski interrupted the proceedings by stating that, in addition to the Declarations of Russia and Prussia on the Dissident question, there were those of Great Britain and Denmark. He asked that they be read to the Diet.

No sooner had the secretary finished than the assembly began clamoring for the reading of the proposal on faith. Chants of "Read, Read, Read" were repeated over and over. Several Deputies wanted to speak but were inaudible because the shouts of "Read, Read, Read," had increased in tempo and volume. Finally the secretary of the Diet rose and began reading the proposal as submitted by the ecclesiastical council. "The Holy Catholic faith," he read, but cries of "Roman!" halted his speech. He began again: "The Holy Catholic faith," but again cries of "Roman!" stopped him. The secretary started once more: "The Holy Roman Catholic faith . . ." and was allowed to continue. The title of the project now announced, he proceeded with the body of the text: "Desiring to secure as most fundamental the Holy Catholic faith . . ." Shouts of "Roman!" interrupted him, but he continued: ". . . in order to block the road to the Dissidents . . ." Interruptions again called for "against the Greek Orthodox and the Protestants." The secretary tried to continue, but constant interruptions made his reading difficult. "All the laws, and particularly of the years 1717, 1733, and 1736, and of the last Convocation Diet of 1764, together with punishments for violations [by persons] of any status or condition, in toto . . ." "For all," "for all," the Deputies shouted. The secretary obliged them: ". . . for all, we reaffirm."

Czaplic asked for a vote, and the proposal was made law by unanimous voice vote. As it was finally put into the statute books, the law "The Holy Roman Catholic Faith" read thus:

Desiring to secure as most fundamental our Holy Roman Catholic

[18] Wroughton to Conway, Nov. 26, 1766, PROSP, 88/92 and ACz, 1984/243.

faith against the Greek Orthodox and the Protestants, we reaffirm all the former laws of our native land, particularly of the years *1717,* 1733, and 1736, and of the last *Convocation* Diet of 1764, *together with punishments* for violations [by people] *of any status and condition, in toto, and for all.*[19]

There were three major results of the closing deliberations of the Diet. First, the General Confederation was dissolved. Second, the foreign courts were given the official answer to their Declarations on behalf of the Dissidents. The Commonwealth promised that it would always respect the rights of the Dissidents according to the laws of the land, especially the Constitution of 1717, and the treaties which had provided for them. Any grievance that might be submitted by the Dissidents would find the Council of Bishops always willing to listen in the hope that justice might be served.

Finally, not submitted as a project but rather as a brochure explaining to the Commonwealth certain freedoms that the Dissidents had, the Council of Bishops announced to the Diet the following points: the rule of tolerance was proclaimed as the law of the realm; where Greek Orthodox and Protestant churches were legitimately maintained, no one was allowed to impede their ceremonies; in accordance with local ordinances these same churches might be repaired and restored but not enlarged; where the ceremonies were lawful and held in a discreet manner, burials for the dead would be allowed to the Dissidents; in accordance with local ordinances, the Dissident clergy were allowed to have dwellings on the grounds of their churches and, where there were no Dissident churches, services might be held in private homes but in a discreet manner; the families of the Dissident clergy were not given any special considerations concerning judicial processes and were subject thereto according to the laws of the land; all matters relating to Dissident church estates and taxes were to be administered under present law; and the Dissidents were not to be hindered in the performance of several of their religious ceremonies which were guaranteed by the laws of the land. Of course,

[19] ACz, 1691/154-69; ACz, 1692/63-64; and VolLeg, VII, 192, 204, 233-36.

these concessions were far from what the Russians had asked for in the Declaration of November 4.[20]

There was no doubt in Wroughton's mind that the position taken by the Commonwealth on the Dissident question was a noteworthy sign of the "fanaticism of the Nation." He believed that Catherine "was too far advanced to stop short, and that there will be no avoiding violent measures."[21]

The Czartoryskis, when asked to intervene on the question and "save their country from impending danger," coldly refused. "They dared not risk even the appearance of mitigation in the [Dissidents'] favour, for it would be certain death to them in the [Diet], and if they should escape there, they would be cut to pieces in the country."[22]

What was to come?

Wroughton, in almost prophetic fashion, reported:

> But if the Empress should resolve to come to hostilities, she might easily find in the innovations that have been introduced since the late King of Poland's death, many plausible excuses for such a démarche, and in that case she would infallibly find three fourths of the Nations willing to Confederate themselves with her, and having them thus in her power, partly by threats, partly by application of promises, and some money, she may find means and opportunities of replacing the Dissidents in ease and authority, and probably the rest of Europe will be afraid, or unwilling to intervene, and may stand aloof, as they did at the time of the Election.[23]

The immediate reaction of Repnin to the law on faith was one of astonishment, but he knew what action Catherine would take in consequence. Panin had already spelled it out to Solms in Petersburg. If the Dissidents were refused admittance to the legislature, then they were to make a formal protest and proceed to form a confederation, which would be under the direct supervision of Repnin.[24] Moreover, the other discontented elements in Po-

[20] ACz, 1691/207; ACz, 1692/70-74, 295-97; VolLeg, VII, 214, 221-22, and BJag, 101/VII/379-80.

[21] Wroughton to Conway, Nov. 26, 1766, PROSP, 88/92.

[22] *Ibid.*

[23] *Ibid.*

[24] Solms to Frederick, Oct. 14, 1766, PC, XXV/16318/280-81.

land were to be called upon and organized into a confederation which would sustain the Dissidents and act against the Czartoryskis. Catherine would support these confederations with money and troops—even 40,000 troops, if necessary.[25]

[25] Solms to Frederick, Oct. 21, 25, and 27, 1766, PC, XXV/16332, 16334/289-295, *passim*, and Macartney to Conway, Nov. 23, 1766, PROSP, 91/77.

It is necessary to resolve the Dissident affair not for the sake of propagating our faith and the Protestant in Poland, but for the sake of acquiring for ourselves, through our coreligionists and the Protestants, a firm and reliable party with the legal right to participate in all the affairs of Poland.[1]

PANIN TO REPNIN

VI

THE DEMENTIA OF POLISH POLITICS DECEMBER 1, 1766—OCTOBER 5, 1767

King Frederick II of Prussia was unhappy about the way the Dissident question was being handled. Though he supported the granting of religious freedom, he opposed the Dissidents' becoming the political equals of the Catholics in Poland.[2] Since Russia had taken the lead in Dissident reform, it was logical to expect that the Dissidents, believing Catherine to be their deliverer, would obediently carry out her wishes in Polish affairs. Catherine would no longer have to seek out groups of discontented Catholic Poles to do her bidding, as she would have established her own political party, the Dissidents. Frederick, therefore, would have little or no influence in determining the course of Poland's history. Moreover, he feared that other European countries would intervene in Polish affairs on behalf of the Catholics. This might lead to serious trouble—even war—and Prussia would be involved. Frederick pleaded with the Russian court to follow a policy of moderation. He wrote to Solms:

> The Dissidents in Poland have their churches, and in Holland the Roman Catholics practice their religion and possess their churches. What would [Panin] say, if France were to invade Holland in order to force the Estates-General to admit the Papists to the public charges, and if on this occasion, England seconded the Hollanders? Would he not say that France had been the aggressor? Apply this to the present situation in Poland. You could not deny that Russia had no right or

[1] Quoted in Sergei Mikhailovich Solov'ëv, *Istoriia Rossii s drevneishikh vremën*, XXVII, 482-83 (Aug. 25, 1767).

[2] Frederick to Solms, Dec. 28, 1766, PC, XXV/16418/345-46.

authority to march her troops into Poland to impose laws on the Poles. . . . The Russians are the aggressors. . . . If Russia involves me in this quarrel, my defensive alliance with her will change into an offensive one; the difference between the two is very great.[3]

Frederick's cautious words had no influence on the vain Catherine and the stubborn Panin. Using threats and relying upon former friends in the Commonwealth had not obtained the desired Dissident reform. But the Russian court was not lacking in other means to gain the same end. A new policy was launched on December 6, 1766, when a leading Dissident publicly protested against the harmful laws enacted by the Diet.[4] The King and the Czartoryskis could no longer be relied upon, and henceforth Repnin would have to seek his support from their enemies—the "traditionalists" and the Dissidents themselves.[5]

There would surely be no objection from the Dissident leaders to such collaboration. However, the "traditionalists," who for a long time had sought to reduce the power of the King and his uncles, would have to be convinced that Russian support was worth their yielding on the Dissident question. The first step in this direction was to obtain the agreement of the leaders of the "traditionalist" group to the establishment of a confederation.

Repnin needed the aid of someone who knew the "traditionalists" well and whose word would be respected by them. This assistant had to be someone whose personal ambition would drive him hard to complete his mission and keep him attached to Repnin long enough to reap his reward. In Father Gabriel Podoski, Repnin found these qualities.

Podoski had a long and sincere friendship with several leaders of the "traditionalist" group, of which he was a member, such as Karol Radziwiłł, Jan Klemens Branicki, Bishops Sołtyk and Krasiński, and the Potocki family. During the interregnum he had opposed "The Family." After the election he, like so many others, returned from exile and became a steadfast adherent of the court opposition. Despite his clerical position, Podoski was willing to

[3] *Ibid.* 16423/348-49 (Dec. 31, 1766). See also Solms to Frederick, Jan. 27, 1767, *ibid.* XXVI/16493/51-52.
[4] ACz, 1694/5-6.
[5] See Wroughton to Conway, May 11, 1767, PROSP, 88/94.

compromise the Catholic faith by allowing for Dissident reform. For his services Repnin promised to reward him handsomely —he could expect money and, more important, the Primateship after Łubieński's death.

Podoski would deserve his reward because his mission was both arduous and delicate. He was to canvass the "traditionalist" group and determine whether they would be willing to become the dominant political party in the Commonwealth under the protection of Russia. He was to tell them that Russia no longer had any faith in "The Family" and wished to elevate another party, whose views were closer to her own. Podoski was to intimate that Russia even contemplated dethroning the King. The less devout would secretly be asked to support the Dissident reform program, while the others would be asked only to maintain the traditional laws of the Commonwealth. As a vehicle to execute these designs, Podoski was to tell them that they were to form a General Confederation in the Commonwealth.[6]

The mission was successful. Podoski visited Bishops Sołtyk and Krasiński, Wessel, Mniszech, Branicki, the Potockis, and many others. All agreed to ask Catherine for her protection and favored the idea of a confederation. They suggested that Karol Radziwiłł, who was in exile in Dresden, be Marshal of the confederated forces. Acting on their suggestion, Repnin offered Radziwiłł amnesty and the restoration of all his estates if he chose to lead the confederated forces and would be obedient to Catherine's wishes. On February 28 Radziwiłł wrote to Repnin that he would accept the amnesty and would lead the confederated forces, carrying out Catherine's wishes to the letter.[7]

With Radziwiłł's acceptance Russia was able, in March, to begin executing her plans. The initiative in forming the confederations was taken by the Russian army officer in the field. Detachments of Russian troops were deployed throughout the provinces, invad-

[6] Henryk Schmitt, *Dzieje panowania Stanisława Augusta Poniatowskiego,* II, 159-63; Solov'ëv, XXVII, 469-70; and Claude de Rulhière, *Histoire de l'anarchie de Pologne,* II, 327-29.

[7] The original of Radziwiłł's letter is not available in the Polish archives. Władysław Konopczyński (See his *Konfederacja barska,* I, 88-90) found it in the Moscow archives. See also Schmitt, II, 163-65, 175-76; Solov'ëv, XXVII, 470, and SAP Mém, I, 554-55.

ing every major Dissident stronghold. Dissidents were called together and finally united in confederations.

An interesting description of the formation of a confederation is given by a town official of Toruń (Thorn). He writes that the Catholics were in fear of their lives. The Dissidents entered the town first but were soon followed by Russian soldiers under the command of General Soltykov. All the gates were put under guard. The printing shops were invaded and could print only what they were told by the Russians. Soltykov then declared to a crowded market square that the confederation which was to be established had the protection of the Empress of Russia and that it was the will of the people. He invited other towns to join. He threatened that anyone opposing the confederations would be treated as an enemy. But in spite of these warnings, the town officials refused to sanction the confederation under the town's name. The officials declared that only the King had such a right. The deliberations continued into the night, but still the manifesto was not signed. "Perhaps, tomorrow!" the writer concludes.[8]

On March 20 the Confederation of Słuck, composed mainly of Greek Orthodox, was established for Lithuania. Its Marshal, General-Major Jan Grabowski, a Calvinist, was ably assisted by Bishop Koniski.[9] Four days later Toruń confederated, representing the Protestants of Little Poland and Greater Poland. Count George von Goltz, a Lutheran and a General-Lieutenant in the Prussian civil service, was elected Marshal.[10] Several weeks later (April 10) Gdańsk and Elbląg acceded to the Toruń Confederation because of the urging of Frederick (who reluctantly supported Catherine's policy in Poland rather than lose her friendship) and the Russian guarantee of independence to the great commercial town on the Baltic, Gdańsk.[11]

[8] ACz, 1694/21-22 (March 22, 1767). See also Wroughton to Conway, March 11, 1767, PROSP, 88/94, and Gibsome to Mitchell, March 28, 1767, BMAddMSS, 6828/164-65.

[9] ACz, 1694/7-12.

[10] See ACz, 1693/CIII-CXVIII.

[11] See "L'Acte de L'Accession . . ." PROSP, 88/94; Wroughton to Conway, April 8, 1767, *ibid.;* Frederick to Solms, Feb. 22, 1767, PC, XXVI/16511/72. The only copy I found of the Russian guarantee of Gdańsk is an English translation dated March 24. "We Catherine 2nd by the grace of God Empress of all the Russias etc., declare & make it known to all whom it may concern, that as the Empress

The demands of the two Confederations, as proclaimed in separate manifestos, were similar. Manifestos usually began with a prologue on the historical development of the injuries inflicted upon the Dissidents and ended with a demand for equality with the Catholics and an alleviation of their present condition. For example, the manifesto of the Toruń Confederation contained the following:

We, the knights and inhabitants of the provinces and the Crown, as Dissidents of the evangelical confession, have, for half a century, endured sorrow because of the appalling fate of birth and the conditions belonging to it. We are opposed to such further distress and affliction and, after suffering such disagreeable and numerous injuries, hope, finally, for only a favorable alternative. Distressed and deprived of consolation, we do not expect to be made happy. At the last three

---

Anna of glorious memory, for herself & her successors has been pleased to grant to the city of Danzig at its humble request by a diploma dated the 29 of April 1736, her most gracious interposition to the end of that city might not be molested in its rights and liberties, possessions, and customs, as well in religious as other matters, but more especially in the rights of its harbour and fortifications under any pretext, but be preserved and guaranteed in the full enjoyment thereof, we renewed and guarantee in most solemn manner in the year of 1764 and do now by this our own diploma again give the city our most gracious word and assurance partly of our natural clemency and generosity, partly that on account of the constant trade with our countries and subjects and its convenient harbour it greatly concerns us that the city remain unchangeably in its present system, that we will most powerfully protect it against all and every demand, claim or pretense already made or that may in future be made on the same, and grant it our most high interposition to the end it may be preserved without any reduction or molestation in the fullest enjoyment of its former rights, liberties, privileges, customs, as well in church as other affairs especially in possession of its lands and territories in its sea—and trade—Port—mint—and fortification rights.

"In case and also on account of the Dissidents in Poland, Lithuania, and the countries thereto belonging whom We have taken under our protection to restore their insulted rights, and liberties, hostilities or a war (which pray God graciously to prevent) sho'd ensue the said city of Danzig making part of the Dissidents in Prussia, if it joins the common good cause, shall not only enjoy the like protection from us, but in case it sho'd on this occasion suffer any damage in its estates, wealth, and incomes, or in rights on setting or making peace and indemnification of all such damage shall be negotiated for it and all its rights and privileges be most strongly guaranteed by us, and those high powers connected with us in the Dissident affairs and sufficiently secured against all demands or requisitions on acco't of the past. Finally if the city sho'd in future be molested or marked by any one in its rights and liberties it shall take its humble recourse to us and our successors as formerly and may be assured of meeting with all possible redress protection, and assistance. . . . Given in Moscow this 24 March 1767 [signed by Catherine, Panin, and Golitsyn]." See the enclosure in Suffolk to Gunning, Dec. 22, 1772, BMAddMSS, 35504/193.

Diets, the Convocation, the Election, and the Coronation, and the one following the last, not only were our petitions refused, but also we remained oppressed Dissidents according to the rigorous and severe laws of the Convocation Diet. Our innocence, fortified by justice, has not found a defense against the above-mentioned universal injuries, and, therefore, in protecting ourselves against many violences, we protest and solemnly manifest, as a matter of honor, that not only were the former laws of the years, 1573, 1576, 1581, 1588, 1627, 1632, 1648, 1660, 1668, 1674, and others concerning the Dissidents, abolished, but that the prerogatives of birth and the *szlachta* estate are inseparable, by virtue of the sacrifice of the blood and lives of our forefathers. This is a basic principle. If from time to time various personal persecutions were inflicted upon us by various kinds of contrivances, they should arouse pity and improvement of our situation. . . . We have been made unequal to our fellow inhabitants of the realm, as to laws and freedoms: these injuries are, without qualification, unjustified. It is difficult not to complain when grieving, and it is difficult to keep silent when deprived of a voice in the protocols of the Tribunals, districts, towns, consistories, and others.[12]

The news of the Dissident Confederations supported by Russian troops quickly spread through the country. A perturbed Sołtyk on March 20 wrote to a friend that in his three conversations with Podoski "nothing was mentioned concerning the Dissidents." "But," he continued, "now all the news assures us that the Dissidents confederate with the assistance of Russia. What was the significance at first of consulting us about a confederation, if the confederation would not be against the Dissidents, and we would not unite with them because they have other aims?"[13]

However disturbing the Dissident Confederations may have been, the only organized opposition came from an unusual quarter of the Commonwealth—the Jews. They confederated in Lublin (Lemberg) on March 26 and published a manifesto, asserting that if any religious group were to be given equality with the Catholics in the Commonwealth it should be theirs. After all, they had a stronger claim; theirs was based on the law of Moses, while the Dissidents had only Martin Luther.[14] The opposition of the

[12] ACz, 1693/CIII-CXVIII, and ACz, 1694/7-12.

[13] Quoted in Kazimierz Rudnicki, *Biskup Kajetan Sołtyk, 1715-1788*, pp. 150-51. See also ACz, 820/347; ACz, 1696/125; Mitchell to Conway, March 28, 1767, BMAddMSS, 6810/97; and Macartney to Conway, March 24, 1767, PROSP, 91/78.

[14] ACz, 1693/364-65.

Jews was but a formality and could do nothing to stop the Dissidents.

Meeting with Repnin on May 3, the "traditionalist" group, led by Franciszek Potocki, Mniszech, and Bishop Krasiński put one question above all others: Did Russia intend to depose Stanislas Augustus? Repnin was evasive. All he would commit himself to at that time was that after their confederations were formed and Catherine saw that they were truly interested in becoming the dominant party of the Commonwealth, they could ask her for anything and she would probably grant them their wishes. Apparently satisfied with this answer and without discussing the religious question, they turned their attention to plans for confederating the country. It was decided that each province would begin uniting its *szlachta* into a confederation. When this was accomplished, representatives of each confederation in the Crown and Grand Duchy lands would meet and confederate. The summit of this pyramiding device would be a General Confederation of the Commonwealth sometime in June.[15]

That evening at an informal gathering of Polish nobles, Stanislas Augustus approached Repnin on several points. At first he asked whether the rumors were true that Radziwiłł was returning to the country under the protection of Russia and that he and Stanisław Brzostowski, the *starosta* of Bystrzyca, were going to establish confederations in the Crown and the Grand Duchy. Repnin answered affirmatively. The King then asked about the intention of the Russian court in doing this. Repnin told him that Catherine desired the calling of an extraordinary Diet to settle the Dissident question once and for all and that this was the best means of achieving such an end. Furthermore, Repnin added, Catherine wanted to guarantee the Commonwealth by a treaty between the two countries.[16]

Activity quickened in the provinces during May. From every corner of the Commonwealth, first in small groups and then in larger ones, the *szlachta* met and united under the bond of confederation. Although their work had the character of frenzy, it was

[15] See Schmitt, II, 186-87, and Ernst Herrmann, *Geschichte des russischen Staats,* V, 415-16.

[16] SAPMém, I, 569-74.

by no means disorganized—the Russian officers made certain of that. The manifestos that each confederation published were almost identical in form, if not in the words themselves. The manifesto of the General Confederation of the Grand Duchy of Lithuania, which elected Stanisław Brzostowski as Marshal, is a good example of the principles contained in such documents.

The opening lines were mere formality, but they were followed by sentence after sentence of grievance. The confederates had been quiet until now, but with the recent changes in the fundamental laws of the country this was no longer possible. Under the pretext of defending the faith, the last Diet wanted to establish absolutism. That was why the malcontents had united under the bond of the General Confederation, to defend the freedoms and laws of the Commonwealth. They would keep the Confederation until an extraordinary Diet was convened under the protection of the Empress of Russia. Catherine was a monarch who was the friend of the confederates, so much so that she wished to help and protect them, to guarantee their laws and their freedoms. They did not organize against the King and sincerely hoped that he would join them in maintaining the ancient laws of the land. The *szlachta* of the Greek Orthodox and the Protestant faiths should be equal to the other *szlachta* in the Commonwealth. It was impossible to be silent when they were unhappy. However, the confederates did not intend to show disrespect for the Catholic faith or remove the prerogatives from the clergy. Eulogies to Catherine filled the closing lines of the manifesto.[17]

Facing the established Confederations, the Senate Council met on May 25 to decide what to do. In reality it had no choice but to call an Extraordinary Diet. Major opposition to this decision came from Archbishop Sierakowski of Lwów, but on the advice of the Senate Council the King announced the calling of an Extraordinary Diet for October 5.[18]

Returning from Dresden, Radziwiłł arrived at Wilno on June 3 and was welcomed jubilantly. Ten days later he reached Ra-

[17] ACz, 1693/315-16, 321-41, 345-50, 353-64, 366-68, 374-84, and ACz, 1694/15-21, 31-32. See also ACz, 962/No. 15.

[18] ACz, 820/352-53; ACz, 1694/23-31; ACz, 1696/129, and ACz, 878/173-80.

dom, a town not far from Warsaw, to arrange the General Confederation of the Crown lands.[19] On June 22 deliberations began at Radom between Colonel Kar and the leaders of the Confederations of the Crown lands. At first several demanded that the Russian troops leave the town in order to facilitate an open and free discussion. Kar refused. He then submitted a manifesto which was to serve as their act of confederation. Except for the dates and places, it was identical with the manifesto of the General Confederation of the Grand Duchy of Lithuania.

By mid-afternoon Russian troops had thrown a cordon about the town, and guards were placed at the main gate—no one could enter or leave without Kar's permission. More than one hundred troops were placed at the town hall; Cossacks patrolled the streets. On the evening of June 23 the signing of the manifesto began. Without mentioning the dethronement of the King, and with one exception, it duplicated the Lithuanian manifesto. Because they had protested so severely, the signatories were permitted to add a clause next to their names. They usually followed the example set by Franciszek Potocki who was the first to accede to "everything, excepting what could be against the laws of the land and the Holy Roman Catholic faith." Karol Radziwiłł's election as Marshal of the General Confederation of the Crown was then saluted by twenty-four Russian guns.[20]

The Russian guns saluted also the successful completion of the first stage of Russian policy—a policy which could hardly be misunderstood by anyone. Even a foreigner just passing through knew the meaning of it all. Malmesbury, an Englishman, recorded:

In consequence of not having paid the least attention to the . . . declarations of the Empress . . . in which the griefs of the Dissidents were set forth, and redress demanded, she had marched near twenty thousand men into the country, and gave out, that she would redress the grievances of the mal-contents who, to the number of sixty thousand, were then confederated, with Prince Radzivil at their head. This Confederation was caused by the jealousy of some of the great. . . . This

[19] See Schmitt, II, 199-200; ACz, 1693/317-19, 384-85, 391-92; and BJag, 101/VII/449-52.

[20] ACz, 1694/33-48, 51-57, 88-89, and ACz, 1693/403-11, 431-37. See also Wroughton to Conway, June 27, 1767, PROSP, 88/94.

gained a great number of Poles to her side, who being bitter enemies, of the Court, flattered themselves that by this means they should overthrow the King; and were so eager on this subject, that they never gave themselves time to reflect that the establishing of the Dissidents was the chief object of Russia.[21]

Like sheep, the spiritual and lay dignitaries of the Commonwealth who had not attended the proceedings at Radom began acceding to the General Confederation. On July 4, from Borzęcin, a town not far from Radom, Sierakowski wrote an amazing letter to the other bishops of the Commonwealth.

Desiring to consider closely the most delicate circumstances continuing in the country, I have approached the environs of Radom . . . to arrive at an understanding as to what to do in this situation. I went to the house of the Prince Bishop of Kraków, where the Bishop of Kamieniec was. We deliberated with due attention whether or not the Spiritual Senators should join the movement of Confederation. On the one hand, it seemed to us that our Estate and vocation should stand as a strong dam defending the approach to the Confederation, which includes in its act the broad and high demands of the Dissidents, for the preservation of the wholeness and prerogatives of the Holy Roman Catholic religion. . . . On the other, we would put ourselves, our estates, our subjects, the clergy, and the government in danger if we stood aloof from the Confederation. The consequence of such a danger would be so much the worse for the religion, the laws, the freedom, and the jurisdiction of the clergy if we would give occasion to the Nation to make resolutions about us but without us according to the fancy of their projects. It seemed to us that our descendants would be astonished with our indifference to action if we were to stand aloof from all these acts. We detect that, when all the Nation is united not for vanity but for splendid achievement, there is more hope for the useful service of our motherland, which is surrounded by dangers to the religion and the church, and that there is more to be gained from our joining the Confederation than standing aloof from it. For this and similar reasons, it is our strong conviction to join the Confederation. . . . I am full of hope that you will not condemn our step but rather, for the same reasons, that you will join your hands with ours. . . . This is being done in order that we shall obtain laws, prerogatives, and deeds useful to the Nation, by this means and not by any other and that by our endeavor of faith, sworn to God and country,

[21] Third Earl of Malmesbury (ed.), *Diaries and Correspondence of James Harris, First Earl of Malmesbury*, I, 13-14.

we shall remove everything which might plot injury to the religion, church and country. I am waiting your reply with anxiety.[22]

Sierakowski did not have long to wait, for on August 21 the leading bishops of the Commonwealth acceded to the General Confederation.[23] To their names were added those of lay dignitaries, including Jan Klemens Branicki. Branicki acceded with the usual reservation that no harm should come to the dominant religion or the ancient form of government and also added something on his own—he wanted the restoration of the privileges of the hetmans of the Commonwealth.[24]

The suggested *quid pro quo* in Branicki's accession was quite understandable, especially in light of Podoski's elevation to the Primateship on July 17. Primate Łubieński had died on June 21, and Repnin immediately suggested to Stanislas Augustus that the Crown of Poland request Podoski's elevation. The King refused. How could he seek the highest spiritual office for a well-known political opponent? Repnin was insistent, and on June 22 wrote to Kazimierz Poniatowski, the King's brother, that he should do all he could to persuade the King to seek Podoski's appointment. "I repeat, very decidedly, and it is well-known to all," Repnin said, "that we do not do anything halfway. Therefore, if you love the King, persuade him to grant [this], to feel that he should not hesitate."[25] Convinced that he would win over the King, Repnin sought support from the clergy. What more influential person could Repnin ask to intercede with the Holy See than Bishop Sołtyk? Repnin's request to a person who had always been his enemy, a person whom he contemplated imprisoning, was an amazing stroke. But more surprising than Repnin's boldness was Sołtyk's affirmative reply. Sołtyk addressed the Papal Nuncio on June 25, stating that Podoski

is not only of upright and excellent birthright, but also has every honorable quality of a prelate, and has the capacity to obtain the respect

[22] ACz, 1694/57-59.
[23] BPAN, 649/210, and ACz, 1693/502.
[24] ACz, 1693/392-95, 417-18, 452, 466-71; ACz, 1694/90-91, 121-25; and ACz, 873/71-73. See Gibsome to Mitchell, July 8 and 11, 1767, BMAddMSS, 6828/231, 233, respectively.
[25] Quoted in Schmitt, II, 197.

of all foreigners and neighboring governments. Because he is my [colleagues'] choice and my good friend, I take this occasion to recommend him most strongly to Your Excellency along with the request that You would condescend to honor him with Your favor and as much as You are able to hasten the arrangement of the usual formalities for his promotion. Your Excellency is well aware of the fact that the Extraordinary Diet is scheduled for October 5, and that it is indispensable to us that, under a new Primate . . . the assembly of Bishops might prove effectual in the sensitive questions over which they will deliberate, and in which Podoski, having the favor of the neighboring powers, will be able with profit to resist the strange imaginary claims of the Dissidents, and without fail he will work with greater effort if Your Excellency would oblige him with Your favor.[26]

Schmitt considers this step of Sołtyk's "an enigma."[27] Rudnicki seems to think that Sołtyk's support of Podoski was founded on his belief that Podoski sought to overthrow the King and that as Primate he would have a better chance for success.[28] There seemed to be no real or understandable reason for Bishop Sołtyk's support of Podoski, and therefore we must attribute his action to poor judgment or to imaginative optimism.

On the other hand, in the forwarding of Podoski's name, the Poniatowski family was not above suspicion. If one can rely on the information of the British agent in Moscow, the Poniatowskis sought to gain the Bishopric of Kraków for one of their party. To justify their claims, they recalled the energy exerted to obtain the Primateship for Podoski, an effort that surely warranted some compensation.[29]

Nevertheless, there should be no doubt as to what role Podoski would play in executing Russian policy in the future. Repnin wrote to his court on June 25:

This accession of Podoski will greatly increase Russia's influence in the Commonwealth. Podoski was openly attached to me and worked . . . as my secretary. After the elevation of [Podoski] to Primate, the entire country will perceive how splendidly we reward, openly and

[26] Quoted *ibid.*, pp. 197-98.

[27] *Ibid.*, p. 198.

[28] Rudnicki, pp. 156-57.

[29] See Shirley to Wroughton, July 13 and 14 and August 19, 1767, BMAddMSS, 37054/24-25, 31-32, respectively; Shirley to Conway, July 16, 1767, *ibid.*, p. 26; Wroughton to Shirley, August 5, 1767, *ibid.*, pp. 5-6. Nothing came of the request.

sincerely, those who serve us. . . . The King would not be able to refuse the foremost dignitary in the Commonwealth, who was the principal coworker for the establishment of this Confederation.[30]

The months of July and August were busy ones and kept the scribes in full employment. On July 3 Stanislas Augustus in a Universal officially called for the convocation of the Dietines on August 24 and the Extraordinary Diet on October 5.[31] Three days later the General Confederation of the Crown, led by Radziwiłł, issued two declarations expressing the desire to maintain the Catholic faith as the dominant religion in the country but at the same time wishing to administer justice to the Dissidents by satisfying them in their grievances.[32] On July 11 the General Confederation of the Crown declared itself the highest authority in the land and declared that everyone was to be obedient to its laws.[33] On July 17 and 20, respectively, delegations from the General Confederations of Lithuania and the Crown addressed Stanislas Augustus and invited him to support their confederations. The replies from the King were perfunctory. The King loved his subjects; he had already called for the Extraordinary Diet; and he requested that the Confederations keep the peace and ensure the security of the country until the Diet convened.[34]

Although the Commonwealth was for the moment commanded by two Dissident Confederations and two General Confederations (the latter two were to be united during the first week of August), which were nominally supported by thousands of the *szlachta,* either by coercion or voluntarily, it was the Extraordinary Diet that would decide all issues. The key to the power of the Diet lay in the Dietines. It was, therefore, important to Repnin that the Dietines return "suitable" Deputies, who would follow the precepts already laid down by the Confederations and not act independently. To this end a lively campaign, characterized by a flood of propaganda and the shadow of the Russian soldier, was begun.

On July 24 Karol Radziwiłł penned a letter to all the Dietines

[30] Quoted in Schmitt, II, 197-98. See Gibsome to Mitchell, July 8, 1767, BMAddMSS, 6828/231.

[31] ACz, 1693/395-96.

[32] *Ibid.,* pp. 397-403, 419-21, and ACz, 873/9-12.

[33] ACz, 1693/396-97, 454-59.

[34] *Ibid.,* pp. 414-19, 423-25.

urging them to support the future acts of the General Confederation.[35] During the same week, Branicki and Bishop Krasiński also wrote. The former outlined a proposed agenda for the Diet, which followed closely the demands of the confederations and stressed the need for the laws of the land to be guaranteed by the Empress of Russia.[36] The Bishop's letter indicated a return to his former views. The Catholic religion, he said, must not be infringed upon—the Dissidents must be limited to their present rights. He opposed the incursion of Russian troops into the Commonwealth. Moreover, the Commonwealth should enter into no alliance, defensive or offensive, with any state.[37] On August 10 Michał Rzewuski followed Krasiński's lead by calling upon the King "to condescend to obtain the evacuation of foreign troops from the Commonwealth."[38] Five days later Sołtyk added fuel to the fire with a vitriolic criticism of anyone attempting to subvert the laws of the land or give the Dissidents more than they already had.[39]

Repnin was not to be outdone in this propaganda campaign. On August 10 he reiterated Catherine's intention not to injure the Roman Catholic faith, but he also stated that equality was the basis of freedom. He called upon the Dietines to send good patriots to the Diet.[40] But Repnin had something more to work with than the quill, and he made this clear to Józef Pułaski, *starosta* of Warka, who had previously played an insignificant role in Polish politics. Apparently Pułaski was also beginning to penetrate the maze of double-talk he had heard at Radom, because he balked at giving the Dissidents anything more than their present position called for. Repnin snapped at him: "I will place 15,000 [troops] at the Diet, and the Diet will be compelled to do what the Dissidents demand with the protection of the Empress." Pu-

[35] *Ibid.*, p. 427, and BPAN, 1144/52-53. See Wroughton to Conway, Aug. 5, 1767, PROSP, 88/94.

[36] ACz, 1694/91-93 (July 29, 1767). See also ACz, 962/No. 52.

[37] ACz, 1694/93-95 (July 30, 1767).

[38] ACz, 1693/426-27. August Czartoryski resigned as President of the Commission of the Army for the Crown. See Wroughton to Conway, Aug. 5, 1767, PROSP, 88/94.

[39] ACz, 1693/513-16; ACz, 1694/97-8; and ACz, 962/No. 53.

[40] ACz, 1693/511-13.

łaski replied with equal vivacity: "One hundred thousand are too few, because a free nation, citizens zealous for the faith and freedom, will attain such courage and desperation, that for the faith and freedom they will be ready to shed their blood and lose their lives."[41]

An example of the pressure Repnin exerted on the Dietines is afforded by the description a chronicler gives us of the Dietine of Wisznia (near Lwów). On August 23 the Deputies of the Dietine, as they were proceeding to church for mass, were halted by a Russian colonel and were invited to his quarters, where they discussed the method of electing their representatives to the Diet. On the following day, before the Dietine session opened, a cordon of two columns of Russian troops were placed around the church in which deliberations were to take place. The Russian colonel then announced that no one would be allowed to enter or leave the town. Censorship was not complete, however, for in addition to Repnin's letter requesting Dissident rights, Sołtyk's letters were also read. On August 26 all the Deputies of the Dietine were supposed to elect the representatives to the Diet. However, at four o'clock that morning a group of hand picked *szlachta* met under the protection of Russian soldiers and elected seven deputies who would follow the bidding of Repnin.[42]

With individual opponents, Repnin acted equally severely, placing them under house arrest and preventing them from standing as candidates at the Dietines. On August 27 Major-General Peter Krechetnikov received orders from Repnin to occupy all the villages of the Bishopric of Kraków (Sołtyk's) and appropriate all the grain and livestock necessary for the army.[43] On the following day Repnin asked Panin for permission to arrest and imprison Sołtyk and a few others, because if they continued their opposition he could not guarantee the results of the Diet.[44]

[41] Władysław Konopczyński, *Kazimierz Pułaski, życiorys,* p. 16.

[42] ACz, 1693/535-37. For similar examples elsewhere see BPAN, 1144/381-86. See also Wroughton to Conway, Sept. 5 and 12, 1767, PROSP, 88/94, and Solov'ëv, XXVII, 486-87.

[43] SAPMém, I, 575; Schmitt, II, 247-48, 260; and Rudnicki, p. 168.

[44] See Rudnicki, p. 166. Wroughton wrote to Conway on Sept. 19, 1767: "I am persuaded [that Repnin] has taken the resolution to arrest [Sołtyk] & convey him down the Vistula in case of necessity, & Your Exc. must not be surprised to hear

In September, the Deputies to the Extraordinary Diet began to arrive, and once again the center of the political activity of the Commonwealth shifted to Warsaw. It was difficult to discern what the Deputies' feelings were toward the faith and the laws of the land—their views had changed so often during the year. The Extraordinary Diet would operate under the bond of confederation, and therefore decisions would be reached by plurality vote, which gave Repnin some assurance that Russian demands would be met. But just to make things more certain, he placed troops about the town.

---

of so extraordinary a proceeding. The ending of this affair is so important, that the Ambassador must not hesitate at formalities, and such a measure if well conducted, will not fail to curb the rest of the Chamber." PROSP, 88/94. See also Wroughton to Conway, Sept. 30, 1767, PROSP, 88/94.

Gentlemen, I warn you not to disturb the Diet session when the bills which you have already approved are read. If any Deputy should oppose or block the bills, restrain him yourselves. If there is any opposition, I shall finish as I have started. I warn you, if it comes to this, I shall order the arrest not only of three but of thirty.[1]

REPNIN TO TREATY COMMISSION

VII

THE CONFEDERATED EXTRAORDINARY DIET OCTOBER 5, 1767—MARCH 5, 1768

Early on the morning of October 5 the Papal Nuncio paid an unexpected visit to Radziwiłł's residence, where the confederate leader and several other marshals had gathered before the session of the Diet which was to open later that day. The Papal Nuncio had with him breves from Pope Clement XIII, and he expressed the deep concern of the Holy See for the preservation of the Catholic religion in the Polish realm. "From time to time the Dissidents have stirred terrible tempests, which are now aimed at your Catholic church," he said. "We should continually appeal to God with ardent prayer in order that this time help will arrive and scatter to the winds these boisterous multitudes and restore the former tranquillity."[2]

The Papal Nuncio quickly departed. Spontaneously the marshals began pledging to each other that they would defend their faith to the death. Then Repnin entered from an anteroom where he had been waiting and listening. He announced that the Diet would delegate a commission to discuss with him questions of faith and freedoms. This precipitated shouting from the marshals, who called for defense of the faith. Repnin declared that nothing would be accomplished by shouting. If there was to be

[1] ACz, 1694/404 (Feb. 26, 1768).

[2] ACz, 825/1-8; BPAN, 1139/49-52; and ACz, 873/91-92. The breves were dated September 12, 1767, in Rome.

a competition of loud noises, he assured them, in the end his voice would be heard above all others. The bells of St. John's announced the tenth hour, and the gathering proceeded to mass.[3]

Outside the holy walls the ominous shadow of Russian soldiers blanketed the streets of Warsaw. About 8,000 soldiers had surrounded the city, while some 2,000 were encamped on the Russian ambassador's garden, which was not far from the Diet Chambers. To an observer, Prince Repnin "for the time being, was in every respect absolute monarch."[4]

After mass the Senators and Deputies returned to the Diet. Radziwiłł and Brzostowski took the seats usually reserved for the Marshals of the Diet.[5] Radziwiłł then had the secretary read a bill entitled "Act of Adjournment."[6]

The opening lines of the bill explained that the Estates of the Crown and the Grand Duchy of Lithuania were united under the bond of the General Confederation for the purpose of "maintaining the national freedom as well as for improving the defects of the motherland." It was to Catherine that the Commonwealth must look for guidance. Therefore, an embassy had already been sent to Catherine to thank her for her friendliness to the Commonwealth and to request that she give her "supreme guarantee" of the laws and freedoms of the Commonwealth. Furthermore, the Confederated Estates also assured Catherine that "their fellow citizens, the Greeks and the Protestants," whom she and her allies supported, would be accorded "justice and satisfaction." What was still lacking was the sincere "declaration of recognition" on behalf of the Commonwealth of Catherine's guarantee of the Commonwealth's "laws and the form of [its] government." In order to do this, it was necessary that a Commission of Deputies and Senators (including delegates from the Confederations of Toruń and Słuck) of the present Diet be chosen and be vested with plenipotentiary power to negotiate and sign a treaty with Repnin. It was therefore necessary that the present Diet be ad-

[3] ACz, 825/4-8.

[4] Third Earl of Malmesbury (ed.), *Diaries and Correspondence of James Harris, First Earl of Malmesbury*, I, 11-12.

[5] ACz, 825/9-11.

[6] *Ibid.*, pp. 11-14.

journed until February 1, 1768, at which time it would reconvene to ratify the decisions of the Commission.[7]

Sołtyk was the first on his feet as the secretary finished reading the bill. He agreed that such a Commission be chosen but not that it should negotiate any treaty with Prince Repnin. "Treaties," he said, "either military or for purposes of maintaining peace, are concluded between powers as new alliances. We are not at war with Russia and we are told of no new demand for an alliance in the Declaration of Her Imperial Majesty. . . . What treaties, I ask, concerning the Dissidents have been broken, and what laws of the Nation concerning the the Dissidents have been abrogated?" The Commonwealth should allow the Commission "only the power of discussion." He reminded the King of his royal promise made at the last Diet to defend the faith with his life.[8]

Sołtyk's remarks were seconded by Wacław Rzewuski, who let it be known that he was prepared to sacrifice his life and property for the defense of the faith and the liberties of the country. "If God were to allow our immortal, noble and illustrious forefathers who gave their blood and lives for the faith and for freedom to arise from their graves and stand here in the midst of the assembly of this Diet of the Estates, they would see awful attempts being made on our faith, the horror of the dismanteling of our ancient laws." They would ask, were these men Poles? But were not Poles ready to sacrifice their lives to defend the faith? What had happened to these people?[9] Sołtyk wanted the floor again, but the session was adjourned until the following day.[10]

The next morning Archbishop Sierakowski, in a clear and logical presentation, began criticizing the premises and claims of the General Confederation and the Confederations of Toruń and Słuck. The King's Universal, said Sierakowski, called only for a discussion of the Dissident question, and therefore no other matter could be discussed—even though the General Confederation thought so. Since the Dissidents had in 1717 obtained a definite clarification of their position, which had been guaranteed by

[7] VolLeg, VII, 244-45, and BPAN, 1139/43.
[8] ACz, 825/15-17; ACz, 1693/572-75; and BPAN, 1139/45-46.
[9] ACz, 825/17-18; ACz, 1693/575-76; and BPAN, 1139/47.
[10] ACz, 825/18. See also BPAN, 649/210.

Peter the Great and had not since then been infringed upon, it was the responsibility of the Dissidents, not the Diet, to prove their claims. He was not opposed to the Empress's guaranteeing the laws of the land. But why, he asked, limit this guarantee to but one power? Why not invite other powers to join—for example, the Catholic powers?[11]

By this time the patience of the Deputies and Senators had worn thin. From all sides of the Chamber they arose and began speaking with undisciplined enthusiasm. Finally, Kazimierz Poniatowski, the King's brother, stated that the important "Act of Adjournment" should be given the customary time for discussion, but since it was so closely linked with the "Plenipotentiary" bill the two should be discussed jointly. Sołtyk agreed, and the secretary was ordered to read the second bill.[12] This bill provided the Commissioners with full plenipotentiary powers to negotiate and conclude agreements with Prince Repnin. When the Commissioners completed their business, the Diet would be obliged to ratify automatically whatever the Commissioners had agreed upon.[13]

During the next few days private and separate meetings of the Deputies and Senators took place, according to the region of the Commonwealth they represented. These meetings were not compulsory and therefore were not always attended by all. The consensus at all the sessions was opposed to allowing the proposed Commission to have decisive power in determining for the Commonwealth its laws concerning religion and civil liberties.[14]

Equally interesting, and perhaps more important, were meetings between Radziwiłł and Michał Czartoryski. On October 8, Michał Czartoryski asked Radziwiłł not to make trouble for him at the courts of the General Confederation. During the lifetime of the General Confederation, these courts held the supreme judicial power in the Commonwealth even over the regular royal courts. Radziwiłł told him that he had nothing to worry about. Two days later Michał Czartoryski paid his respects to Radziwiłł

[11] ACz, 825/19-23; BPAN, 1139/53-56; and BPAN, 649/210-11.
[12] ACz, 825/24-29; ACz, 1693/580-81; and BPAN, 1139/57-61.
[13] VolLeg, VII, 246-48, and BPAN, 1139/44.
[14] ACz, 825/30.

and informed him that if ever he needed his help in the future, he would always be at the Marshal's service.[15]

On October 13 the Senators and Deputies deliberated in their regional assemblies the proposals that had been presented to the Diet. The most vitriolic criticism came from the meeting of Little Poland where Sierakowski and Sołtyk led the campaign. The King was attacked for delaying the votes on the bills because he knew that they would fail, and there was a solid agreement that there was no need for Russian troops to be in the country. The discussions lasted until the evening. Sołtyk, not going to his residence, accepted an invitation to dine with Mniszech, the Crown Marshal for the Court.[16]

When Sołtyk was about to leave Mniszech's residence at ten o'clock, he noticed that Cossacks had surrounded the entire area. A few minutes later Mniszech's servants entered the room in a frenzy, declaring that Russian troops were breaking down the gates. Within minutes Colonel Igelstrom entered. "I have an order for your Excellency's arrest." Indignantly Sołtyk questioned him: "Sir, do you know that I am the Prince Bishop of Kraków and a Senator of the Realm?" "I know, but you, sir, are under arrest." It was useless to argue. Sołtyk agreed to go and said goodbye to Mniszech, asking him to save the country. He entered the waiting carriage, which sped away through the heavily guarded streets.[17] About an hour later Russian troops arrested Bishop Załuski, Governor Rzewuski, and his son, Seweryn. They were all taken to Repnin's residence, where they met with Sołtyk, and eventually were dispatched to Russia.[18]

At noon on October 14 a Declaration appeared, signed by Repnin, which explained the abductions.

The Army of Her Imperial Majesty . . . friend and ally to the Confederated Commonwealth, has arrested the Bishop of Kraków, the Bishop of Kiev, the Governor of Kraków, and the *starosta* of Dolin because in their activities they forgot the dignity of Her Majesty, the

[15] *Ibid.*, pp. 30-31.

[16] ACz, 1693/597-98; BPAN, 1139/68-73; and ACz, 653/529.

[17] ACz, 825/45-47; ACz, 1693/581-82; and BPAN, 1139/72-75. See also Malmesbury, I, 14.

[18] ACz, 825/47-50, and BPAN, 1139/75-77.

Empress, blackening the integrity of her wholesome designs, which are unselfish and truly friendly toward the Commonwealth. Let it be known that the General Confederation, being the united Crown of Poland and the Grand Duchy of Lithuania, is under the protection of Her Imperial Majesty, and is indeed assured of the solemn continuation of this protection.[19]

The following day a delegation headed by the Primate requested the King to appoint a committee to speak to Repnin concerning the release of the dignitaries and the possibility of his guaranteeing the Diet deliberations against interference. The King complied. As the committee departed for the Russian ambassador's residence, Zamjoski entered the King's chamber and submitted his resignation as Grand Chancellor because he could no longer bear the responsibility for the crimes being committed against the Commonwealth. The King retired to his chapel.[20]

The committee returned an hour later and informed a gathering of Deputies and Senators that there was no hope of obtaining the release of the dignitaries. Repnin had stated, moreover, that anyone daring to oppose the General Confederation, would be considered an enemy of the Empress of Russia. In a remorseful voice Stanislas Augustus told them that he believed it was too late to do anything about saving the dignitaries—they must now do everything to save themselves. The path they must follow, the King said, was a very narrow one with great depths on either side.[21]

Angry, frustrated, but also fearful, the Deputies and Senators took their seats in the Senate Chamber on October 17. A score of Deputies and Senators, each in his turn, lamented the abduction of the notables. But this all came to naught. On October 19, the "Act of Adjournment" and "Plenipotentiary" were accepted by the Diet, which was not to reconvene until February 1, 1768.[22]

Sixty-eight members of the Diet had been appointed to the Commission to negotiate with Repnin. However, numbers were of little value, and "negotiate" was just a word in the bill establishing

[19] ACz, 825/50; BPAN, 1139/78; ACz, 1693/567-68; and ACz, 873/101-2.
[20] ACz, 825/54-55.
[21] *Ibid.*, pp. 55-57.
[22] *Ibid.*, pp. 75-78; BPAN, 1139/86, 90; and VolLeg, VII, 245-50.

the Commission. Technically, the meetings, which began on November 4 and closed on February 26, were to be held three times a week with the chairmanship alternating between the Primate and Repnin. Actually, meetings were frequently postponed and subcommittees were appointed to draw up draft bills for later approval by the Commission as a whole.

One of the most important matters, religion, was from the first guided by six points that Repnin presented at the meeting held on November 7. First, the Dissidents were to be accorded complete freedom in the performance of their religious ceremonies. Second, all disputes involving the Dissidents were to be decided by courts made up of jurors of mixed faiths. Third, the Dissident *szlachta* were to be given equal status with Catholics and Uniats. Fourth, Dissidents were under no circumstances to be judged by Catholic clergy. Fifth, wherever they were, Dissidents were to be given the right to build their own churches and were to be free to hold services in them. Last, there was to be equality in the assessment of taxes.[23]

Because the Commission was unable to complete its work by February 1, 1768, the Diet was postponed several times. Finally, on February 27, the Diet convened, and the report of the Commission was submitted in the form of the "Perpetual Treaty Between the Polish Commonwealth and the Empire of All Russia."

The most important parts of the treaty were Articles II, III, and V, and the separate and supplementary sections which served as further explanation of these articles. Article II provided that "both High Contracting Parties agree to mutually guarantee the territorial integrity of their possessions—the land, provinces, and the frontiers—in Europe; most solemnly *et sacrosante* for all times." Article III granted extensive and detailed "lay and spiritual" rights and privileges to those of "the Greek Orthodox faith and the Protestants of both Evangelical confessions" in the Polish-Lithuanian Commonwealth and its annexed provinces. Article V provided for the guarantee of "the constitution, the form of government, the laws . . . the maintenance, the preservation, and the protection of the territorial integrity of the Majestic Pol-

[23] ACz, 1694/325-404, especially 326-27, and ACz, 875/1-112, especially 28-29.

ish Commonwealth" by Catherine and "the successors to the Imperial throne of All Russia."

For several days the Diet, except for one spontaneous outburst of protest, listened quietly to the reading of each article. On March 5 it unanimously ratified the treaty. The General Confederation was dissolved, and the Diet was adjourned.[24]

Catherine had now succeeded in her maximum program for Poland. Never in history had Russia obtained such influence over the Commonwealth. Other foreign powers soon displayed jealousy of Catherine's success—not because they desired Poland to be free and untroubled, but because they could not view with indifference the growing power of a state that might some day endanger their own existence. The first to object was Turkey; she demanded that Russian troops evacuate Poland if Russia wanted to keep the peace. Feeling quite secure in Poland, Catherine ordered Repnin to send the Russian troops home.[25]

[24] ACz, 825/81-101; BPAN, 1139/119-24; and VolLeg, VII, 244-82. See also ACz, 874/5-62, 65-89. The Papal Legate Durini protested against the treaty and declared that the Catholics of the Commonwealth were not bound to obey it. See ACz, 1693/647-55, and ACz, 1694/295-96, 304-7.

[25] See Sergei Mikhailovich Solov'ëv, *Istoriia Rossii s drevneishikh vremën,* XXVII, 511-15; Wroughton to Weymouth, Feb. 24, March 2 and 9, 1768, PROSP, 88/96; Malmesbury, I, 30; and Panin to Repnin, Jan. 29, 1768, Sb, LXXXVII/1631/20-22, and Panin to Obreskov, Jan. 31, 1768, Sb, LXXXVII/1635/28-32.

You are in rout because you began without a plan, without a system, and without negotiation or an understanding with other powers. . . . Time has shown that this project was very short-sighted for such a great work. Meanwhile, the Muscovites who were leaving remained on the pretext of preventing the country from being damaged and plundered. Horses, arms, and all military equipment were seized on the pretext of disarming the nation. Villages were deserted. Those who wanted to come together were scattered to the different ends of the earth. Moreover, the country is now full of brigands.[1]

BISHOP ADAM KRASIŃSKI TO JÓZEF PUŁASKI

VIII

THE CONFEDERATIONS OF THE COMMONWEALTH AND THE OUTBREAK OF THE RUSSO-TURKISH WAR FEBRUARY 29-OCTOBER 6, 1768

Nineteen days after the Extraordinary Diet had adjourned, when it was thought that the "Polish Question" was solved, twenty-eight Senators hurried to a Council meeting called by the King. In reality, it was Repnin who summoned the Senators. There was a sense of urgency in the air; they had been called to discuss a matter of importance—a matter important enough for Repnin to halt the evacuation of Russian troops from Poland.[2] Earlier that week the Commission of the Army for the Crown received reports from local Polish commanders in Podole to the effect that a confederation was being formed at the small fortress town of Bar. The commanders requested instructions and, in the meantime, deployed their troops throughout the area as a precautionary measure.[3]

[1] Quoted in Władysław Konopczyński, *Konfederacja barska,* I, 121-22.

[2] See Wroughton to Weymouth, March 2, 9, and 23, 1768, PROSP, 88/96; Third Earl of Malmesbury (ed.), *Diaries and Correspondence of James Harris, First Earl of Malmesbury,* I, 30; Konopczyński, I, 38-39; and Sergei Mikhailovich Solov'ëv, *Istoriia Rossii s drevneishikh vremën,* XXVII, 514.

[3] ACz, 878/239-48; Benoit to Frederick, March 12, 1768, PC, XXVII/17112/90-91; Wroughton to Weymouth, March 12 and 29, 1768, PROSP, 88/96; and Solov'ëv, XXVII, 515.

The Senate was divided in its opinion. Some did not trust the reports of the local commanders. The Czartoryskis refused to comment because, as they explained, they had been out of touch with the current political situation for so long. Others were disposed to put an end to the apparent conspiracy but did not want to employ Russian troops. Finally, on Repnin's insistence, the Council "agreed" on March 27 to request Russian aid because the Bar incident seemed to violate the recent Russo-Polish treaty. The Commission of the Army for the Crown was instructed to reinforce its local fortresses. At the same time Repnin made preparations for deploying the Russian troops under his command.[4]

When exactly did the Bar conspiracy originate? Who supported it? What was its purpose? As more information filtered into Warsaw and circulated among the small cliques of the politically active, many of the queries were answered. Although there is a paucity of documentation, historians have been able to reconstruct a thin narrative.

It will be remembered that there was considerable opposition to the Polish court and to the Russian policy in Poland even before the opening of the Extraordinary Diet. It centered first in the Radom Confederation, when several of the *szlachta* refused to sign the manifesto, and was then epitomized by Bishop Kajetan Sołtyk and his associates during the election to the Diet. For their opposition, their "defense of the faith" and the "Golden Freedoms," Sołtyk and his colleagues had been rewarded with imprisonment and forced exile, but not before they had succeeded in laying plans for a conspiracy against the King and Russia. Clandestine meetings were held in Warsaw and its suburbs. They were attended by several of the leading figures of state—Sołtyk, Branicki, Mniszech, Wessel, Radziwiłł, the Potockis, the Rzewuskis, Bishop Adam Krasiński, and his brother Michał, Chamberlain of Rozań—and some less important figures, including Józef Pułaski. Various plans and ideas were discussed by the group, but nothing definite was decided upon and therefore only a general idea of their purpose can be ascertained.

[4] ACz, 1696/130-33; ACz, 878/213; Wroughton to Weymouth, March 16, 29, and 30, 1768, PROSP, 88/96. See also Solov'ëv, XXVII, 515-16, and Konopczyński, I, 36-41.

First, all Europe, especially the German courts, was to be awakened to the Russian menace. Poland was to be represented to the Germanies as a "barrier." Deputations were to be sent to Berlin, Versailles, Vienna, and the Porte to request financial and diplomatic support. Under the protection of Turkish troops a confederation was to be established at Lwów. Stanislas Augustus was to be deposed, a new monarch elected, and the crown made hereditary in his line.

The arrests of October 13, 1767, deprived the conspiracy of several of its ablest leaders and frightened others, but did not stop the movement. Two days earlier Bishop Krasiński had left Warsaw disguised as a doctor and made his way to Kamieniec. From there he sent a trusted messenger to the Porte with letters explaining the recent abuses by Russia. Krasiński then departed for Dresden via Wrocław (Breslau), which he reached at the end of January 1768. He wrote his comrades that he was going to seek foreign help and that they were not to do anything until he had secured it and Russian troops had evacuated Poland. The Bishop's plans were totally disregarded, however, by the impatient Józef Pułaski, who decided to take matters into his own hands.[5]

Józef Pułaski had retired to his estates at Winnica before the Diet had opened. There, with his sons and his close associate, Father Marek Jandołowicz, he decided not to wait until foreign support was assured before beginning the confederation. In January he went to Lwów to meet other conspirators, namely Archbishop Sierakowski, Marian and Ignacy Potocki, and Jan Czarnecki, Castellan of Kiev. Their activities were noticed by the local commandant, and they withdrew to the nearby town of Kukizów to continue their discussions. In the meantime, Józef's two older sons, Franciszek and Kazimierz, were sent into the provinces to marshal support. The discussions continued at Kukizów until February 28, when the party went to the small town of Bar in Podole, which would henceforth serve as the base of operations.[6]

[5] See Konopczyński, I, 22-26, 109; Henryk Schmitt, *Dzieje panowania Stanisława Augusta Poniatowskiego,* III, 25-35; and Władysław Smoleński, *Dzieje narodu Polskiego,* pp. 281-82.

[6] See Konopczyński, I, 26-29, and Władysław Konopczyński, *Kazimierz Pułaski,* p. 18.

On the following day Michał Krasiński arrived at Bar, and the Confederation was established. Its principal purpose was announced in the opening lines of the manifesto: "We, the Councils of the Dignitaries, officials of the *szlachta,* and citizens of the Crown, the Wojewodztwa, the lands, and the districts of the Province of Little Poland, assemble to deliver the country, the faith, the liberties, and the national laws and freedoms from impending ruin." The present free and independent Polish nation, the manifesto continued, had been brought to this abject position through the unjust laws enacted during the interregnum. The manifesto then reviewed the history of the last few years, lamenting the fate of the several dignitaries who had been imprisoned by Repnin. The Extraordinary Diet had not been freely held because Warsaw had been surrounded by several thousand Russian troops. Likewise, the Commissioners had been forced to sign a treaty that undermined the ancient faith and liberties. The Barites were confederating in the ancient tradition to liberate the country from oppression and to remove the ominous guard that stood over Karol Radziwiłł and others. The Barites had wanted to elect Radziwiłł as their Marshal, but he was in the custody of the Russians. Therefore, Michał Krasiński was temporarily elected as Marshal of the Confederation, with Józef Pułaski as Regimentary General. The manifesto concluded with several procedural points, including the levy of money, confederation courts, and an intended *levé en masse.*[7]

One ceremony and public announcement followed another. Declarations of allegiance to the Confederation balanced the denunciations of the laws passed and injustices committed during the last few years. On March 4 a formal ceremony took place which established the Army of the Confederation. This was followed by several appeals to all parts of the Commonwealth calling for military support.[8]

[7] ACz, 878/221-27, and BPAN, 1145/126-31, 142-43.

[8] See ACz, 878/229-30, 235-38; BPAN, 1145/121-25, 132-34, 140-41, 151-53, 155, 158-60, 167-93, 201-3; and ACz, 945/40-50. The neighboring Turko-Tartar leaders had repeatedly been asked for diplomatic and military support. See ACz, 945/10-17, 34-35.

A profoundly religious ceremony was conducted on March 6 at the Carmelite monastery of which Father Jandołowicz was prior. A special Confederation regiment was established as the Order of the Knights of the Holy Cross, Józef Pułaski being elected its Grand Master. The Order reflected the extreme religious conviction of this Confederate leader. There was a special oath of allegiance which, among others, contained the following principles: The members were to defend the Holy Roman Catholic faith with their lives; each member was bound to obey commands and to execute orders faithfully, even at the risk of his life; the emblems of the Order were to be Lord Jesus and the Holy Mother, and the motto, "Jesus, Mary, and Joseph"; no correspondence was to be carried on with enemies of the Holy Roman Catholic faith or with those Catholics not committed to the Confederation; a special uniform and equipment were prescribed together with the size of companies; also, the plans of the conspiracy were to be kept secret, and any willful violation of its rules was to be punished by death.[9]

By mid-March Józef Pułaski and Michał Krasiński engaged in battle the local Crown detachments in Podole; on Marsh 23 Sandomierz confederated, echoing the principles announced at Bar; and on March 31 Wawrzyniec Potocki skirmished with the Don Cossacks at Nowy Konstantynów.[10] In April the movement picked up momentum when several important members of the *szlachta* joined the Bar Confederation, and Halicz (Galicz) and Lublin confederated after the example of Bar.[11] On May 2 Joachim Potocki confederated Bracław.[12]

In the first few months the Confederates had the advantage. The suddenness of the move at Bar, the slowness of communications, the delays of the Warsaw councils in calling for Russian intervention, and most of all the disorganization and dispersion of the Crown and Russian armies favored the Confederate position. Major-General Peter Krechetnikov was ordered into Podole to

[9] ACz, 1701/123-27.
[10] BPAN, 1145/543-44, and Konopczyński, *Konfederacja barska,* I, 44-45.
[11] See Konopczyński, *Konfederacja barska,* I, 46-47, 527. See also BPAN, 1145/225-29.
[12] BPAN, 1145/262-69, 280-81.

restore the peace, but it was not until April that he was able to march.[13]

The advantage of the Confederates was short-lived, however, and the Confederates themselves were to blame. They had been warned repeatedly by Bishop Krasiński not to attempt a confederation before a systematic organization had been worked out, until foreign support was forthcoming, and until the Russian troops had left the country. For the conspiracy to be successful, it was necessary that all three conditions be satisfied. But the Confederates did not heed the Bishop, and they were to suffer the tragic consequences.

Although every confederation had announced that it was following the example of Bar, each one maintained a separate and independent marshal and a group of councilors, not to mention a militia that was obliged to follow the commands of its confederation only. There was no mechanism for efficient communication between one confederation and another, and each confederation considered itself the equal of the others. The loyalty of several of the leading adherents was doubtful; for example, Franciszek, Marian, and Teodor Potocki again and again pledged allegiance to the Polish court after having signed the Confederate manifesto. Joachim Potocki did not give his full support to the Confederates until he believed the Porte would support their cause.

Moreover, when military campaigns were planned they were individual undertakings, and sometimes one confederation would compete with another to capture a fortress or a strategic position. The lack of patience, organization, and foresight on the part of the Bar Confederates cost them dearly. They had undermined the conspiratorial movement in the Commonwealth and also suffered the loss of foreign support when it might have been possible to obtain it.[14]

As early as April the Turko-Tartar leaders announced that they would not support the Confederates unless the Confederates could produce a strong and unified organization.[15] On

[13] See Solov'ëv, XXVII, 515-16; Shirley to Weymouth, March 29, 1768, BMAddMSS, 37054/83; and Konopczyński, *Konfederacja barska,* I, 52-57, 90. See also Frederick to Benoit, March 30, 1768, PC, XXVII/17130/104-5.

[14] See Konopczyński, *Konfederacja barska,* I, 48-50, 109.

[15] See ACz, 945/24-26, 36-37, and BPAN, 1145/247-48.

April 26 Bishop Krasiński arrived in Dresden and was told that Saxony had already given Russia its word that it would not negotiate with the Bar Confederates.[16]

The Saxon court's decision to support Russian designs in Poland was based on self-interest. The British Resident summed it up well: "Many, however, here are persuaded the troubles in Poland will hardly cease till the present King is dethroned, nay flatter themselves that the Elector will be chosen in his stead, but not without the Court of Petersburg, the friendship of which this Elector hourly seems resolved to cultivate by all imaginable means, and the nicest attention."[17]

When Choiseul in France received news of the Bar Confederation, he decided to take advantage of it in the hope that it would weaken the Russian position in the Commonwealth. On April 17 he sent the Chevalier de Taulès to the Confederates in the guise of a horse dealer. Taulès was to assure the Confederates that the King of France would favor any means they might employ to free themselves of the oppression to which they had been subjected. Taulès was given letters of credit for the Confederates and was to inform them that, if they so desired, French military officers would be sent to help them. However, under no circumstances was Taulès to reveal his mission and compromise the dignity of the King if he found the Confederates to be nothing more than "one of those ephemeral movements to which Polish flightiness is given." It was precisely this situation that Taulès found and reported back when he arrived in Poland on May 8. The Confederates were in a state of confusion, dissension, ignorance, and disorder. "It did not take me long," he wrote, "to see that the Confederation was lost." He declined to assist the Confederation and burned his credentials.[18]

No help came from Vienna either. Krasiński and Potocki were told that the Empress-Queen did not choose to interfere in the Pol-

[16] See Carroll to Hume, April 30, 1768, PROSP, 88/97; Frederick to Benoit, May 28, 1768, PC, XXVII/17252/186; and Konopczyński, *Konfederacja barska,* I, 115. Ignacy Potocki, who arrived at the Saxon court a day later, was no more successful than the Bishop. See Konopczyński, *Konfederacja barska,* I, 117.

[17] Carroll to Fraser, May 22, 1768, PROSP, 88/97.

[18] See RIDA, V, 272-81, and Baron de Vioménil, *The Private Letters of Baron de Vioménil,* pp. 2-5.

ish affair.[19] Even the Papacy, occupied as it was with the Catholic question in other parts of Europe, did not answer the appeals of the Confederates.[20]

While there was thus no prospect of international intervention at this time, the tumult that the Confederates caused in Poland made a profound impression at the neighboring courts. The Porte was irate and again demanded the evacuation of Russian troops from Poland. It was correctly imagined in Warsaw that the court of Versailles "push'd & animated" the Turks in the hope of engaging them in a quarrel with Russia. Obreskov, the Russian envoy at the Porte, wrote Repnin that the Porte could no longer avoid forming an observation corps on the frontiers of Poland. A magazine had already been set up at Chocim and more than thirty thousand bushels of corn had been requisitioned. Although Frederick wrote to Benoit on April 3 that he believed the "new Confederation which has arisen in the Ukraine [Bar Confederation] will not be of importance and not have any immediate seriousness," ten days later he wrote to Rohd at Vienna that he began to suspect Austria and France of encouraging the Porte to interest herself in Polish affairs. Kaunitz himself, after receiving reports of Turkish troop movements, seemed "much displeased with the appearance of affairs in Poland, averse to the hostile intentions of the Turks, and afraid of the consequences." Frederick became more concerned as the days went by. If the Russian troops remained in Poland, the Turks would take umbrage and meddle in Polish affairs, and this, he thought, would certainly involve the Austrians. Wroughton was perceptive as usual: "For my part, I look on a war to be inevitable, and that Russia will find herself more embarrassed than she imagined, from the troubles of this country."[21]

All this not unnaturally had the effect of depressing Stanislas Augustus. The King told Wroughton that it "cut him to the soul

[19] See Stormont to Rochford, Dec. 1, 1768, BMAddMSS, 35500/50.

[20] Konopczyński, *Konfederacja barska,* I, 120-21.

[21] See Shirley to Weymouth, April 1, 1768, BMAddMSS, 37054/85; Langlois to Weymouth, April 20 and 23, 1768, *ibid.* 35500/37; Wroughton to Weymouth, April 6, 9, 23, and 27, 1768, PROSP, 88/96; and Frederick to Benoit, April 3 and 27, 1768; Frederick to Rohd, April 13, 1768, PC, XXVII/17136, 17192, 17161/108, 146, 126, respectively.

to see his subjects and countrymen [delivered] over to ruin and slaughter," that "the major part [of them] were acting on honest principles of fighting for their laws and Religion." The King was aware that he had lost the public confidence, partly owing to his ignorance of the country's needs and partly from the malice and jealousy of those who had always been his personal enemies. "If he detached himself from, and declared against, Russia, those enemies would be the first to make their peace with Russia and sacrifice him; and what advantage, said he, could I procure to my Nation even supposing this sacrifice was not to happen?"[22]

But it was not Stanislas Augustus who was to make the telling decisions—that privilege had been taken away from him a few years before if, indeed, one can say it had ever been given to him. It was the Russian ambassador who was responsible for the fate of Poland, not the King. In the past, when Repnin wished to quell a disturbance or win over a stubborn opponent, he availed himself of negotiation, bribery, or direct force. In the present situation, there was no question in his mind as to what means he should employ to quiet the country. Obreskov, the Russian ambassador to Turkey, urged Repnin to put an end to the Confederate affair in order to stay on good terms with the Porte.[23] To this end Repnin was sent additional forces. Although there is no exact accounting available, tens of thousands of Russian troops did reach Polish soil during 1768.[24] This force, combined with the loyal Crown forces under the command of Ksawery Branicki, began to entrench itself throughout the whole Commonwealth. By the beginning of May, Repnin was able to direct the entire offensive against the Confederated forces from Warsaw, and he sent out instructions accordingly.[25]

The impatience of the Porte grew. Turkey had given public assurances that it would take no part in Polish affairs and would not place an army upon the borders of Poland, and had sent instructions to all its provincial commanders not to deal with the Confed-

[22] Wroughton to Weymouth, May 11, 1768, PROSP, 88/96, and ACz, 1984/273-74.

[23] Solov'ëv, XXVII, 520.

[24] A plan describing the estimated number, the command, and the deployment of troops for 1768 provided for 95,760 men to be in Poland. See BPAN, 316/1.

[25] See ACz, 945/82-86. See also ACz, 966/77-80, and Wroughton to Weymouth, May 25, 1768, PROSP, 88/96.

erates. But the question still remained as to how long this pacific policy could be maintained. Obreskov was told in no uncertain terms that if Russian troops remained on Polish soil the Porte could not guarantee its policy of noninterference.[26]

Repnin was well aware of the sensitive international situation. From the moment new detachments of Russian troops entered Poland, general orders were issued that they should not go within fifteen miles of the Turkish frontier while executing military operations. However, it became increasingly difficult to pursue the Confederates (who, when in retreat, made for the Turkish border), and this limit was reduced first to ten miles and later to five—a thin margin to respect.[27]

The major battles with the Confederates took place in June, and victory went to the Russian and Crown armies. On June 14 Berdyczów, under the command of Kazimierz Pułaski, fell.[28] Two days later the seat of the confederation movement came under attack, and on June 20 Bar surrendered. Father Jandołowicz was captured, but Józef Pułaski, Michał Krasiński, and Joachim Potocki escaped into Turkish territory.[29]

On the same day a group of Confederates pursued by Russian troops crossed the Turkish border at Bałta. However, they were not safe, because a Zaporozhian Cossack leader razed the village and massacred everyone in sight.[30]

On June 21, before the news of the surrender of Bar had reached them, the *szlachta* of Kraków confederated.[31] But no sooner had they pledged themselves to defend the faith and expel the Russians

[26] See Murray to Shelburne, May 17, 1768, PROSP, 97/44, and Mitchell to Weymouth, May 28, 1768, BMAddMSS, 6810/151. See also Gibsome to Mitchell, June 4, 1768, BMAddMSS, 6828/299, and Shirley to Weymouth, June 6, 1768, BMAddMSS, 37054/98.

[27] See Konopczyński, *Konfederacja barska,* I, 132, and Murray to Shelburne, June 15, 1768, PROSP, 97/44.

[28] See BPAN 1145/309, 311, 312, 335; Wroughton to Weymouth, June 22 and 29, 1768, PROSP, 88/96. On June 9 Poznań and Kalisz confederated. See Konopczyński, *Konfederacja barska,* I, 528.

[29] BPAN, 1145/309, 312, 320-21, 334-35. See also Gibsome to Mitchell, July 2, 1768, BMAddMSS, 6828/301.

[30] See Zegelin to Frederick, July 16, 1768, PC, XXVII/17391/290-91; BPAN 1145/99; Konopczyński, *Konfederacja barska,* I, 136; and N. D. Chechulin, *Vneshniaia politika Rossii v nachale tsarstvovaniia Ekateriny II,* pp. 297-98.

[31] BJag, 101/VII/672-74, and Jadwiga Krasicka, *Kraków, ziemia krakowska wobec konfederacji barskiej.*

than they were put to the test. The city was immediately under siege, and the struggle lasted until August 17, when the Kraków Confederation was forced to capitulate.[32]

The Confederates were troubled from another quarter. During the summer Greek Orthodox peasants, in revolt against their landlords, also began to war against the confederate detachments in eastern Poland. The *hajdamaks,* as the revolts came to be called were not initiated by St. Petersburg and, at most, could be attributed to the individual action of Russian military commanders in the field. Repnin himself, despite the fact that the *hajdamaks* tended to weaken the confederate position, feared the possibility of such a movement spreading to the western provinces of Russia and endeavored to stop the peasant rebellion.[33]

Repnin had not anticipated that the Perpetual Treaty of 1768 and his firm policies in Poland would result in such widespread discontent and revolt. Even though the confederate movement was decidedly disorganized and did not seem to be making progress along the lines it had publicly announced, the offensive against it was expensive for his court and personally irritating. Whatever reputation he may have built up at home by virtue of having concluded the Perpetual Treaty seemed to be swept away in the face of the civil war that was raging in Poland. Repnin had resorted to force to suppress the confederate movement, but no sooner had one provincial confederation been dissolved than another was established somewhere else. Repnin's policy of retaliation had not resulted in speedy victory but had degenerated into a war of attrition. The longer the war continued, the lower Repnin's reputation would fall at St. Petersburg. The consequence of his seeming failure to execute properly the policies announced by his court would also reflect on his father-in-law, Panin, and give his opponents at the Russian court an opportunity to diminish the powerful influence Panin had with Catherine.

[32] See BPAN, 1145/318, 336-37, 377-82. From the end of June to the end of July several other confederations were proclaimed—in Wołyń, Sanok, Chełm, Wieluń, Oświecim and Zator, Sieradz, and Gostyń—but not all lasted as long as Kraków's. See Konopczyński, *Konfederacja barska,* I, 86-88, 526-29, and BJag, 101/VII/664-70.

[33] See Konopczyński, *Konfederacja barska,* I, 68-71; and *Z dziejów Hajdamaczyzny,* Vols. V and VI of *Dzieje porozbiorowe narodu Polskiego w żywem słowie.*

Another means of pacifying the nation had to be found, and it was thought that some of the greater nobles might aid the Russian court. The question that arose, however, was: Which nobles were capable of leading the nation to peace with Russia, and, if they were found, would they be willing to do so? The confederacies of the Commonwealth had divided the *szlachta* into many camps. Several that at one time had sided with Russia—for example, in the Radom Confederation—were now opposing the court of St. Petersburg.

Karol Radziwiłł could not satisfy Russia's desires. Recently he had begun receiving emissaries from the Confederates, and, although the exchange was never made, negotiations for 6,000 of his militia in return for 12,000 ducats were secretly begun. Rumors were current that he would join the Confederates and thus add one of the most prominent names of Lithuania to the movement.[34] There was also Jan Klemens Branicki, whose compromise-tainted past (in 1763 and 1764 he had opposed Russia; in 1765 he was allowed to return from exile but continued his opposition to the court and Russia; in 1767, for personal reasons, he sided with Russia by joining the Radom Confederation but within a few months participated in the councils of Krasiński and Pułaski) qualified him for the task, but he was old and the effectiveness of his present influence in the country was questioned.[35]

Repnin's only alternative was to turn to the neutrals, that is, the Czartoryskis. His court had been at odds with them since 1765 because of their opposition to Dissident reform. The Czartoryskis themselves had for the last three years almost withdrawn from political life. Nevertheless, they still had a reputation that commanded the respect of many and financial resources that ranked them with the richest magnates of the Commonwealth. But Repnin's request for their intervention came to naught. The Czartoryskis wanted the privileges of the Dissidents according to the Perpetual Treaty reduced and Russia's guarantee of the Polish Con-

[34] Konopczyński, *Konfederacja barska,* I, 99-102.

[35] In the Warsaw *News* of May 28, Branicki declared that the Bar Confederation would injure the country and that, if they were to cease their activities, everything would be forgotten and peace could be brought to the nation. But if they continued their opposition to the court and Russia, he would seek them out and punish them. See BPAN, 1145/292.

stitution relinguished, as conditions for their intervention. This, of course, Repnin could not agree to.[36]

While Repnin tried to find the means for bringing about peace in Poland, the international scene lost some of the flavor of tranquillity that had existed during the past five years. Wroughton received word from Constantinople of "the sudden turn of affairs at the Porte, and of the warlike preparations making there."[37] This was understandable considering the effect that the civil war in Poland had on the pro-war group at the Porte, which was ably prompted and assisted by the French ambassador. Simultaneously with news of the Russian incursion at Bałta, reports also reached Constantinople of large numbers of Russian troops at Chocim.

"These reports caused such alarm that a council was immediately called, the result of which was that messengers were immediately dispatched to collect a number of troops to march immediately to Chotchim, Bender, & Orczakow. . . . Constantinople and its suburbs sung with the cry of war," wrote John Murray, the British envoy at the Porte. The Russian ambassador, Obreskov, was at a loss to explain the Russian position and hoped that things could be settled through negotiation. Murray concluded: "I am persuaded that the Porte has not thought of war for the present, but what the march of those troops or the general cry of the people for revenge may produce, no one can determine. By the assiduity of the French ambassador . . . at the Porte, it is to be feared that the French Court trys all methods to kindle a war."[38]

The war cries were unceasing in Constantinople, and the fighting continued in the Commonwealth. The Confederates had suffered one defeat after another, but they continued the struggle. In August Lithuania stirred. Kowno confederated on August 20, and three days later Wilkomirz followed its example.[39] At the same time the defeated and disgruntled exiles of the Bar Confederation argued among themselves. For some time Joachim Potocki had wanted to be the military leader of the Confederation. Now that the defeats of Berdyczów and Bar had seriously undermined the

[36] Wroughton to Weymouth, Aug. 10, 1768, PROSP, 88/96, and ACz, 1984/275-76.
[37] See Wroughton to Weymouth, Sept. 7, 1768, PROSP, 88/96.
[38] Murray to Shelburne, Aug. 1, 1768, PROSP, 97/44.
[39] See BJag, 101/VII/706-11, and 715-16, respectively; and BJag, 1053/213-14.

confidence formerly placed in Józef Pułaski, Potocki found it easy to succeed him as Regimentary General. The formality took place on August 23. Pułaski was nevertheless still respected by some, and several squadrons of troops remained loyal to him. During the following months, Pułaski remained in exile but independently continued his struggle against the Russian and Crown forces along the Polish-Turkish border.[40]

Everyone except France wanted to keep the peace, but all knew that war would soon come. Choiseul wanted the Turks to exert pressure to bring Russia to war. He gave Vergennes, the French ambassador at the Porte, a free hand in Turkey and supplied him with a huge sum of money.[41] Councils were held frequently at the Porte, dignitaries argued with each other while crowds gathered in the streets crying for war, but no decision was arrived at.

"The troops are augmenting daily throughout the Empire, and the bakers are employed in making an immense quantity of bisket," Murray reported during these heated days.[42] Benoit told Wroughton, "It will be very difficult, if not impossible to prevent a rupture."[43] Prince Kaunitz declared that his court was "heartily inclined to peace,"[44] and Maria Theresa disapproved of all France had done to excite the jealousy of the Porte against Russia.[45] Joseph II "would have no war which had not been forced" but he would "defend if attacked."[46]

The anti-war group at the Porte was losing ground. One official followed another into disgrace for opposing the views of the Sultan, who had been won over to a war policy.[47] On September 25 Obreskov told Murray that the Grand Vizier had summoned him to an audience. Obreskov read to Murray a recent dispatch from

[40] BPAN, 318/248. See also Konopczyński, *Konfederacja barska*, I, 210-14, and Smoleński, pp. 286-87. For confederate activity during September, see BPAN, 1145/365, 399, and Konopczyński, *Konfederacja barska*, I, 93-95, 531-33.

[41] See Albert Sorel, *The Eastern Question in the Eighteenth Century*, pp. 24-25, and Francis X. Lambert, "The Foreign Policy of the Duke de Choiseul, 1763-1770," pp. 361, 369.

[42] PROSP, 97/44 (Sept. 1, 1768).

[43] Wroughton to Weymouth, Sept. 7, 1768, *ibid.*, 88/96.

[44] Stormont to Weymouth, Sept. 3, 1768, BMAddMSS, 35500/341.

[45] Rohd to Frederick, Sept. 7, 1768, PC, XXVII/17447/330.

[46] *Ibid.*, 17453/335 (Sept. 10, 1768).

[47] See Murray to Shelburne, Sept. 15 and Oct. 1, 1768, PROSP, 97/44, and Solov'ëv, XXVII, 538-39.

Petersburg containing Catherine's assurance to the Porte that Russia would recall her troops from Poland as soon as peace was restored. He felt, however, that the Porte would no longer listen to assurances of this kind. He feared also that he might never leave the chambers of the Grand Vizier, and he asked Murray to take care of his children in the event something happened to him. After all, their mother was an Englishwoman. Murray agreed but told Obreskov he had nothing to worry about.[48]

The audience was held on October 6. Obreskov repeated the assurance of his court that as soon as peace was restored, Russian troops would leave Poland. The Grand Vizier replied that this promise had been given before but the Russian troops had remained. He demanded a categorical answer on the immediate evacuation of Russian troops. He wanted an answer in "two words, whether you will engage yourself formally, and with the guaranty of allies, to make the troops depart, or have war . . . you must say in two words, you accept the proposal, or war." Obreskov again stated that the troops would leave when affairs were finished in the Commonwealth. Obreskov and his entire staff were then taken into custody.

This act of imprisonment was the Porte's declaration of war against Russia.[49]

[48] Murray to Shelburne, Oct. 7, 1768, PROSP, 97/44. See also Panin to Grand Vizier, Aug. 15, 1768, Sb, LXXXVII/1699/131-35.

[49] Murray to Shelburne, Oct. 7 and 10, 1768, PROSP, 97/44; Rohd to Frederick, Nov. 2, 1768, PC, XXVII/17557/419-20; and Sb, XXXVII/373/166-72.

The declaration of war surprised and disconcerted all men—the Turks who made it, the Russians who had provoked it, the French who had prompted it, the Prussians who had discouraged it, the Austrians who had lived in perpetual dread of it, even the English who pretended to be indifferent to it.[1]

IX

THE CONFUSION WROUGHT BY WAR
OCTOBER 6, 1768—AUGUST 29, 1769

"Impudence and effrontery are scandalous and multiply in all parts of the country; in Greater Poland robberies happen daily, and from time to time new and different parties of robbers appear. Not one złoty goes to the state revenue." Thus Repnin despondently described the condition of Poland to Panin at the close of October. "The mail is intercepted; there is no peace in the villages. . . . It is impossible to have a Diet." "Our army is not able to overtake [the Confederates]—all is in vain."[2]

The defeats suffered by the Confederates during the summer did not end the confederate movement, and the difficulties arising between the Porte and Russia encouraged them. In October a few more confederations were declared in Lithuania, notably that of Nowogródek under Michał Jan Pac.[3] The rebellious fever caught hold of Karol Radziwiłł, too, who had for some months been suspect. Repnin sent troops against him on his estates at Nieśwież, but only minor skirmishes occurred before Radziwiłł made his peace with the Russian ambassador.[4]

At the same time, Bishop Krasiński returned to Podole from France, where he had succeeded in persuading Choiseul that

[1] Albert Sorel, *The Eastern Question in the Eighteenth Century,* p. 28.

[2] Quoted in Sergei Mikhailovich Solov'ëv, *Istoriia Rossii s drevneishikh vremën,* XXVII, 524-25.

[3] See BPAN, 1145/412, and Władysław Konopczyński, *Konfederacja barska,* I, 95, 99, 533.

[4] See BJag, 1053/223-25; Benoit to Frederick, Oct. 26, 1768, PC, XXVII/17608/463n; Wroughton to Weymouth, Oct. 19, and Nov. 3, 1768, PROSP, 88/96; SAPMém, I, 606; and Konopczyński, I, 99, 102-3.

another French agent should be sent to the Confederates in Taulès's place.[5] In Podole Krasiński continued his conspiratorial activity and planned an uprising in Mazowsze, while other Confederates began negotiating with the Turko-Tartar leaders on the Polish-Turkish border for mutual assistance to drive out the Russians.[6]

Warsaw was in confusion. On August 12 Stanislas Augustus issued a Universal calling for the convocation of the Dietines, which would elect Deputies to the Diet scheduled to open on November 7. However, this was an impossibility.[7] The civil war which ravaged the country prevented any kind of orderly constitutional procedure. The few Deputies who arrived in Warsaw decided that it was senseless to try to hold a Diet under the circumstances.[8]

In Petersburg several conferences were held to determine the strategy and tactics to be employed by Russia during the war. Her policy and attitude toward the Porte was summed up in her declaration of war dated November 29.[9] During these conferences Panin was subjected to severe criticism from Gregory Orlov and Michael Volkonskii for his direction of Russia's foreign policy. The outbreak of the Russo-Turkish war was in their opinion the result of a mishandling of the Polish question. In a weak defense, but with Catherine's support, Panin stated that a new project for the pacification of Poland would be presented shortly.[10]

The plan was not really new. Panin was again hoping to end the war in Poland by seeking an accommodation with a leading family—the Czartoryskis. They had at times refused to serve Russia, but never had they betrayed her or promised anything they were not able to make good.[11] This policy, however, seemed

[5] See RIDA, V, 283-93. See also Adolf Beer, *Die erste Theilung Polens,* I, 291.

[6] See Konopczyński, I, 180, 217, 528-29.

[7] See BJag, 1053/174-76, and Wroughton to Weymouth, Aug. 24, 1768, PROSP, 88/96.

[8] See BPAN, 1145/400; Wroughton to Weymouth, Sept. 21, Oct. 5, and Nov. 9, 1768, PROSP, 88/96; and Konopczyński, I, 175.

[9] See AGS, I, 1-13, and PROSP, 91/80.

[10] See AGS, I, 1-18; Solov'ëv, XXVIII, 558-60, 600; and Solms to Frederick, Nov. 18, 1768, PC, XXVII/17631/487n.

[11] See Solms to Frederick, Nov. 15 and 17, 1768, PC, XXVII/17625/480, and Sb, LXXXVII/1735, 1736, 1745, 1746/183-84, 185-86, 201-4, 205-8, respectively. Frederick believed that the pacification of Poland could not be successfully executed unless

doomed to failure, since the Czartoryskis themselves would not co-operate with Russia unless she significantly modified her position. Moreover, Stanislas Augustus was trying to effect a *rapprochement* with his uncles, but on a basis that was totally contrary to Russia. Disregarding the advice of his brother Kazimierz, who believed in a strict alliance with Russia, Stanislas Augustus thought the only way of gaining the confidence of the country was to oppose Russia.[12]

But gaining the confidence of anyone in Poland was an extremely difficult task. Primate Podoski himself conspired for the dethronement of Stanislas Augustus. He corresponded with the Saxon court in the hope that the Elector would succeed to the Polish throne and continually pestered Repnin for the support of Petersburg in this venture. Repnin told Podoski that the basic principle of Catherine's policy toward Poland was the maintenance of Stanislas Augustus on the throne and she would never think of changing her mind. Despite Repnin's warnings Podoski remained obstinate and even sent a private agent to Petersburg, to negotiate for this coup.[13] This move added to Repnin's difficulties, and the outbreak of the Russo-Turkish war made matters worse. Disgusted and embarrassed, Repnin threw up his hands and asked for his recall.[14]

Obviously the action taken by Turkey against Russia affected more than those two countries. Every European country dreaded the possibility that the Russo-Turkish conflict would spread and involve them in a struggle similar to the Seven Years War. Great Britain immediately offered her good offices for mediation.[15] Britain was still seeking a Russian alliance, and she hoped that her friendly attitude would be looked upon with favor by the Russian court. Besides, an end of the war with the Porte would

---

Russia modified several policies, especially the renunciation of Catherine's guarantee of the Polish constitution. He did not believe, however, that Russia would do this. See Frederick to Solms, Nov. 30, 1768, PC, XXVII/17625/482.

[12] See Cathcart to Rochford, Dec. 27, 1768, PROSP, 91/97, and SAPMém, I, 616; and Konopczyński, I, 200-3.

[13] See Konopczyński, I, 197-205.

[14] See Solov'ëv, XXVIII, 600.

[15] M. S. Anderson, "Great Britain and the Russo-Turkish War of 1768-74," *The English Historical Review*, LXIX, 41-43.

release Russian troops and resources from a "rather sterile struggle in the Principalities and on the shores of the Black Sea for use in central or western Europe against France, her allies of the Family Compact, and if necessary Austria."[16]

Entering into a war could not have been further from the intention of the Austrian court. Austria wanted peace, and the Russo-Turkish conflict threatened that desire. Maria Theresa told Stormont that she would be "sorry to see the Turks victorious" but neither would the success of Russia make Austria rejoice. "We cannot wish to see the Czarina more powerful than she is. You see, then, that all the possible events of the Turkish war are against us." She denied that she wished to dispute the validity of the King of Poland's election or to place the Elector of Saxony on the Polish throne.[17]

Maria Theresa's chief minister was indignant that any rumors should be spread that Austria had "contributed to the kindling of this Turkish War."[18] Above all, Kaunitz wanted peace. If the Russo-Turkish conflict were to spread to other parts of Europe, Kaunitz wanted to ensure the neutrality of the Germanies. He instructed Nugent (his envoy to Prussia), who was at that time in Vienna on leave, that on his return to Berlin he should declare to Frederick the peaceful intentions of Austria and her desire to reach an understanding with Prussia on the neutrality of the Germanies.[19]

Frederick desired peace no less than did the Austrians, and, therefore, was very much pleased with the news that Nugent brought him.[20] He had, he said, only one obligation to Russia in this war—the subsidy article of his alliance with that country.[21] Although he reiterrated his long-range scheme of Prussian expansion (which included Saxony, Polish Prussia, and Swedish Pomerania) in his *Political Testament* of November 7, Frederick

[16] *Ibid.*, p. 41.

[17] See Stormont to Rochford, Dec. 1, 1768, BMAddMSS, 35500/49-50.

[18] See Stormont to Rochford, *ibid.*, p. 51 (Dec. 3, 1768).

[19] Alfred Ritter von Arneth, *Geschichte Maria Theresia,* VIII, 144. See also Stormont to Weymouth, Oct. 26, 1768, BMAddMSS, 35500/42.

[20] Frederick to Rohd, Nov. 20, 1768, PC, XXVII/17598/456. See also "Unterredung . . ." Nov. 15, 1768, *ibid.*, 17586/441-445.

[21] Frederick to Finckenstein, Nov. 2, 1768, *ibid.*, 17558/421.

expressed no desire to go to war to obtain these ends.[22] Nugent suggested that the Prussian ruler meet with Joseph II during the time when the Prussian maneuvers were to be held. Frederick agreed, but since the maneuvers would not take place for several months no time or place was fixed.[23]

Frederick was persuaded that the Austrian court would not meddle in the affairs of Poland nor in the Russo-Turkish war. However, he could not promise (nor could Austria) that these peaceful intentions would remain constant if the war continued.[24] Frederick desired this *rapprochement* because it would "reestablish the trust and good harmony between me and the Emperor and will contribute very much toward the maintenance of the peace and toward the general well-being of Europe."[25]

But Frederick's policy was guided as much by his desire to maintain the "ancient rule" of international relations as it was by his desire to keep the peace.

It is certain that the object of France is to stir up a general war in order to fish in troubled waters. But there is an ancient rule that it is necessary to desire the opposite of what your enemies wish. If France wishes only trouble and war, we ought to look for the opposite—that is to say, we ought prudently to prevent the chance of a general war, and to terminate the Turkish war as quickly as possible; that is the way to invalidate all the vast projects which are, at the present, turning over in M. Choiseul's mind.[26]

There were, indeed, many projects turning over in Choiseul's mind. One concerned Poland. Now that the war between Russia and Turkey had begun, it was necessary to use every available opportunity to satisfy the requirements of France's policy in the East. To implement this policy, the Chevalier de Chateaufort was sent

[22] Frederick II, *Die politischen Testamente Friedrichs des Grossen* (ed. by G. B. Volz), pp. 214-16, 219, 222; and Frederick to Finckenstein, Nov. 2, 1768, PC, XXVII/17558/421.

[23] Kaunitz to Nugent, Dec. 28, 1768, PC, XXVIII/17712/16n; "Unterredung(s) . . ." Nov. 15, 1768, *ibid.*, XXVII/17586/441-45, and Jan. 8, 1769, *ibid.*, XXVIII/17712/16-19.

[24] Frederick to Rohd, Jan. 18, 1769, *ibid.*, XXVIII/17742/40-41; and Frederick to Rohd, Nov. 20, 1768, *ibid.*, XXVII/17598/456. See also *ibid.*, XXVIII/17763-17847/62-138, *passim*, and Cathcart to Rochford, Jan. 17, 1769, PROSP, 91/80.

[25] Frederick to Rohd, Jan. 29, 1769, PC, XXVIII/17774/74.

[26] *Ibid.*, 17745/45-46 (Jan. 19, 1769).

to the Confederates. He was given two sets of instructions. By the first, Chateaufort was ordered to continue agitating the Poles against the Russians; to convince them of the necessity of declaring the Polish throne vacant; to assist in forming a general confederation from the several scattered and disorganized confederations which dotted the country; and to encourage the occupation of major fortresses in Poland by Turkish troops, for the maintenance of which Chateaufort was supplied with French funds.[27]

The second set of instructions comprised a secret mémoire, which explained the primary interest of the French court.

> The essential interest of France requires not only that war be waged between the two empires, but that it be waged vigorously and as soon as possible. It is also important that Poland be made the theater of war, and whatever sympathy one might feel for this unhappy kingdom must yield to the necessity of guaranteeing Poland and even Sweden and a great part of Europe from the plague of Russian ambition and despotism. . . . As to the Confederates, in general, their dissensions, their incapacity, their fickleness, merit no confidence from us. They act only for private and personal ends; very few of them consult the true interests of their country. No fixed aims, no system, no common rallying point, no means, no resources. In this condition, we realize that they would merit only contempt and oblivion were not the interests of Poland and the necessity of opposing Russia essentially bound to their cause.[28]

What more could be said for the Confederates? They were a sad lot, chasing and being chased, winning one battle only to be defeated in another. During the winter no less than a dozen new confederations were declared and probably an equal number dispersed. When they retreated they very often sought refuge in a neighboring country. They broke into Austrian and Hungarian territory and threatened Frederick's possessions.[29] These sporadic violations of the frontiers were destined to bring protests.

Austria was the first to protest. In February 1769, the Vienna court proclaimed a military cordon around the county of Spisz (Zips), which comprised a dozen or more towns lying on the Hungarian frontier, and posted its Imperial Eagles. Spisz was Polish

[27] RIDA, V, 284-88 (Jan. 18, 1769).
[28] *Ibid.*, pp. 289-90.
[29] See BPAN, 1145/57; BPAN, 316/6-9, 14-15, 16, 43; and Konopczyński, I, 526-33.

territory. Since 1412, when King Sigismund of Hungary had mortgaged this county to the Polish King Władysław, it had never been reclaimed by the Hungarian Crown—nor was it now. Kaunitz suggested this action because he feared confederate disturbances there might lead to an incident that might involve the Vienna court in the Russo-Turkish struggle.[30]

Simultaneously with Austria's cordon around Spisz, that county became part of the subject of conversation between Frederick and a retired Prussian diplomat, Count Lynar. So much attention has been given to this visit, the matter which they discussed, and its significance, that it is necessary to examine the evidence carefully. All we have at our disposal are the words of Frederick to Solms.

> Count Lynar came to Berlin to marry his daughter to the son of Count Kameke. He is the man who concluded the peace of Kloster-Zeven; he is a great politician and still keeps informed about European affairs from his village [Lübbenau in Spreewald], to which he has returned. Count Lynar has a rather curious idea concerning Russia that might appeal to the interests of the princes and that might improve the present conditions in Europe. He suggests that Russia offer to the court of Vienna for its assistance against the Turks the town of Lwów, with its environs, and Spisz; that Polish Prussia with Warmia and the right of protection over Gdańsk be given to us; and that Russia, to indemnify herself for the expenses of the war, take whatever part of Poland would be convenient; and then Austria and Prussia, neither being envious of the other would, in emulation of each other, aid Russia against the Turks.
>
> This plan has some luster; it appears seductive; I believed it my duty to send it to you. Although it seems to me that it is more brilliant than sound, you know the way of Count Panin's thinking; either you will suppress all this, or you will judge what is opportune to employ.[31]

The Lynar proposal immediately poses several questions which

[30] BPAN, 316/206; and Kaunitz to Maria Theresa, Jan. 9 and 30, 1769, VA, Vorträge; Arneth, VIII, 170-72; and Rohd to Frederick, April 22, 1769, PC, XXVIII/18050/292n. Frederick accepted the reasoning of the Vienna court in taking this action. See Frederick to Solms, April 30, 1769, PC, XXVIII/18050/292. Because of his fear that the commerce with his possessions would be interrupted by the Confederates, Frederick ordered his patrols to increase their surveillance closer to Elbląg and Toruń. See Frederick to Benoit, July 30, 1769, PC, XXVIII/18288/463.

[31] Frederick to Solms, Feb. 2, 1769, PC, XXVIII/17786/84.

warn one against taking it seriously. Would Russia agree to offer Austria Lwów and Spisz? Would Austria content herself with these rewards for assisting Russia against Turkey? If Austria were to receive rewards in Polish territory for her assistance, on what basis would Prussia obtain Polish Prussia, Warmia, and protection over Gdańsk? Certainly not for her subsidy obligation to Russia, which had not as yet been fulfilled. Or was it, perhaps, for initiating the plan? And assuming that the above-mentioned could be settled despite all the previous statements by these three courts never to dismember Poland, what then would be the nature and substance of the "aid" which Prussia and Austria would give to Russia against the Turks? Would this not then contradict the rationale of both the German courts in wanting to restore the peace? Furthermore, if Frederick were really sincere and interested in "pushing" this Lynar plan, would he allow Count Solms to decide to "suppress" it if he thought it were not worth while to proceed? Is not this directive totally out of line with Frederick's single-minded manner of issuing orders when he sincerely felt an issue worthy of his time and energy?

The Lynar plan was most certainly not worthy of his time, energy, or attention. There is no mention of it in Frederick's next eighty-eight dispatches, a marked departure from his habit of repeating to his several ministers abroad even the most unimportant gossip.[32] The next mention of the Lynar plan was made by Solms to Frederick on February 17. Without even mentioning the subject to Panin, Solms doubted its efficacy, because he believed it totally contrary to the Russian minister's way of thinking.

According to Solms the principle upon which the foreign policy of Russia was founded precluded embarking upon negotiations with Austria. It would require mutual faith, and Russia did not trust in the "sincerity of the court of Vienna." Moreover, "The preservation of this republic [Poland] seems really to hold the heart of the court here," at least since Panin had taken control of its foreign policy. Panin "regards Poland as suitable to serve Russia against the Porte, and . . . also the friendship of the republic is advantageous to Your Majesty in a war against Austria." Panin

[32] *Ibid.*, 17787-17874/84-160.

"has accepted the principle that it would be prejudicial to Russia to make conquests." In Panin's opinion, Solms stated, Russia sought to make all Europe respect her and trust in her declarations, and therefore to renounce the principle of preserving Poland's territorial integrity would destroy everything that she was trying to build.[33]

Frederick's reply to Solms all but put an end to any further discussion of the Lynar plan.

As to the project of Count Lynar, you will have perceived beforehand that in my orders of February 2 I regarded it, at first, as very chimerical. This is also why I left you the master entirely in talking to Count Panin or in suppressing it entirely, and you may decide whether to keep that minister ignorant of it.[34]

Panin gave his opinion of the Lynar plan before Solms had received the above dispatch and, for that matter, before Frederick himself had sent it to St. Petersburg. In Solm's words:

The first observation [Panin] made on this was that he found that the county of Spisz was an acquisition very convenient for Austria, but he did not know how the author of the project was able to add the town of Lwów, which was situated in the heart of Poland, distant from the frontiers of Austria and, in consequence, less convenient. He remarked afterwards that he would not hesitate to unite the three great powers but would hesitate to only push the Turks back to the other side of the Dniester; that if this union were to take place, it would then be necessary that it propose not much less than to chase the Turks out of Europe and a great part of Asia; and that this would not seem difficult to execute.[35]

In his reply to this last dispatch of Solms, Frederick made no direct mention of the Lynar plan and it is not to be found in any future dispatches. The Lynar plan was, indeed, "chimerical."[36]

Far more important to Frederick was his forthcoming meeting with the Emperor Joseph. On February 12, hoping to dispel the fears Panin had about the consequences of the meeting, Frederick wrote Solms that the Russian court had no reason to be suspicious

[33] Solms to Frederick, Feb. 17, 1769, *ibid.*, 17875/160-61.
[34] Frederick to Solms, March 5, 1769, *ibid.*, p. 162.
[35] Solms to Frederick, March 3, 1769, *ibid.*, 17917/194.
[36] Frederick to Solms, March 19, 1769, *ibid.*, pp. 194-95.

or jealous of his meeting with Joseph.[37] Panin wanted Frederick to oppose Joseph's idea for the neutrality of the Germanies.[38] But Frederick wanted the neutrality of the Germanies as much as Joseph did, and he was still convinced that the Vienna court at that moment would not meddle in the affairs of Poland or the Russo-Turkish war. However, "unforseen and sudden events" might change Austria's peaceful intentions. It was, therefore, urgent that Frederick meet with Joseph, discuss the present situation of Europe, and search for means to secure Prussia from harm in the future.[39] Moreover, these "unforseen and sudden events" might not come from the East or from Austria. Frederick wrote to Solms on March 15 that in the present situation of Europe "the neutrality [of the Germanies] would be advantageous in the event that France and England engage in a war, because it would make Hanover safe and would prevent France from making a diversion; anything I say on this neutrality is pure conjecture, because I do not know now what the Emperor may say to me, if I see him."[40]

Frederick was anxious to prove to the Russian court that his meeting with Joseph in no way impaired the solid and friendly union he had with it. On March 13 he had received an interesting dispatch from Goltz, his agent in Paris. Based on the information supplied to him by a reliable informant, Goltz told Frederick that France wished to place a different king on the Polish throne. For the aid that Frederick would supply France in this venture, Prussia would receive Kurland and the Bishopric of Warmia. Austria, for her complicity, would be given a part of Silesia. Sweden, financially aided by France, after declaring war on Russia would be rewarded with Livonia and Estonia.[41] Frederick thought it "extravagant and chimerical" that another plan concerning Poland should appear, but he refused to be seduced. "I shall make Russia see how I shall snub it," he declared to Solms.[42]

[37] *Ibid.*, 17812/108.

[38] See Solms to Frederick, Feb. 28, 1769, *ibid.*, 17903/183.

[39] See Frederick to Rohd, Feb. 8 and March 1 and 12, 1769, *ibid.*, 17800, 17863, 17892/97, 152, 176, respectively, and Frederick to Catherine, Feb. 14, 1769, *ibid.*, 17823/119.

[40] *Ibid.*, 17903/184.

[41] Goltz to Frederick, March 3, 1769, *ibid.*, 17899/181n.

[42] *Ibid.*, p. 181 (March 13, 1769).

The question of dethroning Stanislas Augustus was more than once brought to the attention of Poland's three neighbors, and on all occasions it was dismissed. In the early months of 1769, reports again came out of Warsaw that a Saxon party was taking form and that its vigorous supporter was the Primate.[43] Frederick, still firm in his support of Stanislas Augustus, instructed Benoit to make it publicly known in Warsaw that he "would never agree to any prince of the house of Saxony . . . mounting the throne of Poland."[44]

Despite the repeated assurances Frederick had made to the court of St. Petersburg that Austria would not interfere in Polish affairs, Panin would not be satisfied until he had made his own inquiry. He instructed Golitsyn to sound the Austrian court on this matter. Kaunitz told the Russian ambassador that, if Prussia sent troops into Poland to aid Russia, the Austrian court could not view this with indifference. However, Austria had no desire to interfere in the domestic affairs of the Polish state and would not second the idea of dethroning Stanislas Augustus.[45]

The Russian position remained unchanged and was summed up very well by Cathcart, the British ambassador at the court of St. Petersburg: "[Russia] will never consent either to the dethronement or abdication of His Polish Majesty, nor ever encourage the Poles to think that after they have unanimously elected a King they are at liberty to withdraw their allegiance."[46] The Russian position was further clarified in the instructions given on April 10 to Russia's new ambassador to Poland, Michael Volkonskii. He was to maintain the existing Polish government, find a suitable means for the settlement of its troubles, preserve the status of the Dissidents and the territorial integrity of the Com-

[43] See Benoit to Frederick, Feb. 15 and April 8, 1769, *ibid.*, 17847, 18010/138, 264n, respectively.

[44] *Ibid.*, 18010/264 (April, 16, 1769).

[45] See VA, Vorträge, and Beer, *Documente*, pp. 101-4 (May 11, 14, and 15, 1769). Choiseul also proposed a project to Kaunitz similar to the one he offered Frederick, that is, for Austria to take a part of Polish land and replace Stanislas Augustus on the throne of Poland. Kaunitz did not take this proposal seriously and attributed it to Choiseul's inquisitive nature in attempting to get at the bottom of Frederick's and Joseph's proposed meeting. See Arneth, VIII, 198, 571, and Sorel, pp. 56-57.

[46] Cathcart to Rochford, April 10, 1769, PROSP, 91/80. See also Cathcart to Rochford, March 28, 1769, *ibid.*

monwealth as guaranteed by the last Diet, prevent the Poles from joining with the Turks, and secure the King on the Polish throne.[47]

Volkonskii arrived in Warsaw on June 2 and immediately set about finding means for pacifying Poland. Several weeks passed in discussions with the King, the Czartoryskis, and several other dignitaries of state—but the results were all the same. No agreement could be reached while Russia refused to modify her demands regarding the Dissidents and the guarantee of the Polish constitution, two of the most irritating articles of the 1768 Treaty. On each issue, however, Volkonskii refused to budge.[48]

Volkonskii was a friend of neither Repnin nor Panin, and his appointment to Poland was a sharp indication that Panin's dominating influence over the Empress was slipping. When questioned about Repnin's conduct in Poland, his reply was anything but a brief in his defense. "I asked him," Wroughton stated, "[if] what had been done in Poland was upon a plan of Mr. Panin's, or intended to be carried with so high a hand by the Empress?" "It was entirely an abuse of the indiscreet power given Repnin," Volkonskii replied, "and . . . Mr. Panin was ashamed, and unwilling to disavow him, but he could not be ignorant of the [disgrace] and even mischief, he had done to his Court without advantage to it."[49]

But Volkonskii would neither disavow the results of these abuses nor admit their immorality. When Stanislas Augustus requested the scrapping of all the old constitutions and treaties between the two countries, Volkonskii told the King to forget all such ideas because the Empress would never consent to abolishing the treaties.[50]

And so another impasse was reached in Polish affairs, and things

[47] Sb, LXXXVII/1831/372-404, and Solov'ëv, XXVIII, 607-8. Volkonskii was nominated for the position on January 3, 1769, and had the reputation of being on good terms with the Czartoryskis. He had served in Poland in various capacities in 1746, 1757-58, and 1764. See Konopczyński, I, 197-98; BPAN, 316/17; BPAN, 1146/19; and BPAN, 1147/11.

[48] Cathcart to Rochford, Dec. 27, 1768, PROSP, 91/79; Wroughton to Cathcart, Aug. 7, 1769, Wroughton to Rochford, Aug. 8, 1769, *ibid.*, 88/98, and ACz, 1984/283-95; Panin to Volkonskii, July 18, 1769, Sb, LXXXVII/1865/470-72; and SAPMém, I, 617-18.

[49] Wroughton to Rochford, Aug. 19, 1769, PROSP, 88/98, and ACz, 1984/299.

[50] See Solov'ëv, XXVIII, 610 (Aug. 6, 1769).

continued as before. Stanislas Augustus had, on more than one occasion, tried to quiet the country, asking everyone to forgive and forget, and promising that the faith would be protected.[51] But as usual no one paid any heed to what he said. The Confederates continued along the same confused road they had started on in March 1768. Some towns and villages gave rise to as many as three confederations in less than two years. No battle could ever be considered "decisive" by either party. News of Józef Pułaski's death from the plague caused only a few outside his immediate family to mourn. Whatever attempt there was at unifying the several confederations failed almost immediately. Each confederation argued, denounced, vindicated, competed with the other, and it began to seem that the real enemy was no longer Russia. In short, the Polish story of two Poles meeting and giving birth to three political parties has significance here.[52]

East Central Europe was in flames, and there was no hope that they would soon be extinguished. The desire to avoid being involved in a war, which might arise if the flames should spread to the West or if a new war should break out between England and France, was the single theme of the discussions held between Joseph and Frederick. The talks began on August 25 at Neisse in Prussian Silesia and lasted three days. They led to a *rapprochement* between the two German courts. The neutrality of both parties was assured in the event of a future war being brought to their doorsteps. Frederick could, if he so desired, according to Joseph, write to Catherine all that had taken place at Neisse and could also express to her the interest of both German courts in seeing the prompt pacification of Poland and the conclusion of the Russo-Turkish War.[53]

[51] See ACz, 830/97-98, and ACz, 1701/47-49.

[52] See BPAN, 1145/45-56, 59-60, 89-90, 101-109; BPAN, 1146/21; BPAN, 1147/18; BPAN, 316/142; ACz, 944/237-42, 293-95; ACz, 1701/219-21; ACz, 2191/273-75, 277-81; Baron de Vioménil, *The Private Letters of Baron de Vioménil on Polish Affairs,* pp. 49-63; and Konopczyński, I, 245-74, 526-33.

[53] See VA, Vorträge, July 29, 1769, and VA, *Polen III Erste Teilung Polens Akten,* August 17, 1769; "Unterredung(s) . . ." PC, XXIX/18351-18354/41-49; Alfred Ritter von Arneth (ed.), *Maria Theresia und Joseph II, Ihre Correspondenz,* I, 300-15; Arneth, *Geschichte Maria Theresia,* VIII, 198, 571; and Oeuvres, VI, 26-28.

In our last interview, the Emperor of the Romans has given me the most forceful assurances [that he will] not meddle in any manner in the affairs of Poland. . . . I flatter myself that the general tranquillity will not suffer any change.[1]

FREDERICK TO SOLMS

X

THE DIPLOMATIC STALEMATE
AUGUST 30, 1769—OCTOBER 23, 1770

The Russian campaign of 1769 was successful. In September the Russians were at Jassy, two months later Bucharest was occupied, and by the end of the year Moldavia and Wallachia had been overrun. The Russian fleet had set sail for the long journey through the Atlantic and would soon reach the Mediterranean. Catherine's successes were praised, but they struck fear in the hearts of the rulers of Prussia and Austria, not to mention the Porte.

Frederick hoped that her successes would lead to the speedy reestablishment of the peace rather than to further aggrandizement. The appearance of the Russian fleet in the Mediterranean might, in Frederick's opinion, furnish Choiseul the opportunity of engaging Spain in his intrigues. And Frederick was equally fearful that if the Turks were pushed back too far, the court of Vienna would become jealous of the Russian victories, take umbrage, and bring all Europe into the war. However, Solms was to tell Catherine that if she concluded the peace that winter, the glory of Russia would be praised forever and she would gain the gratitude of all Europe.[2] Frederick was willing to help. He told Rohd that if the Porte would request Austria to act as its mediator and if Russia would call upon Prussia to do the same for her, then not only could peace be reestablished, but also the "radical troubles in Poland" could be terminated.[3]

[1] PC, XXIX/18379/65 (Sept. 7, 1769).
[2] Frederick to Solms, Oct. 18 and 22, 1769, *ibid.*, 18506, 18515/153, 160, respectively.
[3] *Ibid.*, 18523/165 (Oct. 25, 1769). See also Frederick to Solms, Nov. 5, 1769, *ibid.*, 18546/183-84.

The "radical troubles in Poland" had annoyed Frederick enough for him to take retaliatory measures. "I have resolved to march troops on the frontiers of Elbląg and Warmia in order to drive away the Confederates from these provinces, which are found enclaved in my Kingdom of Prussia," Frederick wrote to his envoys. Moreover, he stressed the point that when his action was questioned his envoys were to explain very clearly the motive of the Prussian court.[4]

Panin questioned the necessity of Frederick's actions since, as he claimed, that area was no longer disturbed by the Confederates. He hoped that this step on the part of Prussia would not in any manner create a situation which would give occasion to Austria to meddle in Polish affairs. Solms told Panin that Frederick, always aware of the delicate international situation, would not have made this move without first being assured of the passivity of the court of Vienna. Panin seemed to be content.[5]

The Vienna court did not take any notice of Frederick's action. It was convinced that he wanted only peace and agreed to his suggestion on mediation. After all, did it not follow in the spirit of Neisse? Maria Theresa wished for peace, and she would gladly work hand in hand with Frederick toward its fulfillment.[6] This was, for Frederick, "a mark of character and perfect sincerity" on the part of the Empress-Queen.[7] So Frederick instructed his envoy at the Porte to suggest the mediation of the two German powers.[8]

While the two German courts sought to bring an end to the hostilities, Choiseul continued his endeavors to prolong the war as long as possible, in order to sap the strength of both belligerents. He believed that the continuation of the Russo-Turkish struggle

[4] Frederick to Benoit, Oct. 15, 1769, *ibid.*, 18494/145, and Frederick to Rohd, Oct. 15, 1769, *ibid.*, 18495/146.

[5] Solms to Frederick, Nov. 3, 1769, *ibid.*, 18592/212. See also Frederick to Solms, Nov. 19, 1769, *ibid.*, pp. 212-13. On November 25, Frederick wrote Solms that the Confederates were again violating his frontiers and that he had imprisoned two of them. See *ibid.*, 18607/221.

[6] Rohd to Frederick, Nov. 18, 1769, *ibid.*, 18609/222.

[7] Frederick to Rohd, Nov. 29, 1769, *ibid.*, 18620/230. See also Frederick to Rohd, Nov. 26, 1769, *ibid.*, 18609/222.

[8] Frederick to Zegelin, Dec. 7, 1769, *ibid.*, 18634/240. See also Frederick to Rohd, Dec. 7, 1769, *ibid.*, 18633/239.

would eventually serve to strengthen the Franco-Austrian alliance, and he informed Kaunitz of his views. Regarding Poland, it mattered little to the French minister "who will be King of Poland, provided that Poland would be kept in turmoil and that Russia would be kept occupied with her and the Porte for some years."[9]

The Vienna court did not see things in the same light. Kaunitz informed Choiseul that instead of France and Austria working toward a continuation of the war they should employ all imaginable means to accelerate peace between the two powers on the basis of the *status quo ante bellum.* Russia would then gain nothing, and because she would be exhausted she would be unable to resume her aggressive policy in the north. Prussia according to Kaunitz, did not desire war with Austria—Neisse had removed that threat—and the meeting to be held the following September in Moravia would go a long way to solidifying Austro-Prussian relations and securing the peace of Europe. Catherine was the one to fear, not Frederick. If things continued as they were—that is, if Russia continued to defeat the Turks in battle—Austria might make military demonstrations in Hungary and be prepared to act at a moment's notice. With regard to Poland, Kaunitz felt that it would be best if the Poles discarded their idea for declaring the Polish throne vacant.[10] Kaunitz requested his envoy at the Porte, Thugut, to suggest the good offices of the Vienna court for mediation.[11]

Mediation was also desired by the Polish court. On September 30 Stanislas Augustus called a Senate Council, which decided that England and Holland should be asked to intercede on Poland's behalf and that an envoy should be sent to Constantinople to negotiate with the Turks for a cessation of the incursions made by them on the Polish frontier. A deputation should also be sent to Catherine protesting against the consequences of Repnin's activities in Poland, and another request should be made for the re-

[9] "Mémoire du Duc de Choiseul au Compte de Mercy" c. Dec. 1769, in Adolf Beer, *Die erste Theilung Polens, Documente,* pp. 5-7.

[10] *Ibid.,* pp. 7-11 (n.d.).

[11] See Rohd to Frederick, Feb. 10, 1770, PC, XXIX/18807/348; Frederick to Rohd, Jan. 7, and Feb. 18, 1770, *ibid.,* 18715, 18807/285, 349, respectively; and Frederick to Zegelin, Jan. 7, 1770, *ibid.,* 18714/285.

lease of the four dignitaries who had been arrested in October 1767.[12]

Volkonskii was taken aback by this positive attitude of the King and his ministers. He complained to Stanislas Augustus of his shameful protest against Repnin's activities at the last Diet. "You know that all this was approved by the Empress; why, the Diet itself ratified the affair. Even though a part of the people feared the violence of Prince Repnin, nevertheless, he could not decide this without the permission of his court. . . . Why did you keep quiet until this day?" Now, when Russia was protecting the King from the Turks and the Confederates, Volkonskii found Stanislas Augustus ungrateful to Catherine. "You demand the withdrawal of the Russian army, which is supporting you on the throne, and dispatch ministers to such courts as endeavor to ruin you. Until now you called the Confederates fanatics, but now you speak their language."[13]

Toward the end of Feburary 1770, Stanislas Augustus took it upon himself boldly to ask Catherine to recall her troops from Poland and allow him to request the mediation of a Catholic power. This would be the only way a pacification Diet could be held and the confidence of the country restored in the central government.[14] Catherine's answer on April 10 was a firm rejection. "From your letter," she wrote him, "I saw with regret that you still continue to trust insidious people and conceal ambitious projects."[15]

The pacification of Poland was desired by all powers (except

[12] ACz, 1696/134-36, and SAPMém, I, 622-29. See also Wroughton to Rochford, Sept. 27, 1769, PROSP, 88/98, and ACz, 1984/304-5. Stanislas Augustus requested Frederick to help pacify Poland and also said that he and his uncles were seeking the aid of a Catholic power to mediate Poland's difficulties. Frederick suggested Austria: "I am persuaded that her mediation would have a very good effect for the pacification of the troubles of Poland." The difficulty would arise only from Russia, since Frederick "agreed to mediate if that court desired it." See Benoit to Frederick, Dec. 23, 1769, PC, XXIX/18698/276n, and Frederick to Benoit, Dec. 27, 1769, PC, XXIX/18691/271-72. See also Cathcart to Rochford, April 17, 1770, PROSP, 91/84.

[13] Volkonskii to Panin, Oct. 13, 1769, quoted in Sergei Mikhailovich Solov'ëv, *Istoriia Rossii s drevneishikh vremën*, XXVIII, 614. See also Panin's letters to Volkonskii and Stanislas Augustus of Nov. 10, 1769, in Sb, LXXXVII/1886-1890/512-29.

[14] SAPMém, I, 645-49 (Feb. 21, 1770).

[15] Sb, XCVII/1939/50-53. See Cathcart to Rochford, April 13, 1770, PROSP, 91/84.

France and the Porte), but none had a plan or suggestion that would satisfy the others. Russia even made another attempt. For some time she had hoped that a counter-confederation, that is, a Russian-supported confederation on the order of Radom, could be established against the several confederations then rampant in the country. Volkonskii could make no headway with the Czartoryskis and thus turned to Jan Klemens Branicki and Poniński. Measures were discussed and finances estimated. Mniszech was asked to head the confederation but he refused; he had been deceived at Radom and did not wish to trust Russian promises again. The idea was abandoned.[16]

The civil war in the Commonwealth was, therefore, destined to continue without any hope of a settlement or a decisive victory. For a brief moment in late 1769 there seemed to be the possibility of a turning point in the internecine struggle. In the small town of Biała, not far from Teschen, leading representatives of several confederations met and discussed the possibilities and means for uniting the confederate movement. The outcome of the conferences was the proclamation, dated October 31, of a Generalcy. The Generalcy, an executive council, which later came to represent thirty-seven independent confederations, made no significant change in the principles that had been discussed in Warsaw in 1767 or in those laid down by the Bar Confederation. Michał Krasiński, who was serving with the Turkish army, was elected Marshal for the Crown; and Michał Pac, for the Grand Duchy. The Regimentary Generals were Joachim Potocki for the Crown and Józef Sapieha for Lithuania. In late December the Generalcy decided to send several emissaries to other courts in search of aid.[17]

There was only one thing wrong with the Generalcy; no one really took it seriously. Those who joined were in no way representative of the entire confederate movement, and, moreover, they could not agree among themselves. The military undertakings

[16] See Wroughton to Cathcart, Feb. 7 and June 20, 1770, PROSP, 88/100, and ACz, 1984/323; Panin to Volkonkii, Dec. 15, 1769, Sb, LXXXVII/1892-1894/538-42; Solov'ëv, XXVIII, 615-18; and Władysław Konopczyński, *Konfederacja barska,* I, 356-60.

[17] BPAN, 316/509-10, 537; BPAN, 317/389; ACz, 831/303, 315-17; and Konopczyński, I, 340-45.

of the Generalcy resulted in the same continuing failures the confederates had experienced when divided, suffering one defeat after another.[18] One of the French officers assigned to help the Confederates described their weaknesses and strengths: "I must render the Poles the justice which is their due: they are brave and courageous; unhappily they rely too much upon their courage and neglect to study the art of war, while their neighbors, more enlightened and better disciplined, have attained every possible advantage from their study of military affairs."[19] But if at times the Confederates lost faith in themselves, Choiseul, who knew their real value to his political system, did not. More subsidies would be forthcoming—and French officers, too.[20]

By the beginning of April, Zegelin, the Prussian envoy at the Porte, informed Frederick that the Porte was interested in mediation and asked him to ascertain the conditions under which Russia would talk.[21] Frederick, pleased with this news, forwarded it to Solms at St. Petersburg.[22] Mediation seemed all the more important now: Austrian troops were massing on the Hungarian-Turkish frontier, and magazines to support a corps of 40,000 troops were being established in Transylvania.[23] Panin was disconcerted and somewhat confused by this, but Golitsyn told him that he should not worry. It was true, Golitsyn said, that the Austrians were massing troops and establishing magazines, but the number was not large enough to be considered important. Panin asked Frederick if he had any information to offer.[24] Frederick confirmed the troop movement but "it is impossible to say what [the Austrians] will do or not do in order to avoid a new neighbor."[25]

But Frederick endeavored to find out. He said to Nugent, "I

[18] See Konopczyński, I, 360-72, 384-414, 527-34; and Baron de Vioménil, *The Private Letters of Baron de Vioménil on Polish Affairs*, pp. 51-56.

[19] See Vioménil, p. 53.

[20] RIDA, V, 293-96. See also Vioménil, pp. 11-13.

[21] See PC, XXIX/18979, 18980/458, 460n; and Zegelin to Frederick, May 7, 1770, *ibid.*, 18983/465-66.

[22] Frederick to Solms, May 6, 1770, *ibid.*, 18980/460.

[23] See Solms to Frederick, April 20, 1770, *ibid.*, p. 459.

[24] *Ibid.*

[25] Frederick to Solms, May 6, 1770, *ibid.*, p. 460.

know well that you do not wish to have the Russians as neighbors."

"Neither I, nor Your Majesty," Nugent replied, and added, "I dare press to assure you that we will not meddle at the present in the mediation between Russia and the Turks, unless one or the other of the powers makes a convenient request." Austria's neutrality was above all suspicion, Nugent declared. "In regard to the march of troops into Transylvania, perhaps, it has been found necessary in order to protect our frontiers." Nugent then suggested that if Frederick were to acquire Polish Prussia the kingdom of Prussia would have better communication with Brandenburg. Frederick did not reply to this seductive invitation but remained "a little pensive."[26]

The next time Nugent's suggestion was discussed was in a letter written by Prince Henry to his brother Frederick on June 22.

> I admit that my imagination was struck by this idea. . . . But, if this is only a vision of mine, it is nonetheless such a pleasant one that I find it difficult to renounce it. I want to see you lord of the Baltic coast. . . . If this is [only] a dream, it is [at least] a very happy one, and you may well believe that the interest that I take in your glory makes me wish it were true.

Frederick told Henry:

> I see, my dear brother, that in the political field you do not suffer from want of a good appetite; but I, being old, have lost that of my youth. Not that your ideas are not excellent; but a man must have the wind of fortune in his sails to succeed in such an enterprise, and I dare not flatter myself that I can do it.[27]

Frederick was still uncertain of Austria's motives. He began to panic when he received news from Solms that Russia had intentions of liberating Moldavia and Wallachia from the domination of the Turks. If this happens, he told Solms, "war between Austria and Russia is inevitable." Frederick stressed the necessity for making peace now. "If Russia allows this moment to pass, it is to be

[26] "Unterredung . . ." May 6, 1770, *ibid.*, 18982/464-65; and Nugent to Kaunitz, May 25, 1770, in Alfred Ritter von Arneth, *Geschichte Maria Theresia*, VII, 573-76.

[27] G. B. Volz, "Prinz Heinrich von Preussen und die preussische Politik vor der ersten Teilung Polens," *Forschungen zur brandenburgischen und preussischen Geschichte*, XVIII, 151-88, especially pp. 187-88; and Chester V. Easum, *Prince Henry of Prussia, Brother of Frederick the Great*, pp. 262-63.

feared that it would result in a general war." As far as he was concerned, "the treaty of alliance with Russia had not the least bearing in Moldavia and Wallachia . . . only on the affairs of Poland." He instructed Solms to impress the St. Petersburg court with his disposition on this point.[28]

The pressure on Russia to make peace mounted during the summer. Kaunitz told Golitsyn that it was impossible for neutral powers to sit by and see the balance of Europe destroyed by the rapid successes of the Russians. Since the Turks seemed utterly unprepared to save or defend themselves, it would become necessary, if the war continued, for neighbors to interfere.[29] Catherine seemed on the verge of weakening when she requested in July that negotiations be kept open with the Porte.[30] The Sultan, however, had seemed bent on continuing the war, so great was his wrath toward Russia; but when the Turks found themselves repeatedly defeated, on both land and sea, the Porte seriously requested the mediation of both German powers.[31]

Before this request for mediation reached the two German powers, the Vienna court took a step which threatened the future security of the Polish-Lithuanian Commonwealth—Austria extended her military cordon to include Nowy Targ, Czorsztyn, Nowy Sącz, Bochnia, and Wieliczka; this brought the Imperial Eagle close to Kraków itself. At first Frederick did not suspect this action as being anything more than a continuation of the policy of protecting the Hungarian frontiers. He and his envoy at Vienna believed that when the troubles in Poland ended and the danger of Austrian involvement in the Russo-Turkish War was less, these territories would be returned to the Commonwealth according to an amicable agreement. However, when a protest was made by the Polish court against this seizure, Kaunitz declared that before

[28] PC, XXIX/19039, 19045, 19047/498, 502, 504 (June 4, 9, and 10, 1770), respectively.

[29] See Cathcart to Rochford, June 12, 1770, PROSP, 91/84. It was Saldern who informed Cathcart of the Kaunitz-Golitsyn talk.

[30] See Solms to Frederick, July 13, 1770, PC, XXX/19172/48n.

[31] See Frederick to Zegelin, July 19, 1770, *ibid.*, 19148/32-33; Frederick to Solms, July 22, 1770, *ibid.*, 19158/39; Zegelin to Frederick, Aug. 13, 1770, *ibid.*, 19281/133-34. See also Beer, I, 314-15; Arneth, VIII, 208; M. S. Anderson, "Great Britain and the Russo-Turkish War of 1768-74," *The English Historical Review*, LXIX, 47.

Poland could claim injury, she would first have to prove that those districts belonged to the Commonwealth.[32]

The Turkish request for mediation arrived as the rulers of the two German powers were meeting for the second time, at Neustadt. These talks began on September 3 and lasted four days. Kaunitz accompanied Joseph this time and did most of the talking. No documents were signed and only verbal promises given; however, the entire tone and spirit of the Neustadt meeting furthered the consolidation of the *rapprochement* begun at Neisse the previous year. Once again the two courts pledged cooperation and trust in each other. In all things they would be open and considerate of each other's interests. The two courts wanted peace not only for themselves but for all Europe. It was in the interest of others as well as themselves that the Russo-Turkish War end as soon as possible and a suitable pacification be found for Poland. They were now firmly committed to mediation. All they had to do was to persuade Russia that she, too, wanted it. Because Russia had succeeded in overwhelming the Turks, she was entitled to compensation, but not too much. If Russia continued to be obstinate and push her advantage, war with Austria was inevitable.The penetration of Russian troops deep into the Danube basin or the determination of Russia to make Poland a province of her empire would be sufficient cause for Austria's intervention.[33]

[32] See VA, Vorträge, Aug. 19, 1770 (with enclosure of Młodziejowski's of July 28, 1770), and "Imperial Resolution of 19 July 1770," in Beer, II, 327; Rohd to Frederick, Aug. 18, 1770, PC, XXX/19230/85-86; Frederick to Rohd, Aug. 23, 1770, PC, XXX/19230/86; and Cathcart to Rochford, Oct. 30, 1770, PROSP, 91/86. About the same time, but for very different reasons, Prussian troops were ordered into Gdańsk. Gdańsk officials confiscated wagons of rubles minted by Frederick for distribution in Poland. Frederick became enraged and sent troops into Gdańsk to exact compensation. There was no attempt at acquisition; it was never thought of. The troops were removed after Gdańsk had paid an indemnity of 25,000 ducats. See Frederick to Junck, July 4, 1770, PC, XXX/19113/10; Frederick to Finckenstein, July 11, 1770, PC, XXX/19134/23; Frederick to Benoit, July 18, 1770, PC, XXX/19146/31; Cathcart to Rochford, July 6, 1770, and Cathcart to Wroughton, July 27, 1770, PROSP, 91/85; Cathcart to Mitchell, Aug. 21, 1770, BMAddMSS, 6826/212, and BMAddMSS, 6810/284-89. Szymon Askenazy, *Dantzig & Poland*, pp. 34-35, says that Frederick's motivation was the recruitment of troops. While this "recruitment" may have taken place during the Prussian occupation (a not unusual occurrence during the eighteenth century), it does not appear to have been the primary motive for it.

[33] VA, Vorträge, Sept. 3-7, 1770, and "Unterredung(s) . . ." PC, XXX/19257,

Frederick informed the Russian court of his own disposition and that of the Porte and Austria toward mediation of the crises.[34] On October 8 Frederick's letter came before the Russian advisory council. The letter was discussed, and on the basis of Panin's suggestions Catherine wrote to Frederick on October 9 that she greatly appreciated the kind and noble sentiments of her ally who wished only to bring about a good peace for Russia.

However, there were several obstacles which prevented her from accepting a formal proposal of mediation from the two German courts. Great Britain had from the very beginning offered her good services to bring about the cessation of hostilities, and, since Britain had aided Russia by assisting her fleet, Catherine could not think of excluding her from the mediation. If Russia were to allow three powers to enter into the mediation, would not France become jealous and move heaven and earth to interfere? Moreover, Austria presented a problem. Frederick knew the influence that France had at that court. Could Russia be assured of an impartial mediation? Notwithstanding all these considerations, Russia would still be very pleased if the two German courts offered their good services in seeking the peace, but they should not take the role of "mediators."[35]

Frederick had also suggested to the Russian court several ways in which the Commonwealth could be pacified. Most important was that the Dissidents themselves should desist from entering the Senate. If this were accomplished, Frederick pledged that he would endeavor to obtain the promise of the Vienna court to force the

---

19258, 19261/101-14, 116-18. See also Frederick to Rohd, Sept. 5, 1770, PC, XXX/19259/114-15; PC, XXX/19281/134-35; Mercy to Maria Theresa, Sept. 19, 1770, Alfred Ritter von Arneth and M. A. Geffroy (eds.), *Marie Antoinette correspondance secrète entre Marie-Thérèse et le Cte de Mercy-Argenteau,* I, 57-60; and Kaunitz's and Mercy's correspondence, Alfred Ritter von Arneth and Jules Flammermont (eds.), *Correspondance secrète du Comte de Mercy-Argenteau avec l'Empereur Joseph II et le Prince de Kaunitz,* II, 371-78, *passim.*

[34] Frederick to Catherine, Sept. 14, 1770, PC, XXX/19282/138-40, and Sb, XX/63/274-77. See also Frederick to Solms, Sept. 12 and 13, 1770, PC, XXX/19271, 19274/126, 129, respectively, and Frederick to Zegelin, Sept. 14, 1770, PC, XXX/19281/135-37.

[35] AGS, I, 61-62; Sb, XX/64/277-81; PC, XXX/19389/215-17; and Solov'ëv, XXVIII, 686.

Confederates to submit to equitable conditions which the Empress might choose to prescribe.[36] Catherine's answer on this point was somewhat surprising but could not be taken too seriously. She consented to the Dissidents giving up their demand to enter the Senate and the high offices of state in return for a grant of unrestricted freedom of public worship which would afford them, in effect, equality with the Catholic inhabitants. However, these matters could be brought up only at a pacification Diet, and the Empress would take it upon herself to guarantee the constitution "that would be declared fundamental law."[37]

Although the Russian concession involving the Dissidents might satisfy Frederick, it was a far cry from meeting the demands of the Confederates. Besides, it was far easier to declare such an intention than to execute it. Cathcart's appraisal that "affairs of Poland stand at this moment as they did in October 1768" is thus a gross understatement.[38] They were in fact much worse. The Confederates were running helter-skelter now, as they had two years before. But on October 23 they took their boldest step, when the Generalcy proclaimed an interregnum in the Commonwealth.[39] Moreover, the Polish frontiers were now being invaded with impunity—not only by the Russians, but by the Turks, the Austrians, and the Prussians.

As if Poland had not enough troubles already, nature added to them—in midsummer a plague came from the east. By the fall it became serious enough for the Polish government to take precautions by restricting the entry into the country of untested goods. Frederick did the same: "As to the news of the plague, it is becoming more serious every day, and it has forced me not only to reinforce the cordon on my frontier, but to extend my forces up to Marienwerder, in order to preserve the communication of my provinces with Polish Prussia, which without this precaution, would be

[36] Frederick to Solms, Sept. 12, 1770, PC, XXX/19272/127-28.

[37] Solms to Frederick, Oct. 23, 1770, *ibid.*, 19423/244-45n, and Catherine to Frederick, Oct. 9, 1770, *ibid.*, 19389/217-18.

[38] Cathcart to Rochford, Oct. 19, 1770, PROSP, 91/86.

[39] See BPAN, 317/120, 388-89, 567-70, and BPAN, 1149/50-56, 70-73, 95-97, 101-4; ACz, 831/379; and Konopczyński, I, 508-9. See also Stormont to Rochford, Aug. 1, 1770, BMAddMSS, 35500/66-67.

entirely cut off."[40] The cordon was to be explained to the Polish government as only a quarantine against the plague. In no manner of speaking had this cordon a purpose similar to that of the Austrian one. There was no pretension to any territory, and it would last only as long as the plague persisted.[41]

The desire for peace on the part of the several belligerents and spectators had increased from the beginning of hostilities, but each suggestion or invitation was checked by exaggerated demands and by the fear of losing face. The sweeping victories of Russian armies over the Turks were contrasted by the war of attrition in the Commonwealth. The civil war in the Commonwealth had created the delicate situation of neighboring powers taking measures to ensure the security of their frontiers. If the wars continued there was no telling what might occur, but a spark of hope remained—Prince Henry was journeying to St. Petersburg to visit Catherine.

[40] Frederick to Solms, Sept. 19, 1770, PC, XXX/19301/151; BPAN, 317/406-7; and Wroughton to Rochford, July 28, Aug. 11 and 15, and Oct. 11 and 30, 1770, PROSP, 88/100.

[41] Frederick to Benoit, Oct. 10, 1770, PC, XXX/19348/183.

My sojourn in St. Petersburg marked the beginning of negotiations for the agreement between the King and Russia. . . . I have evidence, more than twenty personal letters to the King, that I supplied the suggestion which led to the agreement. But I do not request any reward for this; I seek only recognition . . . from the hand of Her Majesty the Empress of Russia. If after taking possession of Polish land, she will honor me with a letter which will serve as proof that I promoted this great affair, my wish will be fulfilled. . . . I shall look upon this letter as the greatest moment of my glory.[1]

HENRY TO SOLMS

XI

THE PARTITION BEGINS
OCTOBER 12, 1770—MAY 27, 1771

"The King of Prussia has given his consent and I hear that Prince Henry will accordingly set out some time this [September] from the Court of Sweden for Petersburg. There are people who pretend that Prince Henry has no real business either in Sweden or Russia, but that it is a journey of mere ostentation and meant to give occupation to the speculative politicians."[2]

But Henry had "real" business at both courts, and it was somewhat Machiavellian in character. Henry saw the confusion in Europe as a chance for Prussia to profit—perhaps even to divide up the Germanies between Austria and Prussia. He hoped at least that Prussia might gain some territory out of Europe's difficulties. Frederick did not agree with his brother. He believed himself too old for another military adventure, and he did not think Austria financially sound enough to do anything to help. Nevertheless, the first opportunity for bringing about Henry's wishes came when he was invited to St. Petersburg.

It would be more truthful to say that Henry invited himself there—Catherine merely fulfilled his wish. He believed that by

[1] F. de Martens (ed.), *Recueil des traités et conventions, conclus par la Russie avec les puissances étrangères*, VI, 67-68 (April 5 (?), 1772).

[2] Mitchell to Rochford, Sept. 4, 1770, BMAddMSS, 6810/292.

going to St.Petersburg he could further his plans for aggrandizement and that Catherine would help him. Most assuredly, this was for Henry the "boldest stroke" of his life. "Unable to induce the King to take even the first steps toward the seizure of West Prussia, he had decided to take them himself and virtually to make Prussia a present of the provinces."[3] Immediately after Henry learned of his mission to Sweden[4] he arranged to have Golitsyn inform the Russian court that Prince Henry of Prussia would be very grateful for an invitation to visit St. Petersburg. Frederick had no knowledge of Henry's negotiations for getting himself invited to the Russian court.[5]

On July 30 Catherine wrote to Frederick that she would be greatly pleased if Henry, after his sojourn in Sweden, could spend some time with her in Russia. She suggested several means of travel by which Henry could make the trip to St. Petersburg and offered everything at her disposal to make his trip and stay in Russia enjoyable.[6]

From the standpoint of Russia, a visit from Henry would be desirable for several reasons. First, Frederick had already had one meeting with Joseph and a second was forthcoming (September 3-7); these would serve to bring the two German courts closer together. Russia could not afford to have her alliance with Frederick weakened or possibly replaced by an Austrian one. A meeting with Henry would in a sense replace a meeting with Frederick,

[3] Chester V. Easum, *Prince Henry of Prussia, Brother of Frederick the Great,* pp. 256-59.

[4] Frederick to Solms, Dec. 31, 1769, PC, XXIX/18699/277. In 1769, Frederick renewed his alliance with Russia with a secret proviso. He would come to the aid of Russia if Sweden attacked Catherine or if the Swedish constitution of 1720 were overthrown. He would make a diversion in Swedish Pomerania. His reason for sending Henry to Sweden was to inform his sister, the Queen, of this proviso. The personal mission was favored because he did not trust in the mail. See G. B. Volz, "Prinz Heinrich und die Vorgeschichte der ersten Teilung Polen," *Forschungen zur brandenburgischen und preussischen Geschichte,* XXXV, 196.

[5] Catherine to Golitsyn, March 8 and April 20, 1770, Sb, XCVII/1928, 1948/34, 65-67, respectively; G. B. Volz, "Prince Heinrich von Preussen und die preussische Politik vor der ersten Teilung Polen," *Forschungen zur brandenburgischen und preussischen Geschichte,* XVIII, 155 ff.; G. B. Volz, "Prinz Heinrich als Kritiker Friedrichs des Grossen," *Historische Vierteljahrschrift,* XXVII, 390-490; and R. Krauel (ed.), *Briefwechsel zwischen Heinrich Prinz von Preussen und Katharina II von Russland,* VIII of *Quellen und Untersuchungen zur Geschichte des Hauses Hohenzollern.*

[6] PC, XXX/19208/72, and Sb, XX/61/271-73.

since it was believed at the Russian court that Henry had considerable influence with his brother. Furthermore, Catherine was anxious to learn what had happened in Sweden.[7]

Frederick informed Henry that Catherine "requests you with so much eagerness" that he could not refuse.[8] To Catherine he poetically wrote: "Neither the sea, nor the heights, nor the precipice will stop [Henry], and he will overcome all the obstacles . . . to present homage to You, Madam." He went on to applaud Catherine's greatness and to express his thankfulness at being her ally. He pictured "Constantinople trembling at the sight of the Russian fleet and the Sultan forced to sign the peace which Your moderation will dictate to him."[9]

Nearly three weeks later, after he had had time to send Henry a special cipher that would be used only by him, Frederick was able to speak his mind more clearly on the subjects most important to him.[10] Sweden, of course, held a claim on Frederick's attention; he wanted to reestablish the best relations between Catherine and his sister, the Queen. But of more immediacy, he desired to bring about the end of the Russo-Turkish War and the pacification of Poland. Henry was informed of the Neustadt discussions and the Turkish request for mediation. Henry was told to influence Catherine toward a moderate policy with the Turks and the Poles. If Catherine were to show clemency after so many victories, this not only would assure a good and solid peace but would add to Catherine's fame. The Russian court must accept the mediation of Austria and Prussia and not make "untenable conditions" to the Poles. Catherine had to reduce the demands which she had made at the last Diet, otherwise the troubles would never end in Poland. If she would do this, Austria and Prussia would help in bringing the Confederates to "reason, and then the peace would be stable."[11]

[7] See Sergei Mikhailovich Solov'ëv, *Istoriia Rossii s drevneishikh vremën*, XXVIII, 687.

[8] PC, XXX/19209/73 (Aug. 12, 1770).

[9] *Ibid.*, 19208/72-73 (Aug. 12, 1770).

[10] See Frederick to Henry, *ibid.*, 19229/85 (Aug. 23, 1770).

[11] See Frederick to Queen of Sweden, Aug. 30, 1770, and Frederick to Henry, Aug. 30 and 31, Sept. 9, 13, and 18, and Oct. 8, 1770, *ibid.*, 19243-19245, 19266-19267, 19276, 19298, 19343/92-95, 121-24, 130-31, 149, 179-80, *passim*. See also Henry to Frederick, Sept. 17, 1770, *ibid.*, 19329/169.

Henry arrived in St. Petersburg on October 12.[12] Several days later he wrote Frederick that every day he had been having "familiar conversations with the Empress, and, as M. [Gregory] Orlov has a higher position here than one can imagine, I am confident that . . . I shall be able to use him." He talked to Panin, who told him that Catherine desired the pacification of Poland, that Volkonskii had already been advised to negotiate with the nobles of the Commonwealth, that the Dissidents would yield in their demands, and that an accommodation would be reached with the Confederates. Panin explained that "his sovereign desired the peace, that she hoped to have it, and that she worked for it."[13]

When Frederick received Catherine's letter of October 9, which, according to him, neither refused nor accepted the mediation, he wrote Henry: "I am resolved not to meddle either in the peace or in the affairs of Poland and to be only a simple spectator of events; while those people there are able to accept or refuse us as mediators, it is not necessary that they openly mock us."[14]

As the days passed Frederick became more irritable and more pronounced in his views.

> The whole Kingdom [of Poland] is alienated from the Russians. If the Empress of Russia believes she has partisans, she deceives herself very much. The question is to pacify these troubles. If the peace imposes laws that the Poles believe they are not obliged to observe, [the troubles] will begin again in three months. I ought to add another consideration. The court of Vienna regards the affairs of Poland with the greatest discontent; and, although I hesitate to say it, if the Russians, after the peace is made, do not recall their troops from this kingdom, then the Austrians, in the end, will become impatient.
>
> . . . Russia should make a tolerable pacification plan for Poland and communicate it to me and to the court of Vienna. If this plan is found reasonable—that is to say, in maintaining the King on the throne and compromising a little on the other [formerly announced demands]—

[12] See Cathcart to Rochford, Aug. 24, 1770, PROSP, 91/85; Cathcart to Mitchell, Oct. 9, 1770, BMAddMSS, 6826/216; Cathcart to Rochford, Oct. 16, 1770, PROSP, 91/86; and Mitchell to Rochford, Nov. 3 and 10, 1770, BMAddMSS, 6810/296.

[13] PC, XXX/19415-19416/239-40. (Oct. 18, 1770). Two years later, Robert Gunning, the British ambassador to Russia, wrote to Suffolk about Henry's visit to St. Petersburg: "Prince Henry of Prussia in his visit to Petersburg treated the favorite Orlov with indifference, at the same time living with, and shewing the utmost attention to the [Chernyshevs]." BMAddMSS, 35502/8 (Aug. 8, 1772).

[14] PC, XXX/19391/219 (Oct. 26, 1770).

I should be able to convince the court of Vienna to reprimand, jointly with me, the Confederates and force them to submit. That would provide a stable peace and a new reign. But the Empress does not wish to follow my advice. I fear that sooner or later the smoldering fire will ignite a blaze which will devour all Europe.

Besides, I renounce the title of mediator.[15]

Henry, as yet unaware of Frederick's change of mind, urged the pacification of Poland before peace was made with the Porte. He suggested a general confederation which would command the obedience of the malcontents and further suggested that the Austrians would assist in this venture. He was informed by the Russian court that, although Russia would welcome the idea of Frederick's encouraging the Austrians to engage themselves in this action, she did not want that power "meddling directly in the affairs of Poland."[16]

Henry's idea was not new. Russia had for some time been trying to effect such a policy. Whether her new attempt was influenced by Henry's suggestion is not known, but she tried again. Russia as before, was not successful. Nevertheless, this new failure revealed the lack of trust the Poles had for the promises of the Russians.

Wroughton reported that Volkonskii "received a refusal from every quarter he has applied to." The Potockis told Volkonskii:

Their family had been notoriously deceived at Radom, where with bayonets at their throats, they had been obliged to sign the General Confederation, on conditions quite contrary to those, on which they had undertaken it, on the most solemn engagements with Russia; that having been thus forced to acts, which had driven the Nation to their present state of despair, and failed in their engagements to their friends, and society, they now saw the difficulty, if not the impossibility, of the Nation's trusting again the promises of Russia; that as to their promising in order to ruin the Czartoryskis, it was true their family were long rivals, and even enemies, but, if Russia was capable of acting thus violently with people, whose greatest crime with the Nation was for forty years past having been connected with the Court, what hopes could new friends have, of being treated better, whenever their conscience should put them under the necessity of refusing to comply with every demand of that power; that likewise it would be

[15] Frederick to Henry, *ibid.,* 19404/230 (Oct. 30, 1770).

[16] Henry to Frederick, *ibid.,* 19437/256 (Oct. 27, 1770).

deceiving Russia to make her believe that the affairs of the Dissidents could possibly be maintained.[17]

During the remaining weeks of November nothing significant took place in the negotiation between the two northern courts. At the same time that Frederick announced that if the war continued between Russia and the Porte he would not continue the subsidies, Panin informed Henry that very soon the Russian court would present a definite program concerning the war and the pacification of Poland.[18]

Early in December the Vienna court formally proclaimed the reincorporation of Spisz into the Crown of Hungary. It was the beginning of the dismemberment of Poland.[19] Whatever plans Russia and Prussia might have had for Poland would have to be adjusted to this fact.

Within the next two weeks, reports came from Vienna and Warsaw describing the advance of the cordon of Imperial Eagles and other acts of incorporation into the Crown of Hungary of the territory already occupied by Austrian troops.[20] The Austrian court claimed more territory extending to Austrian Silesia and including no less than nine towns and ninety-seven villages. The inhabitants of this area would be treated as subjects of the Empress-Queen, and they would not pay more taxes now than they had before.[21]

The Prussian court did not at first show any concern: "I do not regard of great consequence," Frederick wrote to Rohd, "the seizure on the frontiers of that republic by the court where you are. . . . I am persuaded rather that once the peace is made, she will

[17] Wroughton to Rochford, Nov. 10, 1770, PROSP, 88/100, and ACz, 1984/346-48. It is interesting to note that at the same time that the Potockis announced their position vis-à-vis the Russian court and their disappointment at Radom, Bishop Krasiński wrote the Generalcy the same thing. See ACz, 944/447-53. See also Wroughton to Rochford, Dec. 12, 1770, PROSP, 88/100.

[18] See PC, XXX/19410-19515/234-317, *passim.*

[19] See VA, Vorträge (Dec. 27, 1770); and Maria Theresa to Stanislas Augustus, Jan. 26, 1771, in Adolf Beer, *Die erste Theilung Polens, Documente*, pp. 86-87.

[20] See Rohd to Frederick, Dec. 19, 1770, PC, XXX/19555/347n, and Benoit to Frederick, Dec. 19, 1770, *ibid.*, 19556/349.

[21] Rohd to Frederick, Dec. 22, 1770, *ibid.*, 19555/347-48. See also Stormont to Rochford, Dec. 22, 1770, BMAddMSS, 35500/70.

not delay in abandoning this possession and confine herself to her boundaries *ante bellum*."[22]

Golitsyn, however, told Rohd that his court would not view the Austrian seizure with indifference.[23] During the first week of 1771 one discussion followed the other at Petersburg concerning the Austrian court's seizure. Solms wrote to Frederick on January 8 that the Russian court believed that "if Austria gave the example for the dismemberment of Poland, Your Majesty and the Empress of Russia would not be wrong in doing the same; that in the archives in Berlin and Petersburg could easily be found the right to lay claim to the Bishopric of Warmia for Your Majesty and to Polish Livonia for Russia." Russia would then extend her boundaries along the Dwina (Dvina) as far as Połock; and if a line were to be drawn as far as the Dnieper, the incorporation of the territory lying on the eastern side of those two rivers would give Russia her "natural" boundaries. This would be considered a just compensation for the six years of war in Poland and with the Turks. Prussia would receive by her acquisition an adequate recompense for the expenses she had suffered during this time in fulfilling the alliance with Russia. "The removal of these provinces from Poland," Solms continued, would not, according to the Russian court, "render her king less able or less recognized than he had been."[24] From the Russian side, this proposition was, in general, the substance of the secret project which General Chernyshev had submitted in 1763.[25]

On the evening of January 8, Henry was approached directly by those at the Russian court who favored this revolutionary change in Russian policy toward Poland.

This evening I have been with the Empress, who told me in fun that the Austrians were seizing two starostas in Poland and that they

[22] PC, XXX/19555/348 (Dec. 30, 1770). See also Frederick to Benoit, Dec. 30, 1770, *ibid.*, 19556/349.

[23] See Rohd to Frederick, Dec. 22, 1770, *ibid.*, 19555/348. Cathcart wrote to Halifax: "The conduct of Austria in possessing herself of the Polish district, the moment she has taken, and the answer she has given to the King of Poland, have given surprise and concern for the example it may give to princes not reckoned so scrupulous, when acquisition comes in question." PROSP, 91/87 (March 12, 1771).

[24] PC, XXX/19615/405.

[25] *Supra*, Chapter II

have placed Imperial troops on the frontiers of those starostas. She added: "But why does not everyone take such action?" I replied that although You, my very dear brother, have a cordon drawn in Poland, You have not occupied the starostas. "But," the Empress said smiling, "why not occupy them?" A moment later, Count Chernyshev approached me and spoke to me on the same subject, adding: "But why not occupy the Bishopric of Warmia? It is necessary, after all, that everyone have something."

Although this was only a discourse of pleasantries, it is certain that it had a purpose, and I have no doubt that it will be possible for You to profit from this occasion. Tomorrow Count Panin comes to my house. I shall tell him what You have written me on the subject of the Austrians.[26]

It is perhaps significant that not only Chernyshev (who had long been an advocate of extending the frontier of Russia into Poland) but now also Catherine favored the idea of dismemberment. It meant that Panin's influence over Catherine in foreign affairs was waning again, as it had after the outbreak of the Russo-Turkish War and with Volkonskii's succession at Warsaw. It meant, moreover, that the "Northern System" was being discarded.

But Panin opposed any idea of partition and made this clear to Solms and Henry. "He is very much against the imitation of [the Austrian seizure]," Solms wrote to Frederick on January 11. If anything were to be done, Panin told Solms, it should be made known that the King of Prussia and the Empress of Russia oppose such ideas. Panin would "never give his sovereign counsel to seize for herself that which did not belong to her."[27]

There was an apparent division in the Russian advisory council. "All those who are supporting aggrandizement wish that everyone would take something in order that Russia might profit at the same time, whereas Count Panin is for tranquillity and peace." Henry, of course, wanted Frederick to involve himself in the partition. "I believe You risk nothing in seizing something for Yourself," he urged his brother; a "plausible pretext" could be found to seize the Bishopric of Warmia.[28]

The influence of the "partition" party at the Russian court was

[26] PC, XXX/19616/406-7; Oeuvres, VI, 39, XXVI, 345; and Solov'ëv, XXVIII, 698.
[27] PC, XXX/19622/410.
[28] Henry to Frederick, *ibid.*, 19635/417 (Jan. 11, 1771).

soon felt in other quarters. Volkonskii told Benoit that he desired very much that Vienna persist in occupying Polish territory, and that Frederick and Catherine both agree to dismembering Poland.[29] But Frederick was still not convinced that the seizure by the Vienna court would be permanent. "I believe," he wrote to Benoit on January 23, "that [Maria Theresa] only did it in order to keep the states of Hungary safe against the plague and that the intention of the Imperial Court is not to try to appropriate the starostas."[30] But there was a change in Frederick's tone when he wrote to Solms the same day: "If they pretend to keep them, they surely authorize the other neighbors of Poland to think about declaring their rights to do the same." But he believed there was sufficient time to think about such things.[31]

On the following day he wrote to his brother, saying that he would not give "six sous in order to acquire" the Bishopric of Warmia. Besides, it was an "unpardonable mistake in politics . . . to contribute to the aggrandizement of [Russia], who will be able to become a dreadful and appalling neighbor for all Europe."[32] Frederick considered the conclusion of the Russo-Turkish War the most important work that had to be done, and the affairs of Poland nothing more that "trifles."[33]

However, on January 31, after having received a report that the Vienna court was massing 30,000 troops along the Hungarian frontier,[34] Frederick seemed interested in the idea of obtaining Polish land, but he was convinced that Panin's view would stand the test of all criticism. He wrote Henry : "Concerning the matter of the seizure of the Duchy of Warmia, I am abstaining because the game is not worth much. This piece is [cut] so thin that it would not compensate for the clamors that it would excite; but Polish Prussia, even excluding Gdańsk, would be worth the trouble, for

[29] *Ibid.*, 19613/403 (Jan. 12, 1771).
[30] *Ibid.*, 19613/403.
[31] *Ibid.*, 19615/405.
[32] *Ibid.*, 19616/407.
[33] Frederick to Solms, *ibid.*, 19622/410 (Jan. 27, 1771).
[34] See Frederick to Rohd, *ibid.*, 19633/416 (Jan. 30, 1771), and Stormont to Sandwich, Jan. 16, 1771, BMAddMSS, 35500/72. See also Joseph to Leopold, Dec. 18, 1770, and Jan. 31, 1771, Alfred Ritter von Arneth (ed.), *Maria Theresia und Joseph II* . . ., I, 316-19, 330-31, respectively.

we will have the Vistula and free communication with the kingdom [of Prussia]."[35]

The reports about Austrian troop movements continued. Calls were sent out by the Austrian court to Italy and the Low Countries. Rohd rightly interpreted this move as having a double intention—to frighten Russia into not extending her conquests and to add force to the extension of the Austrian cordon in Poland.[36]

Frederick was still not overly disconcerted by Austria's activities; he believed that they would "accelerate rather the reestablishment of peace between Russia and the Porte." He did not believe that the "small parcels" of territory that the Vienna court had taken possession of in Poland were of "much consequence." However, he felt that if Austria formally incorporated these territories [the incorporating had already taken place], the neighboring powers would be able to follow her example and similarly renew some old claims on Polish territory.[37]

Everything changed when Henry returned home. He left St. Petersburg at the end of January and arrived in Berlin on February 17. The following day he went to Potsdam, where he stayed the week—persuading Frederick of the necessity for partitioning Poland. In the words of Chester Easum, who has written an excellent biography of Henry: "No other of his servants was ever able to persuade Frederick to reverse himself so completely or so suddenly on a matter of such major importance; and none was ever permitted, even temporarily, so to take play out of the King's hands."[38]

Frederick's change of policy is significantly noted in his letter to Solms on February 20.

> The seizure which the Austrians have made along the frontiers of Hungary . . . appears sufficiently interesting to merit the attention of neighboring powers. . . . The court of Vienna has already exercised several acts of sovereignty. Prince Kaunitz has answered the complaints

[35] PC, XXX/19635/418.

[36] Rohd to Frederick, *ibid.*, 19675/455 (Feb. 9, 1771). See also Oeuvres, VI, 38; Frederick to Rohd, Feb. 10, 1771, PC, XXX/19660/437; Solms to Frederick, Feb. 15, 1771, PC, XXXI/19719/1; and Burnet to Halifax, Feb. 16, 1771, PROSP, 90/90.

[37] Frederick to Rohd, Feb. 17, 1771, PC, XXX/19675/455-56.

[38] Easum, pp. 270-71. See also Burnet to Halifax, Feb. 23, 1771, PROSP, 90/90.

of the republic of Poland in a vague manner, and he clearly indicates the intention of [the Vienna court] to assert its ancient rights. . . .

To several persons at the court of Russia, the news of this seizure gave birth to the idea that all of Poland's neighbors could make similar seizures. . . .

The real issue is to preserve Poland in its entirety, but since the Austrians wish to dismember one part, [it is necessary] to prevent this dismemberment from upsetting the balance of power between Austria and Prussia. . . . I see no other means . . . than to imitate the example that the court of Vienna has given me; to assert my ancient rights, which my archives will furnish me; and to take some small province of Poland. This will make the Austrians desist in their enterprise, or, if they wish to assert their pretentious claims, it will restore [the balance of power]. . . . An acquisition of this nature would not give umbrage to anyone; only the Poles have the right to cry, but their behavior does not merit either Russia's or my sympathy. Once the Great Powers are in accord and work for pacification, they will not be checked. . . .

Above all, I would wish to know the true sentiment of the court of Russia on this affair. . . . If you succeed in making the Empress and her ministers see my point of view, you will render me a service. [It is] the only way to maintain equality between my [court] and the court of Vienna.[39]

A week later Frederick wrote Solms that he was convinced that only force would make Austria desist from occupying Polish territory. But Frederick did not want war.[40] At the same time, Finckenstein and Hertzberg, Frederick's two trusted and reliable ministers of state, were requested to investigate the claims the Prussian court could make on Poland with regard to pretensions in general, districts that would be convenient for the King of Prussia to annex, and the necessary means for bringing this affair to a happy ending.[41]

The ministerial reply was disheartening. It presented Frederick with an uncertain legal pretension. "Your Majesty will see by this memoir that the pretensions of the house of Brandenburg on Poland are neither important nor strong."[42] But Frederick would not let that bother him. He agreed with his ministers that the most advantageous acquisition would be Pomorze (Pomerania) and the land extending along the River Noteć as far as the Vistula. But if

[39] PC, XXX/19687/466-68.
[40] *Ibid.*, 19710/483 (Feb. 27, 1771).
[41] *Ibid.*, 19716/487.
[42] *Ibid.* (Feb. 27, 1771).

this should fail, equal compensations should be found on the other side of the Vistula, for example, Malbork (Marienburg), Chełmno (Kulm), and the Bishopric of Warmia. The example of the court of Vienna's seizure would be followed. A cordon would first be drawn as a means for taking into possession the desired territory, and then a vague explanation of the pretensions would be made to support the occupation. "If the Russians and the Austrians take their part, [the Poles] will not be able to cry more against one than the other, and besides their clamors are powerless." Frederick instructed his ministers to draw up a statement of these pretensions and have it sent to the court of Russia.[43]

The detailed statement, drawn up and presented on March 5, drew from Frederick the simple but precise comment: "This piece is good."[44] Finckenstein and Hertzberg had worked hard; they found that Frederick could also claim territories in Posnań, Oświęcim, Zator, and Siewierz. They gave Frederick a brief that explained the strategy and tactics, the objections which should be anticipated, and the necessity for a flexible policy.[45]

The ambitious and hard-working ministers at Berlin found their counterpart in Solms, who displayed a never-ending determination to win Panin over to the idea of partitioning Poland. Panin was the only minister at St. Petersburg who still opposed the idea, but he was also the most influential. Solms discerned, however, that Panin was weakening under the pressure of those who desired the partition, especially Chernyshev and Orlov. "There are persons who have stated in the Council that Russia ought to imitate these examples [of Austria] and who are only leading Count Panin step by step to convincing himself that he should no longer oppose the dismemberment of Poland."[46] Panin, according to Solms, did not deny the rights of the Prussian court to certain territories in Poland, but only raised doubts and objections to the manner of executing them. Panin hoped that Frederick would defer for some time the execution of the partition. The principal reason for such

[43] *Ibid.*, pp. 487-88 (c. Feb. 28, 1771), and Frederick to Finckenstein, c. Feb. 28, 1771, *ibid.*, 19717/488.

[44] Frederick to Finckenstein and Hertzberg, *ibid.*, XXXI/19728/9.

[45] *Ibid.*, p. 8.

[46] Solms to Frederick, March 8, 1771, *ibid.*, 19772/38, Solov'ëv, XXVIII, 755. See also AGS, I, 74 (Feb. 18, 1771).

a request was that Russia would be totally embarrassed if she were to agree upon a scheme of partition that would violate every promise and treaty that she had made with the Commonwealth.[47]

But once Frederick had committed himself to the idea of partition, he was unwavering. He challenged every argument Panin offered. He wrote to Solms on March 24, "I know very well that [Russia] has given her assurance that she will help preserve in entirety the provinces of that kingdom. But after the Confederates have openly taken arms against her, it seems to me that Poland would not deserve this kind of guarantee."[48] It would not be difficult to justify a change in Russia's policy toward Poland if Russia was reminded that the Russo-Turkish War arose from the anarchy which persisted in Poland. Since the Austrian court had seized Polish territory and was not likely to relinquish it, were not Russia and Prussia obliged to restore the balance of power? Moreover, if the Prussian alliance was worth having, should not Russia do everything to keep it?[49]

Panin did not change his mind, but it became increasingly difficult for him to repeat his former statements and yet remain on a good footing with Frederick. He needed time, and he requested that Frederick find out the intentions of the Austrian court regarding the occupation of Polish territory.[50] The urgency of the situation increased when reports circulated that Austria had continued her policy of entrenchment in Poland and her massing of troops along the Hungarian frontier.[51]

[47] Solms to Frederick, March 12, 1771, PC, XXXI/19787/51-52.

[48] *Ibid.*, 19772/39.

[49] Frederick to Solms, March 25, 1771, *ibid.*, 19781/45-46. Benoit wrote to Frederick on March 27 that Volkonskii had told him that on his return to Petersburg he would urge the Empress and the Council to accept the partition of Poland as a matter of policy. Volkonskii had requested his recall in order to go to Spain. His replacement was Saldern. See *ibid.*, 19802/65n; Henry to Frederick, Jan. 25, 1771, *ibid.*, XXX/19659/436; Wroughton to Halifax, Feb. 16, 1771, PROSP, 88/102; and Cathcart to Rochford, May 1, 1770, PROSP, 91/84.

[50] See Solms to Frederick, April 5, 9, and 12, 1771, PC, XXXI/19853, 19862, 19869/102-3n, 108-9, 119, respectively.

[51] See Kaunitz to Swieten, March 1, 1771, VA, PreusWeis; AGS, I, 75-76 (March 4, 1771); Rohd to Frederick, March 13, 1771, PC, XXXI/19764/33; Stormont to Halifax, March 9, 1771, BMAddMSS, 35500/75; Wroughton to Halifax, March 13, 1771, PROSP, 88/102; Cathcart to Halifax, March 29, 1771, PROSP, 91/87. See also Cathcart to Halifax, April 16, 1771, PROSP, 91/87.

The visit of Prince Henry to Russia and the subsequent negotiations between the Prussian and Russian courts added to the rumors at Vienna that a partition of Poland was afoot. These rumors alarmed Kaunitz.[52] "What causes us most worry is the very suspicious Russian and Prussian aggrandizement schemes in Poland," Kaunitz informed Lobkowitz, the Austrian ambassador to Russia. Austria, therefore, must thwart "such extremely dangerous plans," and "let the King of Prussia know, politely but firmly, that we will not be indifferent to his designs of aggrandizement." Kaunitz was fearful that "an open rupture" might result between the three powers.[53]

This was sheer hypocrisy. Austria had been the first to incorporate Polish land and by moving troops into Hungary had not diminished but increased the possibility of "an open rupture" between the three powers. Notwithstanding the fact that Kaunitz was speaking for the Vienna court, and there was never a question of his loyalty, he did not favor his court's embarking on this policy. Even after Austria had launched the policy, Kaunitz attempted to dissuade his court from executing it. Because of this attitude, it is sometimes difficult to distinguish between his personal feelings and court policy. A good example is his letter of April 10 to Swieten, the new Austrian envoy to the Prussian court: "As soon as peace between Russia and the Porte is established; Poland pacified and her future peace guaranteed by the Empress of Russia, the King of Prussia, and our court; and when the King of Prussia and Russia have withdrawn their troops from that kingdom, then will also their Imperial and Royal Majesties withdraw their army to restore the occupied territory."[54]

On the other hand, it may be argued that Kaunitz only said this to impress the Prussian court (and therefore also the Russian court) that Austrian acquisitions in Poland were merely temporary and that no corresponding action should be taken from their side. It is also not unknown that an envoy has been kept in the dark about the exact nature of his court's policy in order to deceive the court

[52] See Halifax to Stormont, Jan. 29, 1771, BMAddMSS, 35500/73, and Stormont to Halifax, Feb. 20, 1771, *ibid.*, p. 74.
[53] VA, RussWeis (March 7, 1771).
[54] VA, PreusWeis, and Arneth, *Geschichte Maria Theresia,* VIII, 590-91.

where he was. However, Kaunitz' brief to Maria Theresa on April 18 seems to support his opposition to Austria's Polish policy. He stated his opposition to the Austrian incorporation of the Polish districts because the Austrian claim was not proved valid. The only reason that Austria occupied these districts was to safeguard her own frontiers, and until the claims for incorporation could be proved beyond a doubt nothing should have been done. He insisted, but was unsuccessful in convincing his mistress, that the governor of the districts be called *Administrator Districtuum Territorii,* rather than *Administrator Provinciae Reincorporatae.* Furthermore, in order not to whet Frederick's appetite, Kaunitz also suggested that the income derived from these districts during the occupation be turned over to Andrzej Poniatowski, a General in the Austrian army, but also the brother of the King of Poland.[55]

In any event, Kaunitz was fighting a losing battle not only with his court but with Prussia, and at the Russian court Panin was the only important minister who wanted to preserve Polish territorial integrity.[56]

But, for the moment, there was nothing to fear from Frederick, because as usual he would not make a move without the consent and advice of Russia. On April 24 he wrote to Solms: "But as to my taking possession [of Polish land] Count Panin can be certain that I shall undertake this only after there is perfect accord with his court."[57] However, if Austria increased her holdings in Poland, this might be just enough to persuade Panin that it was necessary that his court join in the spoils. "Search in your archives and see if you will not find titles to something more than that which you have already occupied," Frederick told Swieten on April 27, "to some palatinate that should be pleasing to you; believe me, it is necessary to profit from this occasion; I also shall take my part and Russia hers."[58]

The first major change came in May. Solms wrote to Frederick

[55] VA, Vorträge.

[56] See Frederick to Solms, April 21, 1771, PC, XXXI/19853/102-3, and Cathcart to Halifax, April 2, 1771, PROSP, 91-97.

[57] PC, XXXI/19862/110.

[58] Swieten to Kaunitz, April 27, 1771, VA, PreusBer; "Unterredung . . ." PC, XXXI/19868/115-18 (especially 116–17); and Frederick to Solms, April 28, 1771, PC, XXXI/19869/120.

on the seventeenth: "I regard the matter of an acquisition by Your Majesty in Poland as something that will encounter no more obstacles here."[59] On May 27 Panin for the first time reported to the Council the suggestions and requests of Frederick for the acquisition of Polish land. Panin stated that "in consequence of the news of the seizure by the Vienna court of Polish starostas on the Hungarian frontier, the King of Prussia told this court that he does not intend to be a peaceful spectator of such an act." Frederick, Panin continued, "also has the right to adjacent possessions of Polish land and intends to take them; if Russia also has such demands and wants to profit from the opportunity, she could act in common cause with him." Here was the opportunity for the "fulfillment of all the desires" of Russia. In a general way Panin outlined the provinces that would devolve upon the two courts. Prussia would get what she wished (except Gdańsk), and Russia would extend her frontiers westward to include Polish Livonia. The Council agreed.[60]

[59] PC, XXXI/19946/173n.
[60] AGS, I, 83-84, and Solov'ëv, XXVIII, 763.

With regard to Poland. . . . The affairs of that unhappy country are still so perplexed and their issue so doubtful, that I do not know how to form an opinion concerning them. But they are not properly occasions of jealousy among the neighbouring powers for I can hardly accuse the one and acquit the other of designs to take advantage of the disorders and if attempts should be made to dismember the Republick, neither of them will object to give the rest their shares in the partition.[1]

SUFFOLK TO STORMONT

XII

THE PRUSSIAN AND RUSSIAN SHARES MAY 28, 1771—FEBRUARY 17, 1772

The dismemberment of the Polish-Lithuanian Commonwealth had begun with the Austrian seizure of Polish districts. For several decades the idea of dismembering the country had been considered. Most recently partition had been advocated by Zachary Chernyshev, who based his recommendation on military considerations, and by Frederick and Henry, both of whom considered the addition of certain Polish land as a means of rounding out and connecting the estates of Brandenburg-Prussia. Had not Austria "reincorporated" several Polish districts into the Crown of Hungary, it is highly unlikely that the dismemberment idea would have been accepted so completely by the Russian and Prussian courts. The idea having been accepted by them, Russia and Prussia now had to decide on their respective portions and the reaction to be expected from the Austrian court. It was a matter simply of tedious negotiations.

On June 1 Solms reported that Panin had informed him of the decision of the Russian court to join Frederick in partitioning Poland. Solms explained to Panin, in a general way, the various pretensions which the Prussian court had on Polish land, land that was taken from the Hohenzollern house by the kings and seigneurs of Poland. Prussia's share should include Pomorze and all the ter-

[1] BMAddMSS, 35501/11-12 (Aug. 28, 1771).

ritory along the Noteć river from Drezdenko to Bydgoszcz (Bromberg) and Fordon on the Vistula and then along the Vistula up to and including Gdańsk.

Panin was unhappy with this arrangement. Gdańsk could not be included within the Prussian share. Not only would the town itself complain, but also the commercial powers would not tolerate Frederick's taking Gdańsk. Solms brushed aside this objection as a mere "matter of speculation," but Panin was firm. Panin requested that Frederick submit a convention which would include his pretensions, modified as above, and the manner of realizing them. The Russian pretensions were not as yet clearly defined, Panin told Solms, but they would generally extend into Poland along the rivers Dnieper and Dwina penetrating the palatinates of Witebsk and Połock.[2]

On June 14 Frederick sent to Solms a "Draft of a Secret Convention between His Majesty the King of Prussia and the Empress of All the Russias," which comprised a preamble and five articles. The preamble declared that both courts had made common cause in announcing that they each had ancient claims to certain districts of the Polish-Lithuanian Commonwealth and that they were "concerting at present on measures" which would reunite "to their states these provinces which had been detached." The first article explained that the Russian court would take possession of Polish Livonia *et cetera.* The Prussian share, for the most part, remained the same. It included Pomorze and all the territory along the Noteć river from Drezdenko to Bydgoszcz and Fordoń on the Vistula and along the Vistula up to Gdańsk. In exchange for Gdańsk, Frederick now wanted the palatinates of Malbork (including the Bishopric of Warmia but excluding Elbląg) and Chełmno (including Toruń).

The second article provided for the reciprocal guarantee of the above-mentioned acquisitions. The third article provided for the secrecy of the negotiation, but "when it will be time" Russia and Prussia would offer the court of Vienna the "same convenience by allowing it to enter into the partition plan." The fourth article stated that a definite agreement would have to be arranged with

[2] PC, XXXI/19969/189-91. See also Panin to Saldern, June 22, 1771, Sb, LCVII/2068/335-37.

the Commonwealth and for that purpose the Russian and Prussian ministers at Warsaw would be instructed to work together. The fifth concerned the ratification of the convention.[3]

A courier was immediately dispatched with the draft and by June 28 it was in Panin's hands.[4] Within a few days, Panin consulted with Solms on the convention and praised Frederick for his moderation. He expressed the necessity for explaining more fully the reasons for the concert of the two courts to dismember Poland—such as the example set by the Austrian court, the troubles in Poland, the indocility of the inhabitants, the friendship that existed between the Russian and Prussian courts. With regard to the actual possessions Prussia was to receive, Panin had another reservation: he wished the town of Toruń to be excluded from the list of acquisitions. Frederick's pretensions would then appear less an "arrangement of convenience." At the end of the conference, Panin glanced once again at the map and commented on the power the Prussian court would have over the commerce of Poland by virtue of its control of the Vistula. Solms suggested that this was not Prussia's intention but "did not wish to promise anything positive."[5]

Frederick was flexible—he would give up Toruń provided he could have Elbląg. He was generous—he was willing to reimburse the King of Poland for the loss of revenues from those territories he would lose. Frederick was not ambitious—"I have no interest in traversing the commerce of Poland and the town of Gdańsk."[6]

The Russo-Prussian negotiation was to continue along these lines until both parties were satisfied, and then they both would present their case to Austria. Everything was to be kept secret until then, but this was difficult. Already, in June, the Austrian court was certain that something was afoot between the two northern courts. "The Empress intimated," Stormont wrote of his conversation with Maria Theresa, "a strong suspicion of Russia's having formed a deep project of ambition—not less than an intention to

[3] PC, XXXI/19969/191-94; Frederick to Finckenstein, June 14, 1771, *ibid.*, 19970/193; and Oeuvres, VI, 42-43.

[4] Solms to Frederick, June 28, 1771, PC, XXXI/20036/243-44.

[5] Solms to Frederick, July 5, 1771, *ibid.*, 20052/255-56.

[6] Frederick to Solms, July 21 and 23, 1771, *ibid.*, 20052, 20058/256, 260-61, respectively. See also Frederick to Henry, *ibid.*, 20054/258 (July 21, 1771).

dismember Poland." This "we can never suffer," she declared. "I do not wish to keep a village that does not belong to me; I will make no encroachments, and as far as I am able will suffer none to be made. No project of partition however advantageous will tempt me a moment. I shall reject all such projects with disdain. I claim no merit from this; as I should act thus from principles of prudence and policy as well as from motives of equity and justice." Then in a most determined manner, Marie Theresa turned to the immediate danger of the war and said that "if this war does continue beyond this campaign, I must engage in it."[7]

Austria did not want war; this had been a firm policy since the conclusion of the Seven Years War. However, if she were forced into a corner, that is, if Russia continued to drive deeper into the Danube basin and demanded peace conditions that were intolerable, Austria would have no choice. The questions of how to stop the Russian advance, how to make that court come to reason and modify its demands, and how to keep other powers than Austria from dismembering Polish territory were the uppermost considerations at the Vienna court. It had mobilized its troops in Hungary, but this did not seem to be enough of a threat. An alliance with Turkey might turn the tide; but, better still, the semblance of an alliance might be enough, as Austria had no genuine intention of allying herself with a natural, temporal, and spiritual enemy.

During the first week in July a treaty was signed in Constantinople between the two courts. Austria promised to aid the Porte, diplomatically or by arms, in regaining those provinces and fortresses which Russia had taken in the war. Austria would further endeavor to gain a speedy and just peace, which would also provide for the independence and the security of the liberties of the Polish-Lithuanian Commonwealth. In return, Austria would receive a sizable sum of money, to be paid in installments, and, most important, would obtain certain territories lying close to Transylvania. Austrian subjects were to receive commercial privileges according to the most favored nation principle. Everything would be kept secret—especially from France. A ratification was neces-

[7] Stormont to Suffolk, July 1, 1771, BMAddMSS, 35501/11. See also AGS, I, 90-91.

sary, but, with the Turks delivering the first installment of money, the Vienna court was pressed for its approval. On August 6 Maria Theresa put her name to the treaty, but Thugut, the Austrian envoy at Constantinople, was not to produce the ratified instrument until he had further orders. If Russia yielded in her demands, decided on a speedy and just peace, and gave up the idea of partitioning Poland with Prussia, the treaty could easily be scrapped and neither party would have a complaint, as that had been the purpose of concluding the treaty in the first place.[8]

The spread of the war seemed to be the only remaining catastrophic threat, since the plague had ceased. On July 1 the Financial Commission of the Crown of Poland issued an ordinance that all restrictions would be lifted, beginning on July 15.[9] There was no need then for the cordons that had been set up specifically for meeting the danger of pestilence. Swieten informed Hertzberg that Austria was removing her cordon,[10] and Frederick said he would do the same at the earliest opportunity. He had already given orders for the reduction of his posts; only a few would remain for communication purposes with the kingdom of Prussia after the autumn.[11]

Frederick had no desire to keep his troops on Polish soil before the partition convention was agreed upon. When Saldern, Volkonskii's successor in Warsaw, suggested that he "take into his cordon the town of Poznań with its palatinate," Frederick flatly refused. From Saldern's viewpoint it would lessen the pressure on the Russian troops in that area, who were still pursuing the Confederates. If the Austrian court took umbrage at this action, Saldern offered a solution that on the surface seemed highly undesirable—Austria could take Kraków into her cordon.[12]

[8] See Albert Sorel, *The Eastern Question in the Eighteenth Century,* pp. 154-69, and Adolf Beer, *Die erste Theilung Polens,* II, 119-21. See also Joseph to Maria Theresa, Sept. 2, 1771, Alfred Ritter von Arneth, *Briefe der Kaiserin Maria Theresia an Ihre Kinder und Freunde,* I, 4n.

[9] BPAN, 318/195. See also Wroughton to Suffolk, Aug. 2, 1771, PROSP, 88/102, *et seq.,* and Suffolk to Wroughton, Jan. 31, 1772, PROSP, 88/104.

[10] See Hertzberg to Frederick, Aug. 1, 1771, PC, XXXI/20079/274.

[11] See Frederick to Seyditz, July 28, 1771, *ibid.,* 20068/267, and Frederick to Hertzberg, Aug. 2, 1771, *ibid.,* 20079/274-75.

[12] See Saldern to Frederick, July 31, 1771, *ibid.,* 20101/293n. See also Panin to Saldern, Sept. 8, 1771, Sb, LCVII/2099/431-32. It should not be thought, however,

Frederick was of a different mind. "It is impossible," he wrote to Benoit on August 4, "that I advance as far into Poland as [Saldern] desires. This would attract too much attention from the other powers and would give cause, perhaps, for a war with the court of Austria." When the peace was concluded, then Prussian troops could enter Poland to "bring the Confederates to reason by force," in order that they accept the conditions imposed upon them. He suggested that Saldern request more Russian troops (about 8,000 or 10,000) because, according to him, there did not seem to be enough.[13]

On August 13 Panin presented to the Council for the first time Frederick's convention, with the revisions Panin thought necessary. The acquisitions to go to Prussia were the same ones that Frederick had suggested in Article I of his "Draft" but without Toruń. Elbląg was not expressly named as the substitute for Toruń, but this was "understood." Panin did not add an article on the security of commerce for the town of Gdańsk or the Commonwealth as a whole.

The acquisitions which would fall to Russia were the rest of Livonia, part of Połock, and all of the Witebsk Palatinate that lay on the eastern side of the Dwina. This river was to be the natural boundary between Russia and Poland. From the point where the three palatinates (Połock, Witebsk, and Mińsk) met, a line would be drawn to the headwaters of the River Drucz to a place named Ordva, and from there, following this river to the Dnieper, so that all of the Palatinate of Mścisław, on both sides of the River Dnieper would be included in the territory to be ceded to Russia.

Panin added another article marked "separate and secret" concerning Austria. The warlike demonstrations of the Vienna

---

that Saldern confused the enclosure of Poznań or Kraków in the cordons as a permanent step which would lead to the further dismemberment of the country. It was merely a temporary measure, as Saldern, unlike his predecessor or others at the Russian court, was opposed to the dismemberment of Poland because, according to him, it would cause endless troubles. See Frederick to Solms, July 17, 1771, PC, XXXI/20048/252.

[13] PC, XXXI/20085/280-81. See also Frederick to Benoit, July 17, 1771, *ibid.*, 20049/252-53; Frederick to Saldern, and to Benoit, Aug. 11, 1771, *ibid.*, 20101-20102/293-94, 294, respectively; Frederick to Solms, Aug. 25, 1771, *ibid.*, 20131/318; and Wroughton to Suffolk, Aug. 31, 1771, PROSP, 88/102.

court had been noted, but the result was different from what that court had expected. Instead of frightening the court of Russia into a moderate policy toward the Porte, it caused Russia to take precautions. The substance of this new article provided for Frederick to assist Russia with 20,000 troops, if Austria attempted to prevent the partition of Poland by the two northern courts or compel Russia to restore to Turkey the provinces of Moldavia and Wallachia. The *casus foederus* would be Austria's sending her troops either into Poland or into the conquered provinces with the intention of operating hostilely against Russia.[14]

Surely there was no reciprocity in this separate and secret article, Solms told Panin. Prussia gave all and received nothing. Panin was sensible about this and admitted the difficult position that his court faced, but something had to be done in view of the Austrian threat. "If the court of Vienna did not wish or was unable to make war," Panin told Solms, then why its "menaces and demonstrations?" The Russian court, convinced of the necessity of protecting itself, needed Prussian assistance. If Frederick wanted to insert or add something of his own to this secret article, the Russian court would be glad to consider it.[15]

More than three weeks elapsed before Frederick replied to the Russian court concerning the secret article. It was a simple equation. Since Russia now requested more assistance from Prussia owing to the additional outlays that the war with Austria might bring, Frederick believed himself entitled to increase the number of his acquisitions.[16] He wanted Gdańsk.

The settlement of this article alone was to cause more difficulty than the other parts of the convention. In several respects the Rus-

[14] Solms to Frederick, Aug. 13, 1771, PC, XXXI/20144/330-31; AGS, I, 99-100 (Aug. 13, 1771); and Sergei Milkhailovich Solov'ëv, *Istoriia Rossii s drevneishikh vremën*, XXVIII, 773.

[15] Solms to Frederick, Aug. 17 and 27, 1771, PC, XXXI/20150, 20169/337, 353-54, and AGS, I, 101 (Aug. 17, 1771). See also Panin to Saldern, Sept. 8, 1771, Sb, LCVII/2091/411-18. On September 2, the Council, upon Chernyshev's suggestion, decided to strengthen by 50,000 troops Russian forces in the Commonwealth. They were to be used against Austria in the event of that country's invading territory occupied by Russian troops and also against the Confederates. See Solov'ëv, XXVIII, 773-74, and Solms to Frederick, Sept. 10, 1771, PC, XXXI/20212/398.

[16] Frederick to Solms, Sept. 25 and 30, 1771, PC, XXXI/20212, 20223, 20224/399-401, 410-11, 411-14, respectively.

sian and the Prussian drafts were identical or similar in purport —both countries agreed on the necessity of protecting themselves against possible attack by Austria. It was the means of executing this article and the specific provisions concerned with the deployment and duration of their respective corps of occupation troops that proved for a time the major stumbling block. In face of the warlike gestures the court of Vienna was making, it became urgent that the article be agreed upon in order to conclude the convention regarding the partition itself.

During the month of October (and the entire winter) report followed report out of Vienna of the massing of Austrian troops and the call for still more to be mobilized.[17] The action of the court of Vienna started things in motion at Berlin. Frederick ordered several thousand troops to be ready at a moment's notice to enter Poland, and more battalions were being mobilized.[18] At the same time, Panin himself requested that Frederick occupy Poznań in order to relieve the Russian garrisons in that palatinate. Frederick did not refuse this time but made it clear in all his dispatches that his action was precipitated by the Russian court's request.[19]

In the meantime Frederick's request for Gdańsk provoked "great embarrassment" at the Russian court. Panin had been under the impression that Frederick had renounced this town forever. The Russian minister feared that Prussia's acquisition of Gdańsk would create many difficulties for Russia by making it appear that Russia contributed to making Prussia "so powerful on the Baltic and master of all the commerce of Poland. Moreover, Russia had recognized this town as free and independent, and, since Peter I, all his successors had guaranteed it the preservation of this independence."[20]

[17] See *ibid.*, 20234, 20261, 20286, 20344, 20357, 20399, 20433, 20435, 20461/425, 448, 466-67, 512, 521, 522-53, 582-83, 584, 603-4. See also Joseph to Maria Theresa, Sept. 2 and 4, 1771, Arneth, *Briefe der Kaiserin Maria Theresia . . .*, I, 4, 5-7, respectively; and Stormont to Suffolk, Oct. 12 and 19, 1771, BMAddMSS, 35501/3-4.

[18] See Burnet to Suffolk, Oct. 12 and 19, 1771, PROSP, 90/90.

[19] Solms to Frederick, Oct. 4, 1771, PC, XXXI/20285/465n; Frederick to Solms, Oct. 20, 1771, *ibid.*, p. 465; Frederick to Rohd, Oct. 23, 1771, *ibid.*, 20295/472; AGS, I, 103 (Aug. 27, 1771); Burnet to Suffolk, Oct. 26 and Nov. 2, 1771, PROSP, 90/90; Wroughton to Suffolk, Dec. 24, 1771, and Jan. 4, 1772, PROSP, 88/102, 88/104, respectively; and Cathcart to Suffolk, Jan. 28, 1772, PROSP, 91/89.

[20] Solms to Frederick, Oct. 15, 1771, PC, XXXI/20315/486-87. See also AGS, I, 112-13 (Oct. 17, 1771).

Frederick did not consider this "a formal response to the draft of the convention." He was somewhat disturbed by the stubbornness of Russia in not giving him Gdańsk. History had proved, he declared to Solms on October 30, that guarantees made in one era were never binding in another, that additional towns and territories were taken by successors of the guarantors. He again firmly stated that he must receive something for the increased dangers he was asked to shoulder.[21]

The outlook seemed bleak at the close of October for a speedy agreement on the partition convention and also for the restoration of peace between the Porte and Russia. Russia still demanded rewards that seemed extreme to the Porte, to Austria, and even to Prussia. Prussia had for the last several months asked Russia to modify her demands, especially concerning the independence of Moldavia and Wallachia. Austria and the Porte wanted more concessions, and Russia's hope that the Vienna court would accept her demands and cease its own warlike preparations came to nought. The war, and thus, too, the negotiations, continued.[22]

In November an event in Warsaw demonstrated in dramatic fashion the state into which Poland had fallen during these troubled times. The King was kidnaped and had to manipulate his own escape. It will be remembered that almost a year before, the Generalcy had declared the throne vacant. As with other declarations of the Confederates, nothing was done immediately, and, in this case, most of the major powers of Europe frowned upon the Generalcy's declaration of an interregnum in Poland. Nevertheless, on the night of November 3, as the King and some twenty dignitaries of state were leaving the palace of Michał Czartoryski, about forty Poles stole along the opposite side of the street in back of the King's party. Suddenly the King was set upon and carried away, with no resistance by his companions. Supposedly, he was to be brought to Kazimierz Pułaski and then killed. Fortunately, Stanislas Augustus was able to bribe the leader of the kidnapers, Jan Kuzma, and was allowed to escape. His return to War-

[21] PC, XXXI/20315/488.

[22] See VA, PreusWeis (Oct. 25, 1771); Beer, *Documente,* pp. 32-38; Solov'ëv, XXVIII, 781-82; Sorel, pp. 169-72; and Frederick to Thulmeier, Oct. 3, 1771, PC, XXXI/20236/427.

saw the following day caused a stir; everyone was astonished that this could have happened.[23]

When the King's brother, General Andrzej Poniatowski, in sorrow lamented this tragic event to Maria Theresa, she sympathized and told the General he should inform his brother that the Vienna court would entertain a reasonable pacification plan for Poland. The points she considered "reasonable" were:

1. That the King of Poland should remain in the peaceful possession of the throne.
2. That all the territories of the Republick should remain entire, and no part of them dismembered by any neighbouring power, under any pretence whatever.
3. That the article with regard to the guaranty of Russia should be repealed in the Diet.
4. That the priviledges granted to the Dissidents in the same Diet should be lessened.
5. An act of oblivion and indemnity—not to extend to private crises, not to include any of those who had been engaged in the attempt on the King's life [—should be proclaimed].
6. That in case of a vacancy of the throne the choice of a King should be left to the Poles alone, without the interference or influence of foreign troops or princes.[24]

In the circumstances, these provisions would have met with stern rejection from both Russia and Prussia.

On the one hand, besides the provisions concerning the Dissidents and the Russian guarantee of the Polish constitution, Russia could not accept the modified terms of peace which Austria demanded as a basis for ending the war with the Turks, nor could she accept Kaunitz' demand that Russia "give him positive assurances as preliminary [to any form of cooperation] that she did not desire to subject Poland to dismemberment."[25]

On the other, Frederick, although he would agree with several of the points set forth by Maria Theresa, could not and did not want to retreat from his policy of partitioning Poland. Negotiations

[23] See BPAN, 318/259-89, 320-25; BPAN, 1149/579-86; Wroughton to Suffolk, Nov. 6, 1771, PROSP, 88/102; and SAPMém, I, 673-83.

[24] Stormont to Suffolk, Nov. 23, 1771, BMAddMSS, 35501/9-10.

[25] Solms to Frederick, Nov. 22, 1771, PC, XXXI/20432/579-80.

had been carried too far to stop now, when the morsels of Polish land he had always dreamed of obtaining were at last within sight.

However, the stumbling block, the settlement of the secret article to the convention, had not been removed. Had not Russia feared the possibility of an Austrian attack, the partition convention could have been arranged, agreed upon, and ratified before the year was out. Despite Panin's stubborn refusal to yield Gdańsk, Frederick remained confident. "I have learned from you," he wrote Henry, "the secret of dealing with these people, that is, of repeating to them so frequently and so diversely the same thing that in the end they listen to it without being startled."[26]

Yet the attitude of Panin did not change. He reiterated that Russia had given her guarantee to Gdańsk and would not break faith, and, perhaps more important, that the commercial powers would raise every objection and would "find a hundred ways of taking revenge on Russia" for allowing Prussia to become so powerful on the Baltic.[27] This latter reason seemed to influence Frederick himself in his position on Gdańsk. His envoy in London wrote to him that "of all the things that [the English] seem to dread the most, it is that Your Majesty put himself in possession of all the commerce of the Baltic."[28]

It was obvious what the British position would be on this matter. At St. Petersburg, Cathcart made known to Panin his court's feelings on the subject: "I told him [the] commercial powers could not look . . . with indifference" upon Frederick's gaining control of the Baltic trade. Panin, however, played dumb to the fact that Frederick "had any such real intention."[29]

On December 6 Solms forwarded Russia's new counterproposal on the secret article. It arrived in Berlin on December

[26] *Ibid.*, 20360/524 (Nov. 10, 1771). See also Frederick to Solms, Nov. 3, 6, 10 and 15, 1771, *ibid.*, 20329, 20341, 20358, 20373/ 501-2, 510, 510-11, 522, 535-36, respectively.

[27] Solms to Frederick, Nov. 26, 1771, *ibid.*, 20444/591n, and AGS, I, 119 (Nov. 18, 1771), p. 121 (Nov. 26, 1771).

[28] Maltzan to Frederick, Dec. 3, 1771, PC, XXXI/20458/602n. See Frederick to Solms, Dec. 11, 1771, *ibid.*, 20444/591-92.

[29] Cathcart to Suffolk, Dec. 10, 1771, PROSP, 91/88. France even took heart at the possibility of Gdańsk going to Prussia. See Sorel, p. 179, and Duc de Broglie, *The King's Secret: Being the Secret Correspondence of Louis XV with His Diplomatic Agents from 1752 to 1774*, II, 343.

18, but Frederick could not digest its contents and reply to it before the following year.[30]

Russia in the meantime let the Austrian court know her disposition concerning the dismemberment of Poland. During the previous month, Kaunitz had made this a firm condition for any cooperation in arranging a peace between Russia and Turkey. Lobkowitz was advised to inform Vienna that both Russia and Prussia had well-founded claims to Polish land, as had Austria. Panin vaguely asserted that if the court of Vienna saw fit to join with the two northern courts in concerting "an accord," he would "listen" to what it had to say. The guiding principle would be to maintain the balance of power.[31]

This step surprised Frederick. "I do not know why they are eager to request permission at the court of Vienna to assert their rights in Poland," he wrote to Solms on December 28. Notwithstanding this annoyance, he was confident that Austria would adhere to her formerly stated policy and not choose to dismember Poland any further.[32]

On January 4, 1772, Frederick sent to Solms his reply to the Russian counter-proposal of December 6. A further explanation of Article II of the convention was made by both courts as well as a revision of the "separate and secret article." Regarding Article II, both courts agreed to send their troops into the Polish territories which they intended to "reunite" with their realms in late spring. Once the occupation was completed, the Russian draft announced, the Austrian court would be officially informed of the partition, and Austria would have to recognize and acquiesce in the partition before it could become effective. The Prussian draft called only for a joint declaration to be made to Austria that the partition was accomplished and then "allowing her to enter into the plan of partition" if she so wished. However, the partition would not have less effect if Austria did not agree to recognize or support the partition. The "separate and secret article" provided for several meas-

[30] See PC, XXXI/20511/641n; Solms to Frederick, Dec. 6 and 10, 1771, *ibid.*, 20460, 20484/ 603, 620n, respectively.

[31] Solms to Frederick, Dec. 16, 1771, *ibid.*, 20492/625.

[32] *Ibid.*, p. 626.

ures to be taken in the event that Austria chose to oppose the partition by force.[33]

In another dispatch to Solms that same day, Frederick renounced Gdańsk for the second time. He requested at the same time that this town be "declared free and entirely independent of the Crown of Poland."[34] Notwithstanding this provision, it should not be thought that Frederick renounced Gdańsk and the mastery of the Baltic forever. "I will be able to return, when circumstances are favorable," he wrote to Solms two weeks later.[35]

Panin, at least, was satisfied that Frederick had given up his demand for Gdańsk. Concerning the request that it be made a "free and independent town," he foresaw no objection from the Russian court. But if this were to take place it would be better to wait until after the partition convention was settled. Moreover, he did not know whether Gdańsk itself would desire this new status. In addition, before Panin would occupy Polish territory, he preferred knowing the disposition of the Vienna court concerning the partition.[36]

Panin and Frederick did not have long to wait since discussions concerning the Russo-Turkish War and the dismemberment of Poland were taking place at Vienna. On January 17 Kaunitz drew up a dismemberment proposal and submitted it to Maria Theresa for consideration. The introduction read:

> After the extraordinarily successful . . . campaign of Russia there is no hope of prevailing upon her to grant the Porte any better peace conditions, and as Russia and Prussia have already agreed upon their shares in Poland, there is . . . nothing left . . . for us to do but to join . . . in the partition agreement, on the principle of . . . equality between . . . the three powers. Herewith are enclosed seven partition proposals with the proper explanations. . . . Your Majesty is to decide . . . whether the agreed-upon proposal is to be submitted first to Prussia or

[33] *Ibid.*, 20511/644-46.

[34] *Ibid.*, 20512/646-55. Frederick wrote to Solms on January 8 that "as to the matter of Gdańsk . . . it is England to whom I owe all the difficulties that I have encountered in making this succeed." Frederick believed that Russia would have given in to his request for Gdańsk if it had not been for England. *Ibid.*, 20521/662.

[35] *Ibid.*, 20545/682 (Jan. 19, 1772).

[36] Solms to Frederick, January 10 and 17, 1772, *ibid.*, 20570, 20584/702, 713-15, respectively, and AGS, I, 137-38 (Jan. 20 and 21, 1772).

Russia, or to both at the same time, and also what representations are to be made to the Porte.

Kaunitz really desired that Turkey be partitioned instead of Poland, for this would cheat Prussia out of her share. Three of the seven proposals were directed toward this end. Kaunitz' remarks on the partition of Poland contained the principle of equality, based on considerations of territory, population, and resources, among the three powers. The best arrangement would be for Frederick to take Austria's share in Poland and return Glatz and part of Silesia to their former owner, Austria. If he refused, Austria should then ask for Ansbach and Bayreuth; and if he refused this, Austria should ask for all of Wallachia and the part of Bessarabia that bordered on the Black Sea. Poland should then get the other parts of the Danubian principalities. If everything failed, Austria should be content to take Polish territory, but only on the principle of equality.[37]

Maria Theresa consulted Joseph on the partition proposals, and he disagreed with Kaunitz on almost every point. The very fact that Prussia and Russia were asking for peace and dismemberment gave Joseph the impression that the two powers were arguing from a weak position. War with Russia would be a gain for Austria, because it would weaken both northern courts. "Only fear and necessity," Joseph wrote, would have brought these two courts to venture this policy of partition. In view of this, Austria should prepare for war; he thought Austria could be ready for the struggle by 1773. In the meantime, Austria should occupy Kraków, Sandomierz, Lwów, and Częstochowa, and declare herself "willing to relinquish them and to withdraw the troops as soon as . . . Russia and Prussia did the same."[38]

Maria Theresa was hesitant. She cared for neither plan and wanted more discussion. Kaunitz bit into Joseph's criticism of his proposals, declaring that the longer the war continued between Russia and Turkey, the more victories there would be for Russia. Once the Porte realized the uselessness of continuing the war, she would seek an accommodation with the Russian court but

[37] VA, Polen III, Erste Teilung Polens Akten.

[38] VA, Vorträge, and Beer, *Documente*, pp. 39-42 (Jan. 19, 1772).

on terms favorable to Russia, and then peace would be made. If the Porte were allowed to continue the war and suffer the defeats, Russia could continue asking for greater concessions, and the end result would be to destroy further the balance of power, the maintenance of which was then so desperately sought by Austria. No matter which way Austria was to turn, her interests were "tied up with those of Russia and Prussia." It was necessary for Austria to come to some understanding with those powers concerning the partition agreement. Military demonstrations were worthless because they had not frightened Russia into reducing her demands. Besides, they had been and would be a worthless expense. If Austria were to follow the step asked for by Joseph and occupy the above-mentioned territories in Poland, she might cause Frederick to declare war on Austria. This would be catastrophic. Joseph could not argue against this barrage of sound reasoning, and deferred to Maria Theresa to make a decision.[39]

Maria Theresa again expressed her dissatisfaction with both her son's and Kaunitz' proposals. She discounted the proposals regarding Turkey because of the recently concluded convention she had made with the Porte. Concerning Poland, it would be most desirable if Frederick took Austria's portion and in return ceded Glatz and part of Silesia. She believed that nothing would come of Austria's asking for Ansbach and Bayreuth, and she did not consider as useful the acquisition of Wallachia and part of Bessarabia. Austrian participation in the partition of Poland, according to Maria Theresa, was unjust. Therefore, everything depended upon Austria's coming out of the complicated affair *mit Billigkeit,* and it might even be advantageous if Austria put an end to the whole business without any gains. What must be avoided was the combination of Russia, Turkey, and Prussia against Austria. Maria Theresa wanted to end hostilities, but, in the last analysis, if Russia and Prussia partitioned Poland, she "could not view that with indifference." She did not want to share in the dismemberment of either Turkey or Poland, but if Prussia were to take some provinces in Poland, Frederick should recompense Austria. "It is not a question of more or less, but of how to get out of the

[39] VA, Vorträge, and Beer, *Documente,* pp. 42-48 (Jan. 20, 1772).

whole affair with the least harm. This, however, must take place without any loss of time."[40]

On January 25 Kaunitz wrote to Swieten of the Austrian court's decision—its share of Poland for Glatz and a part of Silesia. Kaunitz added in a postscript: "If His Royal Majesty cannot be persuaded to exchange our share in the partition for Glatz and a part of Silesia . . . then you had better suggest . . . Ansbach and Bayreuth either in whole or in part." If this proposal failed, Swieten was then to ask for the Turkish provinces, especially Belgrade and a part of Bosnia. Kaunitz concluded that "if this is not to be gained either, then it is better that Moldavia go to Poland as a compensation for the latter's loss of territory to Prussia and Russia, and we can take Wallachia and Bessarabia, which would serve as a barrier against Russia."[41]

When Swieten received his instructions on January 31, he went to see Finckenstein in Berlin the same day. Finckenstein was shown a copy of the "response of the Emperor and Empress-Queen to the personal response of the Empress of All the Russias." It contained richly embroidered prose declaring the peaceful and friendly intentions of the house of Austria. It expressed the hope that in Austria's answer to the court of Russia, Frederick would also be satisfied. The Vienna court believed it was necessary to act in concert with the courts of Prussia and Russia in dismembering the Polish-Lithuanian Commonwealth. But before the formal response was forwarded to Russia, Austria wanted to concert with Prussia on the subject. Perfect equality would be necessary in the dismemberment. The promise would be made in writing. The portion to go to Austria would be directly and equally proportional to the share that Prussia would take; great or small, Austria would follow the example of Prussia. Swieten explained that he was authorized to negotiate this convention for his court and that he hoped all talks would follow the principles laid down at Neustadt.[42]

Frederick read Finckenstein's report of his talk with Swieten

[40] VA, Vorträge, and Beer, II, 340-41 (Jan. 22, 1772).

[41] VA, PreusWeis; Vorträge, Jan. 23, 1772; and Beer, II, 341-43.

[42] See Finckenstein to Frederick, Jan. 31, 1772, PC, XXXI/20582/711-12, and VA, PreusWeis, Jan. 25, 1772.

with "infinite pleasure,"[43] and informed Solms of the change in the Vienna court's attitude. He now believed there would be no difficulty in arranging the partition convention. To make things easier he agreed to the minor modifications in the "separate and secret article" and withdrew his request that the convention declare Gdańsk a free and independent town. He was indifferent to either May or June as the month for occupation of the provinces and stressed the necessity of Solm's signing the convention as soon as possible.[44]

On February 4 Swieten and Frederick met and discussed the dismemberment of Poland. Swieten asked Frederick what Prussia and Russia had decided on as their shares in Poland, since the Austrian share would depend upon what they were to receive. Frederick accommodated him and suggested that Austria could take as much as she wanted of the territory lying along the Hungarian frontier, excepting Kraków.

Swieten told Frederick that his portion was "admirably well situated to round out His states" and that it could not be purchased even after a long war. "It follows that ours ought to be equal, not only in the extent of land or in its intrinsic value, but also by its importance and political value." Austria would be hard pressed to "find anything in Poland that can give us the same advantages which the possession of Polish Prussia will give You, Sire."

Swieten then suggested that Frederick take Austria's portion in Poland. "But," Frederick queried, "why do you wish that I take your portion?" "Because then, Sire . . . Your Majesty would cede Glatz and a part of Silesia." Frederick snapped: "No. . . . I request nothing more than Polish Prussia; you take your part where you please, but it should not be at my expense." "This would not be at Your expense, Sire," Swieten said, "You will find a perfect compensation, and it is a matter of exchange only."

Swieten tried to persuade Frederick of the advantages to him in this exchange. From the Austrian side it was a matter of great util-

[43] Frederick to Finckenstein, Feb. 1, 1772, PC, XXXI/20582/712.

[44] Frederick to Solms, Feb. 1 and 2, 1772, *ibid.*, 20583-20584/712-13, 715-17, respectively.

ity that Glatz be restored to her. "Glatz is the key to Bohemia . . . You do not need it for defense purposes as much as we do." "But the Emperor has promised me himself that he would never dream of recovering Silesia or Glatz, and Prince Kaunitz has formally and solemnly repeated it to me," Frederick cried. Swieten assured Frederick that his court "has certainly renounced all idea of conquering Silesia and Glatz," but this was not the point; it was an exchange that Austria had suggested, not conquest.

Frederick was annoyed: "I have believed, and still believe that you will be able to find what you want in Poland. . . . But, as for me, I declare to you flatly that neither am I able nor do I wish to agree to any dismemberment of that of which I have actual possession." Frederick then intimated that if Austria could not find anything satisfactory in Poland, she ought to look elsewhere. The subject turned to Turkey. Swieten alluded to the possibility of Austria's obtaining Belgrade and Bosnia and Serbia. This appeared reasonable to Frederick, but he was doubtful of its success. Swieten suggested that it still could be arranged at the forthcoming peace congress between Turkey and Russia. He hinted that Frederick might inquire at the Russian court concerning the feasibility of the matter, but refused to take the responsibility himself for such an overture. Frederick agreed to write to Petersburg, saying that, of course, he would not involve Swieten in the negotiations. The audience was closed on that note.[45]

Frederick wrote to Solms all that had happened between him and Swieten and instructed him to tell Panin everything.[46] But before this news reached Solms, Panin had already received word from Golitsyn that Austria had decided to enter into the partition agreement with the two northern courts.[47]

This promise on the part of the Vienna court was sufficient assurance for Russia to go ahead with the signing of the partition convention with Prussia. With a few changes in language, which however did not alter the substance of the partition clauses, the convention was signed in Council on the night of February 17. The

[45] "Unterredung . . ." *ibid.*, 20591/722-29.

[46] *Ibid.*, 20592, 20622/730-31, 751 (Feb. 5 and 12, 1772), respectively.

[47] Solms to Frederick, Feb. 14, 1772, *ibid.*, 20686/802-3.

convention bore the date of January 15, 1772, only because it was thought necessary to show that there was an agreement prior to the Austrian announcement to enter into the partition.[48]

All that remained now was for Austria to state her equal share, and the occupation by Prussia and Russia of Polish provinces would take place sometime in June. Following that, a formal declaration and announcement would be made to the Polish government for her acceptance of the *fait accompli.*

[48] AGS, I, 146-48, and Solms to Frederick, Feb. 18, 1772, PC, XXXI/20686/803-5.

By Jove, Monsieur, from what I see, you are not at all particular. You have a good appetite. Your part alone is greater than mine and that of Russia taken together; in truth, you are not particular.[1]

FREDERICK TO SWIETEN

XIII

THE LION'S SHARE
FEBRUARY 12—AUGUST 5, 1772

"He believes himself an oracle in politics and the others schoolboys whom he wishes to teach," Frederick criticized Kaunitz after their meeting at Neustadt.[2] Frederick had reason to be annoyed again—Kaunitz in the partition negotiations outmaneuvered him, although both together clearly outshone Panin. Panin no longer initiated the moves; Frederick was too anxious to conclude the affair; but Kaunitz was ever patient. In the end, this was his winning quality.

"Even if the whole thing were necessary, I am by no means convinced that it is just," Maria Theresa commented on the proposed partition of Turkey. "We allied ourselves with the Porte, we have taken money from her. . . . There can be no question of our enriching ourselves at her cost." The only thing that remained, therefore, was to take more Polish land—it was, for Maria Theresa, the "lesser evil." Austrian aggrandizement would be directed not against her natural enemy but against her Catholic sister.[3]

On February 19 Kaunitz sent to Swieten and Lobkowitz the following declaration, which was signed by Maria Theresa and Joseph:

[1] "Unterredung . . ." April 19, 1772, PC, XXXII/20865/130-31.
[2] Frederick to Rohd, Sept. 5, 1770, PC, XXX/19259/114.
[3] Alfred Ritter von Arneth, *Geschichte Maria Theresia,* VIII, 358-60, 595-96 (c. Feb. 12, 1772). Joseph disagreed with his mother. He believed it "detrimental, unjust, and unfeasible." He insisted (without success) that Austria's boundary should be the Prut River and that all of Moldavia, Wallachia, and Bessarabia, in addition to "the town of Orsowa and Belgrad," should go to Austria. See Adolf Beer, *Die erste Theilung Polens,* II, 343-44, c. Feb. 14, 1772.

His Majesty the King of Prussia and Her Majesty the Empress of All the Russias have rights and pretensions to certain palatinates and districts in Poland, as we, on our part, have; in order to prevent any difficulties that might arise in this connection, which might change the friendship and the good understanding happily existing between us, we declare . . . that whatever the extent of our respective pretensions, the acquisitions . . . should be perfectly equal, that the portion of one should not exceed that of another, and that, far from putting any obstacles in the way of the measures which each might find it necessary to undertake for realizing her pretensions, we should, in the case of need, mutually and in good faith aid each other, in order to facilitate our success. We promise at the same time the most perfect secrecy concerning the present reciprocal engagements.[4]

On the same day Kaunitz informed Swieten that he was to disavow all former proposals concerning the exchange of shares. Austrian policy had changed, and former proposals were to be relegated to oblivion.[5]

On February 28, after being handed the declaration, Frederick questioned Swieten on Austria's intentions to seek compensations in Turkey. Swieten told Frederick that, after some reflection, he had decided to give up the idea because it involved breaking faith with the Turks—something his court could not do. Frederick then suggested that Austria could take Lwów and part of Ruthenia, except Kraków, and the land extending to Teschen. To this suggestion Swieten made no comment, because, as he explained, he had no instructions from Vienna.[6]

Several weeks passed, but Austria did not state her claims. Frederick became impatient with Vienna and cross with Kaunitz. "The more I observe the conduct of Prince Kaunitz, the more I notice the finesse and duplicity of it. In effect," he wrote to Edelsheim, the Prussian ambassador to Vienna, on March 29, "after having acceded to the plan of partition of Poland resolved between me and Russia, it seems to me that it would have been very simple and natural that this minister should have declared with more precision the intentions of his court relating to this object, and that he should have described more clearly the provinces it desires for its portion." Kaunitz' reserve gave Frederick "furious

[4] VA, Vorträge, and PC, XXXI/20680/793n. See also AGS, I, 151-54.
[5] VA, PreusWeis, and Beer, *Documente,* pp. 177-80.
[6] "Unterredung . . ." PC, XXXI/20680/793-98.

suspicions." "It is important for me to draw this matter to a close as soon as possible," Frederick emphatically told his envoy. "You tell [Kaunitz] plainly that I made known my surprise at the delay."[7]

But Kaunitz believed it not expedient to inform Frederick and Catherine of Austria's claims. For him it was a sensible policy. The longer Austria was able to delay the execution of the partition, the more anxious Frederick and Catherine would be to conclude the affair and, because of their impatience, the less opposition they would make to Austria's claims.[8]

Kaunitz also believed that Austria had more to gain in the end if the initial demands were high. On April 11 he informed Lobkowitz of Austria's staggering claims, and even hinted that these were "tentative"—they might in the end be still greater because the court at Vienna was as yet not well acquainted with Polish geography. Lobkowitz was not to modify the Austrian claims if the Russian court complained that they were exaggerated. He was, on the contrary, to do everything possible to put them through, without at the same time allowing the Russians to increase theirs. If this became impossible, however, Lobkowitz was not to sign the agreement until further notice from Vienna.[9]

Austria's demands were embodied in a document entitled "Projet d'Article" and a copy was sent to Swieten and Lobkowitz. The boundary line ran from Biała along the Vistula up to but not including Sandomierz and then north to Zwoleń (which lies east of Radom) but not including Zwoleń. From that point the boundary line went east to Parczew (which lies above Lublin) and then southeast along the boundary of the Palatinates of Bełz and Wołyń in such a way as to include in the new frontier not only Lublin, Chełm, and Włodzimierz Wołyński, but also the entire Palatinate of Bełz. The boundary line then continued southeasterly, passing by and including Tarnopol until it reached the Zbrucz River, along which the boundary line continued until it reached Moldavia at Chocim.[10]

[7] PC, XXXII/20785/63.
[8] See Kaunitz to Swieten, March 30, 1772, VA, PreusWeis.
[9] VA, RussWeis.
[10] *Ibid.*, and PC, XXXII/20865/130-31n. See also Joseph to Leopold, April 1772, Arneth (ed.), *Maria Theresia und Joseph II . . .*, I, 367-68.

The Austrian eagle had spread its wings very far indeed. Edelsheim wrote to Frederick after learning of this communiqué: "This will be neither the smallest of the three portions nor the least important, by the considerable number of towns and mines . . . that find themselves enclaved."[11]

Prussia and Russia were to find Austria always one step ahead of them, as had been the case with the initial occupation of Polish territory in 1770. On April 12 Kaunitz informed Swieten that he intended to send troops into the provinces outlined for Austria's share in the partition,[12] which action, according to Edelsheim, would prevent a modification of Austrian demands.[13] On April 15 Stormont wrote to Suffolk that orders had already been given for 20,000 Imperial troops to march from Hungary into Poland.[14]

The Austrian envoy formally presented Frederick with the "Projet d'Article" on April 19, and Frederick at once expressed his amazement over the Austrian claim. Swieten was calm: "I do not believe that our acquisition would ever equal the advantages which Your Majesty will obtain. . . . The situation of Polish Prussia is unique for the rounding out and the free communication it gives to Your States, Sire, and, whereas we will acquire only land, Your Majesty acquires, that is to say, a kingdom." Frederick claimed that it was "a poor country of sand," which lacked "fertility and population." Unimpressed, Swieten maintained that it was "the political value" of the acquisition which was important. This was where the lack of balance presented itself. Swieten even questioned the lack of fertility and population of the lands going to Frederick. After all, he said, would not Frederick enjoy a "double advantage" from the Bishopric of Warmia? Frederick, irritated by the Austrian ambassador, suggested that Austria take her compensation elsewhere. "From whom, Sire?" "From the Turks," Frederick replied. "Your Majesty knows that the idea of taking our part from the Turks came only from me and that it has been re-

[11] PC, XXXII/20855/123 (April 11, 1772).

[12] VA, PreusWeis.

[13] PC, XXXII/20874/143n (April 15, 1772).

[14] BMAddMSS, 35501/26. When the French ambassador at the Vienna court confronted Kaunitz with the rumor which had been circulated that the three powers were concerting to partition Poland, Kaunitz had but one answer for him: "When you took Corsica, we said nothing." *Ibid.* See also Frederick to Edelsheim, April 15, 1772, PC, XXXII/20846/115.

jected by my court." Frederick seemed to be getting nowhere with Swieten. "You have a good appetite," he muttered.

The conversation then turned to the details involving the occupation, which would take place in June, and to the manifesto, which would later be presented by all courts to the Commonwealth. Frederick did not expect Stanislas Augustus to accept the partition with ease and thought he would resort to "some romantic scene." "How, Sire? Will he put himself at the head of an army?" "Oh, no," Frederick stated. "You will see that he will wish to abdicate, and this would be troublesome, because it would create new troubles. But I believe, however, that after having played his scene, he will sober up; the King of Poland is a good, gallant man, but he has a feeble head and is full of romantic ideas, and he will certainly show some on this occasion." Frederick did not fear the Poles themselves: "I do not believe that they will dare stir, and, in any event, one would box their ears for them." He hoped that Poland could be easily pacified, that the Dissidents would demand less, that that the *Liberum Veto* would remain fundamental law.[15]

Frederick could not persuade Swieten to recommend a modification of the Austrian claims. His last hope lay with the Russian court. Austria wanted as much in "quantity" and "quality" as Prussia and Russia combined. He hoped that Russia would support him in demanding a modification of this claim, especially the territory near Kraków, where the rich salt mines were. They alone exceeded the revenues that Frederick hoped to gain from his acquisition. The principle of equality was in question; "the frontier that Prince Kaunitz has traced almost touches Warsaw." It would be necessary, according to Frederick, "to evaluate our possessions according to population, or to the extent or yield of land."[16] But something had to be done soon, since Austria had already sent 20,000 troops into Poland from Hungary and another 70,000 would soon cross over from Austrian Silesia.[17]

[15] "Unterredung . . ." PC, XXXII/20865/130-35.

[16] Frederick to Edelsheim, April 18, 1772, *ibid.*, 20855/123, and Frederick to Solms, April 20, 1772, *ibid.*, 20866/136-37. See also Frederick to Henry, April 20, 1772, *ibid.*, 20869/139.

[17] Frederick to Solms, April 22, 1772, *ibid.*, 20872/142, and Joseph to Kaunitz, May 2, 1772, in Beer, II, 344-45. See also Wroughton to Suffolk, May 9, 1772, PROSP, 88/104, and Joseph to Lacy, May 25, 1772, quoted in Arneth, *Geschichte Maria Theresia*, VIII, 604.

Russia needed no prompting from Frederick to recognize the extraordinary claim that Austria had made. On April 24 the Council decided that it was necessary to exclude the salt mines and Lwów from the Austrian share. Russia could not stand by and allow the major revenues to be taken from the Polish King, nor could she allow Austria to seize one of the richest towns in all Poland.[18] When Frederick received word of this decision, it became his policy also, and he instructed Edelsheim to urge the Vienna court to agree to this modification.[19]

Kaunitz's reply was less than satisfying to both northern courts. He wrote to Lobkowitz on May 30, "I am not yet in a position to give you any positive instructions . . . but cannot refrain . . . from communicating to you certain considerations." Lwów and the salt mines were for Austria the only part of her claim that had any "real value." Without them Austria's share would be a "narrow . . . and exposed strip of land." The balance of power was the primary consideration of the Vienna court, and to deprive the court of these acquisitions would be to upset this balance to the disadvantage of Austria.[20]

The occupation of Polish provinces by Austrian troops and the refusal of Austria to modify her demands greatly angered Frederick. He believed the only recourse Prussia had was to follow the Austrian example and occupy with its own troops the provinces destined for it.[21] Panin, however, begged Frederick to wait until Austria had given her formal declaration on the convention.[22] Frederick acquiesced and informed Solms that he would not occupy the provinces unless it was formally agreed to by Panin.[23] In the meantime, both courts would await the formal declaration of the Vienna court on the partition convention.[24]

[18] AGS, I, 164 ff. Sergei Mikhailovich Solov'ëv, *Istoriia Rossii s drevneishikh vremën*, XXVIII, 853; Solms to Frederick, April 28, 1772, PC, XXXII/20942/192n; and Lobkowitz to Kaunitz, May 1, 1772, VA, RussBer.

[19] PC, XXXII/20958, 20967/204, 211 (May 17 and 20, 1772, respectively).

[20] VA, RussWeis, and Beer, *Documente*, pp. 217-19. See also Lobkowitz to Kaunitz, May 28, 1772, VA, RussBer, and Beer, *Documente*, pp. 115-20.

[21] Frederick to Solms, June 1, 1772, PC, XXXII/20991/229-30.

[22] Solms to Frederick, June 19, 1772, PC, XXXII/21086/305n. See also Frederick to Edelsheim, June 11, 1772, *ibid.*, 21005/243, and Frederick to Solms, June 24, 1772, *ibid.*, 21051/278.

[23] *Ibid.*, 21086/305 (July 5, 1772).

[24] See *ibid.*, 21000, 21005, 21067/238, 243n, 290-91, respectively, and AGS, I, 172 ff.

At the beginning of July the Vienna court finally modified its demands. Lublin, Chełm, and Włodzimierz Wołyński would be relinquished, but the salt mines and Lwów would remain in the Austrian claim. This was the final word.[25] On July 12 Swieten informed Frederick of these conditions. Frederick was complacent: "My advice on all this, after having carefully reflected," he wrote to Solms the same day, "is that if one wishes to terminate this affair pleasantly, it will be necessary to yield to these conditions and acquiesce."[26]

Lobkowitz received these new instructions on July 24. Two days later he informed Panin of their nature, and the Russian minister was pleased by the modification. Panin stated that he would bring the matter before Catherine, and, if she agreed, the convention would be signed in a week.[27] Panin told Solms of his talk with Lobkowitz and expressed his desire to follow Frederick's advice and accept the Vienna court's proposal as the basis for the final conclusion of the partition. "All those whom I have been able to speak to on this affair," Solms stated, "are of the same sentiment. Her Majesty the Empress has frankly made known to me that she was very much content, and the others here all regard the cession of the two important provinces as a triumph over the court of Vienna."[28]

A few days later Panin told Solms that Catherine was entirely

[25] VA, Vorträge, July 3 and 5, 1772; Kaunitz to Swieten and Lobkowitz, July 5, 1772, VA, PreusWeis and RussWeis; Beer, *Documente,* pp. 115-20, 127-32; and Joseph to Leopold, June 17, 1772, Arneth (ed.), *Maria Theresia und Joseph II . . .,* I, 360-70.

[26] PC, XXXII/21102/325-26. See also Frederick to Solms, July 19, 1772, *ibid.,* 21124/340.

[27] Lobkowitz to Kaunitz, July 28, 1772, VA, RussBer, and AGS, I, 186-87, July 27, 1772. See also Joseph to Leopold, July 20, 1772, Arneth (ed.), *Maria Theresia und Joseph II . . .,* I, 375-76. On July 10 Gunning wrote to Suffolk: "Count Zachar Czernichew (the author of the Partition Treaty in Russia, and a professed enemy of Count Saldern [sic])." BMAddMSS, 35502/3. Four days later Gunning wrote to Suffolk and commented on Prince Henry's visit the previous year. "There can be no doubt but he inspired the Empress with very different sentiments from those he found her in possession." PROSP, 91/90. On July 24 Gunning wrote: "Panin and [Chernyshev] have from the beginning differed in opinion with regard to Polish affairs, but the sentiments of the latter, being more conformable to those of the Empress, have prevailed." PROSP, 91/90.

[28] PC, XXXII/21199/401 (July 28, 1772). Frederick wrote to Solms on July 29: "If Russia shows some condescension to [Kaunitz's] propositions, the success of this important negotiation is assured; if, on the contrary, she does not accept it, one can be assured that we will never finish with Prince Kaunitz." *Ibid.,* 21152/362.

in accord with Frederick on the whole affair and that she had resolved to follow Frederick's advice by accepting the latest conditions of the court of Vienna. In a week, Panin said, the triple convention could be signed.[29]

On August 5, 1772, the solemn ceremony of signing the partition conventions between Austria, Russia, and Prussia took place in St. Petersburg.[30]

[29] Solms to Frederick, July 31, 1772, *ibid.*, 21215/414.
[30] See F. de Martens (ed.), *Recueil des traités et conventions, conclus par la Russie avec les puissances étrangères*, II, 21-29, VI, 65-71, and AGS, I, 187-88.

For pride, gluttony and hidden hates, Hungary perished—take care that the same does not happen to you Poles.[1]

DEPUTY PRZYIEMSKI AT THE DIET

XIV

THE PARTITION MADE LEGAL
AUGUST 6, 1772—SEPTEMBER 30, 1773

The ratification of the conventions by the Diet was the last step in making the dismemberment of the Polish-Lithuanian Commonwealth a formal act. Indeed, at the turn of the year the partition had already taken place, the feudal homage had been obtained, the scattered small groups of Confederates rendered ineffective, and the respective provinces occupied by the three powers. The protests of the Commonwealth went unheard.[2]

On February 8, 1773, Stanislas Augustus called the Senate Council to discuss the most important and pressing problem ever put before the Commonwealth. The three powers had demanded that a Diet be convoked to ratify the partition conventions. There was nothing the Senate Council could do—the Diet was called for April 19.[3]

This last step, the convocation of the Diet of the Commonwealth and the ratification of the partition conventions, was not expected to cause trouble. Each of the three powers had had considerable experience in dealing with these Diets, and force had always been the most effective means of getting things done. Legal institutions were not overlooked as valuable assists, and Prussia, Austria, and Russia agreed that if the Diet could be confederated in the ancient tradition, which would provide for plurality instead of unanimity in the decision-making process, the entire course of the Diet deliberations would run more smoothly. The temporary abolition of the

[1] ACz, 825/204.
[2] See BJag, 101/VIII/41-42, 45-46, 81-83; BPAN, 319/160-61, 166, 187.
[3] See BPAN, 319/335; BPAN, 320/166, 184; ACz, 878/299-301; and ACz, 1696/138.

Liberum Veto in this case would, as in 1767–68, prevent the usual rupture caused by a single dissenting voice. Therefore, several days before the Diet opened, discussions were held in Warsaw with the primary aim of establishing a confederation.

At one such meeting, on April 15 at the palace of Chancellor Młodziejowski, which was attended by several dignitaries of state and the ministers of the three powers, it was announced that the Diet should be confederated. Quarrels followed between the Deputies and the Senators present—no one wished to take the responsibility for this act, since they knew its purpose and its end. Poniński, an old hand at such politics, insisted that the confederation must be established, and he was supported by Michał Radziwiłł (the Sword Bearer of Lithuania) and Bishop Massalski. The small group of Senators and Deputies, by no means representatives of the Commonwealth or the Diet, were forcefully told by the foreign envoys that if they did not sign the act of confederation they would perish. Finally, the Deputies agreed to sign an act of confederation, and the Senators and ministers of state promised to support it and establish their own act after the Diet convened. The act expressed the time-honored platitudes the Polish estates were so used to hearing—"because of the disturbances in the land and in the hope of reestablishing order and the general tranquillity, we confederate." Poniński and Radziwiłł were designated respectively as Marshals for the Crown and Grand Duchy.[4]

The day the Diet opened witnessed the usual ceremonial garb of a mass at St. John's and a procession to the Chamber of Deputies. In the absence of the last Marshal, Karol Radziwiłł (who had fled the country), the senior Deputy and the Chamberlain of Kraków, Łętowski, presided over the assembly. His first announcement was that the confederation was already established and the two Marshals elected. As he was about to hand Poniński the mace, an objection was raised by Reytan, the Chamberlain and Deputy from Nowogródek, who declared that he had never elected any Marshal and did not know of anyone else who had. Poniński defended himself, declaring that he had seventy-six signatures attesting to the establishment of the confederation and his election as Marshal.

[4] BPAN, 670/191, and ACz, 825/121-32.

This statement provoked a chorus of objections from several Deputies, who cried that they had come to a "free Diet" and not to a confederated one. The jeering continued, but Poniński had already taken the Marshal's chair. Reytan approached Poniński, who rose to talk to him. Before Poniński realized what had happened, Reytan had taken Poniński's seat, was given a Marshal's mace and declared that he, too, could be a Marshal. The spectators applauded. Then Reytan in a biting and sarcastic manner cried out to Poniński: "I recognize you, I saw you at Radom during the last confederation. I was there, but I did not take anything from the Russians." Reytan declared the session dissolved, and several Deputies began to leave. Poniński, still very confused, also declared the session dissolved.[5]

On the following day at nine o'clock in the morning the Deputy Chamber filled again with the representatives of the Commonwealth and spectators. Poniński was not present. Almost immediately after being seated, Korsak, also from Nowogródek, took the floor and demanded that a free election of a Marshal take place. He was interrupted several times, and quarreling continued for two hours, but it stopped suddenly when Poniński entered the Chamber. Without hesitating, Poniński declared the Diet session dissolved. Several Deputies left the hall immediately with the elder Łętowski.[6]

That afternoon Russian and Prussian troops placed themselves in strategic positions in Warsaw. A cordon was thrown around the Chamber, and only Deputies were allowed in. A delegation of the confederates went to the King to announce the establishment of the confederation and requested him to join. Reytan also went to Stanislas Augustus's chambers but was refused audience. By noon most of the Deputies had arrived at the Chamber, only to be greeted with the news that Poniński had postponed the session. Only thirty Deputies remained—Reytan and his adherents. More than ten stayed until late evening.

That same evening a conference took place between Stackelberg (the Russian ambassador), the King, and his Chancellors.

[5] BPAN, 670/191, and ACz, 825/133-37.
[6] BPAN, 670/192-93, and ACz, 825/139-44.

Stackelberg declared that a meeting of the Senators would be held the following day at which the King would accede to the confederation. If the King did not, Stackelberg said he would order 50,000 troops toward Warsaw and have them lay waste the countryside, the blame falling on the King.

News came in during the night that more Deputies and Senators had acceded to the confederation. At one o'clock, on the morning of April 22, Stackelberg sent his secretary to the Chamber to summon Reytan and the others who were still with him for a conference. Every one except Reytan came. Orders were then given that the Chamber door be bolted from the outside. The recalcitrant Deputies could not be persuaded to forego their opposition. They returned to the Chamber but could not enter.The next morning, the servant of the King who was ordered to open the Chamber found Reytan sleeping on the floor on one side of the door and his compatriots on the other.[7]

Later that morning the activity shifted to the audience room in the King's palace, where the Senators had gathered. The King explained the difficult position he was faced with: ruin for the country, if he did not accede to the confederation. He had no army to defend the country, which was now occupied by several thousand foreign troops. He asked the Senators what he should do—military rule might be put into effect if a favorable decision were not forthcoming. By two o'clock the meeting dissolved, the King having acceded to the confederation on the advice and with the consent of the Senate.[8]

That evening the opposition gave in. Reytan was asked to leave the Chamber; he did not have to join the confederation, only leave Warsaw. He would not be punished by the confederation court and would even be given a guarantee of safe conduct out of the city. The bargain was struck. He had proved his point, but courage alone was no match for armed force.[9]

Poniński, now more convinced of his authority, opened the session of April 24. Several Deputies and Senators added their names to the Act of Confederation. This orderly procedure was broken

[7] BPAN, 670/193-94, and ACz, 825/145-58.
[8] BPAN, 670/194, and ACz, 825/161-63.
[9] ACz, 825/164.

by Bishop Wodziński of Smolensk and Bishop Turski of Łuck, who announced they would agree to a confederation only if it established laws and constitutions against any infringement of the Holy Roman Catholic faith and placed the Dissidents in their pre-1768 position and if it guaranteed against partition of the country. In all this they were supported by several other Senators and Deputies. A new opposition seemed to be forming.

Poniński was angry. He gave the two bishops or anyone else who favored their position the choice of being for or against the confederation. They were not allowed to continue speaking—in fact, no one was. Poniński requested that his "Draft for the Constitution" be read; it stated that the Diet had confederated itself on April 16, 1773, and the confederation would last as long as the Diet. The Diet was to resolve all state affairs before dissolving. The session was then adjourned until Monday, April 26.[10]

Several more Deputies and Senators acceded to the confederation when the Diet session opened. Several names were conspicuous—Michał Czartoryski, who had given up the Chancellorship of Lithuania; Teodor Wessel, Treasurer of the Crown, who on more than one occasion had changed his political affiliation, the last being his association with the Confederates of the Bar days; and even the Bishop of Łuck. Bishop Massalski was asked to sign the document, but refused and left the Chamber amid shouts reminding him of his promise to do so. The session was later closed without resolving anything into law.[11]

Hope for an early decision seemed impossible; the discussions seemed to have no purpose except as a delaying action. Poniński's temper changed from anger to depression.[12] Finally, on April 30, after the King had told the Diet that he had been threatened in the most violent manner by the foreign ministers, Poniński's "Draft for the Constitution" was made law.[13]

On May 10 it seemed that the lethargic attitude of the assembly would have to come to an end. Poniński received word from the

[10] BPAN, 670/194-95, and ACz, 825/165-72.

[11] BPAN, 670/195, and ACz, 825/173-81.

[12] BPAN, 670/197-99, and ACz, 825/183-221. On April 28, Bishop Massalski and several other Deputies and Senators acceded to the confederation.

[13] BPAN, 670/199-200; ACz, 825/225-30; and VolLeg, VIII, 5.

three foreign ministers that an "Act of Adjournment" and an "Act of Plenipotentiary," similar to those of 1767-68, had to be submitted and approved by the Diet. Anyone who opposed such measures, he was told, would receive a quick and severe punishment.

The obedient Poniński followed his orders to the letter. He opened the session and declared that the only hope that Poland had for extricating herself from the present terrible situation was to limit the Diet sessions and appoint a delegation with full power to negotiate with the foreign ministers of the three powers. The delegation would be empowered to discuss and decide everything relating to the pretensions made on Polish land by Austria, Russia, and Prussia; the internal government of the country had to be arranged; complete justice for the Dissidents must be reaffirmed; and the peace and tranquillity of the country had to be restored.

It was at this point that Stanislas Augustus entered the discussion. For him the situation seemed impossible, and the only hope he had was that his own "Act of Adjournment" and "Act of Plenipotentiary" would be enacted into law instead of Poniński's. The King's program provided that the delegation would not be given unlimited power to decide all questions. The Diet would instruct the delegation on how and what to discuss with the foreign ministers. The final decision would remain with the Diet. The King made it clear that he could not be a friend of the partition, since it deprived him of three-fourths of his royal estates and incomes. The hour was late, and the session was dissolved without a resolution having been made.[14]

The following day discussion opened on the two proposals. Poniński declared that his was the one which Austria, Prussia, and Russia wanted and, therefore, must be passed. Several Deputies and Senators, knowing the force that could be exerted by the foreign powers, supported the Marshal although their sympathies lay with the King. The arguments continued for hours, and when the session closed there was no decision in sight.[15]

[14] BPAN, 670/200-4, and ACz, 825/237-310.
[15] BPAN, 670/204-5, and ACz, 825/311-35.

On the morning of May 12 Stackelberg called several Senators and Deputies to his residence and told them that they must accept Poniński's proposal. If they did not, their estates would be confiscated.[16] The next day several conferences were held throughout Warsaw. Bishop Ostrowski of Kujawy told some of the Deputies that the King's proposal could be agreed upon a hundred times, but in the end it would have no effect—Poniński's was the only one the foreign ministers would accept. Poniński and several other representatives met with Stackelberg. The Russian ambassador announced that those who would support Poniński's proposal would be relieved of quartering and requisitions and would be paid for everything taken from them. This promise was enough for some, and they quickly drew up documents providing for the security of their estates. Afterwards, Poniński went from one Deputy and Senator to another, offering the same *quid pro quo*.[17]

Finally, on May 18 Poniński announced to the Diet that the majority of Deputies and Senators wanted a temporary adjournment of the Diet and a delegation plenipotentiary established. Without taking a vote, a delegation was appointed and the Diet was adjourned.[18]

The conferences with the foreign ministers were prefunctory. Frequently the ministers did not appear, and the Deputies and Senators of the delegation argued among themselves. The longest delays were due to the slowness of the printing presses, which labored over one declaration after another. The results were known before the first conference opened on June 2, and no one was surprised to find that by September 14, the last meeting, everything Russia, Prussia, and Austria wanted had been acceded to. The arrangement of the internal government would await further meetings. During the conferences, the Confederation announced to all remaining recalcitrants the opportunity of adhering to the new Confederation as the highest authority in Poland. The partition was accepted by the delegation, and, therefore, the normal ratification by the Diet was a mere formality.[19]

[16] BPAN, 670/206-7, and ACz, 825/347-52.
[17] ACz, 825/359-60.
[18] BPAN, 670/207-8; ACz, 825/366-85; BPAN, 1154/95-8; and VolLeg, VIII, 5-9.
[19] BPAN, 1154/1-373; BPAN, 323/30-123; BPAN, 670/209-10; and VolLeg, VIII, 9-65.

On September 15 the delegation submitted its report to the Diet, and on September 21 the partition treaties were read. While the secretary labored over the reading, Deputy Dunin from Łęczyca shouted that the proceedings of the delegation were illegal and he condemned the entire Diet as acting without authority. He almost touched off a disturbance in which several Deputies and Senators seemed eager to take part.[20]

The following day the Diet clamored its disapproval of all that had happened. Poniński warned everyone against taking any foolish step.[21] On September 25 he began shouting at the assembly that the report of the delegation, the partition of the Polish-Lithuanian Commonwealth, had to be signed without delay. He asked for approval—there was silence. He asked a second time, but heard nothing. He condemned them all, and asked a third time, and only a few murmured, "Agreed." The session was closed until Monday, September 27.[22] The following two sessions were nothing more than an untiring harangue against the partition treaties and the rights of the delegation.[23] But in the end, on September 30, Poniński won out. No vote was taken; he claimed a plurality in favor of the partition treaties and a proposal proroguing the Diet until January 22, 1774.[24]

The Diet session came to an end.

[20] BPAN, 323/134, and ACz, 825/599-606.
[21] BPAN, 323/148, and ACz, 825/607-40.
[22] BPAN, 323/149, and ACz, 825/641-52.
[23] BPAN, 323/150-51, and ACz, 825/653-81.
[24] BPAN, 323/185 ff, and VolLeg, VIII, 9-10. The official date of the partition treaties as entered in the statute books is September 18, 1773.

CONCLUSION

Weaknesses—social, economic, and political—within the Polish-Lithuanian Commonwealth were to blame for its decline and ultimately were responsible for its partition. The Commonwealth was an elective monarchy, but the locus of authority lay with the *szlachta,* which was controlled by an oligarchy of magnates whose fidelity to king, country, and religion was doubtful. There was no uniform concept of patriotism or liberty to guide the political consciousness of the *szlachta.* There was no adherence to an ethical standard which prevented the *szlachta* from falling prey to bribes from one of their own number or from a foreign power. Their courageous spirit was expressed in vitriolic oratory or manifesto, but infrequently on the battlefield in defense of an idea or property outside their own household.

The weakness of the central government made itself manifest in an ineffective executive and a procedurally crippled parliament. The absence of a professional civil service prevented the necessary administrative communication desired by all states during the eighteenth century. The standing army, small by comparison with the armies of Poland's neighbors, was inadequate for the defense of frontiers against invasion. These internal weaknesses offer the obvious explanation for the decline and eventual partition. But this explanation is too simple and too general to answer the queries, "How did it happen?" "Why did it take place?" and "Were there any alternatives?"

The weaknesses of Poland in the eighteenth century prevented her being counted a great power, but her location made her important. Complex diplomatic intrigue frequently involved her as the pawn of France, Austria, Prussia, Russia, and Great Britain, and, more tragically, as a battlefield, as in the Seven Years War. The death of a king brought serious troubles, because the constitution provided for election of a new king. The election, important as it was to the Poles, attracted wide attention among the powers of Europe, and the election contest often changed into a struggle of one power vying with another for ascendancy in Poland. Such conflicts occurred in 1697, 1733, and 1764; tumult accompanied each election. The Poles and the interested foreign powers each had one or more candidates for the throne, and force of arms resolved the problem. After each election contest the Commonwealth suffered internal and external pressures which sometimes added to its glory or sometimes undermined its strength. The events following the election of 1764 resulted in the amputation of vital territories at the hands of Russia, Austria, and Prussia.

Catherine sent her troops into Poland in 1764, because she wanted to ensure the successful election of her candidate. Russian troops had entered Poland before for expressly the same purpose, and therefore Catherine, although she was prompted by the Czartoryski request, needed no excuse for this action. Any evaluation of the ethical and political role of the Czartoryskis must be viewed in this perspective. By seeking the aid of a foreign power during an interregnum they were doing no more than other political factions in Poland had done. Moreover, the invitation to foreign powers to take an interest in Polish affairs was not peculiar to the Poles of the eighteenth century, but had long been a common practice. A noticeable feature of Polish aristocratic politics was the tendency to seek the clandestine aid of foreign powers in support of ventures. More often than not, a Polish domestic program was conditioned by the commitments made to foreign powers.

Nevertheless, the statesmanship and diplomacy exercised by the Czartoryskis in the election of 1764 are open to severe criticism. The Russians were called into Poland to restore order and to facilitate the execution of the Czartoryski reform program, which in itself was beneficial to Poland. But the Czartoryskis miscalculated in believing that the Russians would go home and take a disinterested view toward Poland as soon as the election was over.

After April 1764, when Russia and Prussia concluded their treaty and the French and Austrian courts withdrew from the scene, no one doubted that Stanislas Augustus would be elected King of Poland. In the eyes of Europe, the safeguarding of Poland's independence was not worth a war. Moreover, the European powers had been reassured that Poland would undergo no dismemberment; this influenced their immediate policy. Catherine, counseled chiefly by Panin, did not desire to partition Poland but wanted rather to keep her in a state of vassalage and as a member of the "Northern System." This conclusion is reaffirmed by the Russian advisory Council's disregard in 1763 for Chernyshev's military expansionist program. Polish Livonia was not incorporated into the Russian Empire as Catherine had said it would be if she had to use troops to execute her policy. Catherine's intervention in Kurland could not be considered an act of partition, since Russia did not incorporate Kurland. The Russian protectorate over Kurland should be viewed as a dynastic struggle (a struggle which had been going on for several decades) in a peripheral area that facilitated Russia's access to the Baltic, and it should be treated separately from the dismemberment. Without foreign aid the Poles in their anarchic condition could not successfully oppose Russo-Prussian designs. At the end of 1764, in the eyes of Europe, Poland seemed to be exclusively dominated by Russia and Prussia.

Within two years, however, this image changed radically. The deeply rooted traditions of the Commonwealth conflicted greatly with the politics of the Russian Empire. The Diet of 1766 climaxed the struggle between state and state, religion and religion, and monarch and monarch, but did not satisfy the maximum programs of either of the leading protagonists. Repnin had succeeded in clarifying the acts of 1764, but failed miserably on the Dissident question. Sołtyk and his adherents, although not completely satisfied on the Dissident question, were able, at least, to keep the *status quo*. They also relished the fact that the *Liberum Veto* was restored and the power of the court significantly weakened by the clarification of the laws of 1764. The most disappointed was, of course, the King. Any moderate program of Dissident reform which Stanislas Augustus may have hoped for became impossible when Sołtyk and Repnin put forward their extreme and uncompromisingly contrary programs.

For Catherine, success in Poland became as much a matter of

pride as desire for fulfillment of her maximum program toward Poland. The Dissidents had to be made the equal of the Catholics in all temporal and spiritual matters. Had Panin not pressed by force for this equality it is more than likely that the events following the election of Stanislas Augustus would have taken a different course—that the dismemberment of the Polish-Lithuanian Commonwealth might not have taken place when it did. The results of the Diet of 1768 resolved the Dissident question, made Catherine and her successors guarantors of the constitution of the Commonwealth, and reduced Poland almost to the status of a Russian province. No foreign power could expect to negotiate with Poland without first anticipating Russia's disposition. If a foreign power chose to act otherwise, it might be considered an enemy by Russia. On the other hand, if the Poles themselves decided to act independently, they might be considered rebels and be treated accordingly. It took six years and required considerable force, but Catherine had succeeded in her maximum program, and Russia now commanded a greater hold over the Commonwealth than ever before.

Was her victory worth her efforts? Were not the consequences of such a success implicitly dangerous for Russia? Peter I had been faced with a similar problem, but he was able to foresee the consequences of a strong and aggressive policy to restore the Dissidents to their ancient rights and liberties. Equality for the Dissidents in his time would have evoked an intolerant cry of protest from the Catholics, on whose support Russia had to depend, and would have given other powers an opportunity to interfere in Polish affairs. Catherine was aware of those dangers, and her ally, Frederick, frequently reminded her of them. While it was necessary for Russia to have a political party to follow her bidding in Poland, necessity did not demand that the party be the Dissidents. Russia could have always found a group of Catholic Poles to follow her commands. This conclusion is confirmed by the success Catherine had in obtaining the services of Karol Radziwiłł and several other Polish nobles in 1767-68. Moreover, manipulation of the ramshackle Polish constitution had never been difficult for Russia.

Several powers looked enviously upon Catherine's ascendancy, and she could rest assured that at the first opportunity they would try to remove her grip on the Commonwealth—not because they sought peace and independence for Poland but because they could not be indifferent to the growing power of Russia. Turkey was the first to voice disapproval. She demanded that Russian troops evacuate Poland in order to ensure the permanency of the peace. Russia, feeling secure in Poland, obliged the Porte and gave orders for the removal of her troops.

The explosive reaction to the Perpetual Treaty of 1768 by the self-appointed Confederates, who had decided to defend the Holy Roman Catholic faith and expel the Russians from Poland, clearly showed the lack of political insight the Russian court had about Polish traditions. The Confederates, naive and unequipped for the challenge they had set for themselves, precipitated events which brought ruin to Poland—the outbreak of the Russo-Turkish War and the dismemberment of their country. Had not the Russians been faced with a civil war in Poland, which again demanded the occupation of the country by Russian troops, it is probable that the Porte would not have found sufficient cause for declaring war on Russia at that time, despite the prodding of the French. The Russo-Turkish War and the sweeping victories of the Russian armies struck fear in the hearts of the rulers of Austria and Prussia. They immediately set about to reconcile their differences, which had been widened at the close of the Seven Years War, and resolved to do the same for Russia and Turkey. But the desire for peace on the part of the several belligerents and spectators was checked by exaggerated demands and by the fear of losing face. The civil war in the Commonwealth created the delicate situation of neighboring powers taking measures to ensure the security of their frontiers. The Austrian military cordon was the first, and when it was extended deeper into the small but rich territory lying south of Kraków, and the Imperial Eagle became permanently fixed, the first step in the partition of Poland had been taken.

There was no legal or moral basis for the Austrian court's claim of "reincorporating" territory which had passed out of its hands approximately three hundred and fifty years before. Nor was there any legal or moral basis to the claims of Russia and Prussia. It was a simple issue of aggrandizement executed by the force of arms. However, its achievement was not a simple matter.

According to their previously announced policies, Russia and Prussia were opposed to partitioning Poland. The dismemberment of Poland was contrary to Panin's "Northern System." And, although Frederick had stated in his *Political Testaments* that some Polish territory would be desirable, after 1768 he announced emphatically that dismemberment of Poland was not a venture he wished to undertake. Why then did Russia and Prussia agree to dismember Poland?

The answer is to be found in the Austrian seizure, reinforced as it was by Austria's partial mobilization of troops; Prince Henry's visit to St. Petersburg and his return home; and the efforts of Chernyshev and Orlov to undermine Panin's dominant position in directing Russian foreign policy and their desire to execute their long-desired military expansionist program.

Austria's initial occupation of Polish land was sufficient cause for the other two powers to give thought to doing the same. Austria had upset the balance of power; Russia and Prussia decided to redress it. The forces at the Russian court opposed to Panin's handling of the entire Polish question gained support with the outbreak of the Russo-Turkish War and with Prince Henry's arrival at St. Petersburg. The outbreak of hostilities convinced Chernyshev and Orlov of Panin's inability to cope with foreign affairs. Had he not allowed Polish affairs to get out of hand, and his son-in-law Repnin to invite the enmity of the Polish nobles, Russia might have been spared the expensive struggle with the Poles and the Turks. Even with the decisive victories of the Russian armies, other powers not directly involved in the struggle had prevented Russia from reaping her rewards. Prince Henry desired that his brother acquire Polish territory, thus connecting the Brandenburg estates with the kingdom of Prussia and making Frederick dominant in the Baltic area. After collaborating with Chernyshev and Orlov to turn Catherine toward partitioning Poland, Prince Henry took it upon himself to persuade Frederick of the feasibility of executing the old idea of rounding out his realm. In spite of Frederick's reluctance to undertake a new venture, he could not deny the probabilities of success—part of the Russian court urged it and Austria had already taken her share. Simultaneously with Prince Henry's pleading, the pressure on Panin increased in the Russian advisory Council for his acquiescence in, if not his approval of, the further dismemberment of Poland. Moreover, Panin's attitude on the Polish question was influenced by the threat of Austria's intervention in the war. The Austrian bluff did not work; it only reinforced and made necessary the Russo-Prussian alliance. But Austria frightened Russia enough to prevent Catherine from executing the plan to dismember Poland further without first obtaining the approval of Maria Theresa. And Frederick was not bold enough to act without Catherine's approval. At this crucial moment Austria had several alternatives. She could remain at peace or choose to launch an aggressive policy; she chose the latter, and directed it not against her natural, temporal, and spiritual enemy, Turkey, but against her Catholic sister, Poland. Hypocritically, Austria never regarded as an act of partition her seizure of Spisz, Nowy Targ, Czorsztyn, Nowy Sącz, Bochnia, and Wieliczka. Therefore, the Austrian court reasoned that it could not allow Russia and Prussia to obtain any land in Poland without first acquiring more for itself. In the whole tragic affair of dismemberment Panin lost the initiative, Frederick was too impatient to bring the affair to an end, and Kaunitz won a resounding diplomatic victory.

Before the Diet of 1773 opened, no one doubted that it would ratify the partition conventions. Indeed, it was a formality. In 1764, when Stanislas Augustus came to the throne, the Polish-Lithuanian Commonwealth comprised 759,910 square kilometers and contained 11,420,000 inhabitants. Eleven years later, the Commonwealth's territory was reduced by 29.5 percent and its population by 35.2 percent, leaving to Stanislas Augustus 535,736.5 square kilometers and 7,400,000 inhabitants.

Although in 1775 it was too early to measure the full impact of the dismemberment in terms of political, cultural, and economic effects, certain things were clear. Austria had gained the most by depriving Poland of 11.8 percent of her land (89,669.4 square kilometers) and 18.6 percent of her population (2,130,000). The Austrian share included the richest salt mines in all East Central Europe and a rich soil that promised a significant increase in the agricultural produce of the lands ruled by Maria Theresa and Joseph II. The Russian acquisitions (12.7 percent of the land, 96,508.6 square kilometers, and 11.5 percent of the population [1,310,000 inhabitants]) did not contain the wealth of the Austrian share. However, it did provide Russia with the natural boundaries between the two states which had been desired by the ruling military circles at St. Petersburg. Prussia received much less than Austria and Russia in land (5 percent, 37,995.5 square kilometers) and population (5.1 percent, 580,000 inhabitants), but gained almost as much in political and potential economic value. The estates of Brandenburg and Prussia were now more compact, and greater communication and protection was provided for by the Prussian acquisition. Gdańsk was cut off from the rest of Poland, and Frederick, if he so desired, could easily control the commerce on the Vistula.

Poland was the loser, but she was not the only one. Russia's gain in Polish territory and population was the symbol of Catherine's and Panin's failure to maintain their original exclusively dominant position over the Commonwealth. Their failure was of their own making. The argument that Russia benefited more now that she had complete and unreserved control over a smaller portion of Polish land, rather than a nominal overlordship over the entire Commonwealth as she had before, loses force when one considers the advantages obtained by Austria and Prussia. An unrealistic approach to the Polish question and a lack of diplomatic shrewdness on the part of Russia allowed Austria and Prussia to share in an influence in Poland which had never before been accorded to them. For the Poles the partition was not necessarily the end of their troubles—they had no assurance that partition would not take place again and again.

APPENDIX

DECLARATION ON BEHALF OF THE DISSIDENTS, FROM EMPRESS CATHERINE II OF RUSSIA, PRESENTED BY REPNIN AT THE DIET OF THE POLISH-LITHUANIAN COMMONWEALTH ON NOVEMBER 4, 1766.

The unity of religion and the glory of contributing to human happiness are not only the reasons that induce Her Imperial Majesty to reiterate, in a most pressing manner, her intervention in favor of the Greek and Protestant subjects of the Kingdom of Poland toward ending their oppression, under which they groan, and toward returning them to the condition of equal citizens and as free members in the State.

The undersigned, in order to clarify all which was expressed, submits this point which is attested by the laws of the Polish nation: that the Greeks and the Protestants, in the most prosperous times of the Commonwealth, always received the prerogative they demand today and that they received them peacefully without any restriction as other inhabitants of the Nation obtained them.

This prerogative was assured by all that constitutes the bond of nations, namely by solemn agreements which established law between them and their compatriots. This law, however, can be claimed at all times to be fulfilled and cannot be violated or abolished by civil constitutions of only one part of the State.

One cannot avoid acknowledging as an invariable principle that a constant refusal to do justice to the claims of the Greeks and the Protestants would necessarily lead them to extricate themselves from all obligations toward a community whose advantages they did not share; that a prolonged refusal would make of them a community of completely free people and give them the right to choose judges among their neighbors who would judge between them and their equals; and, if unable to avoid persecution, no law, either human or divine, could condemn them if they were to ally themselves to these neighbors.

In times past, the Commonwealth had been in danger of this, but had happily succeeded in preventing it by the sanction which treaties formed with foreign powers gave to the domestic policy of Poland.

Now, the maintenance of the tranquillity of the Commonwealth belongs not only to the inhabitants of the land but also to the neighbors, who, treating with the Commonwealth, contracted with her members.

It is thus that Russia, in virtue of the Treaty of 1686, and the other powers in concert with her, in consequence of the Treaty of Oliva, engage in watching over the security of each part of the Commonwealth to prevent discord between them, to procure exact justice, and the enjoyment for each and all that which constitutes reciprocal and common rights.

Therefore, it is for the reason of executing the provisions of the treaties, that the Empress desires to regain for the Greek and Protestant subjects all their rights and the security of their preservation. [The Empress] cannot place any limits on the protection she grants to the Greeks and Protestants without compromising the glory and the dignity of her Crown and the confidence of her friends.

Without any expectation of obtaining a reward but merely for the purpose of emphasizing the necessity of the Commonwealth's agreeing to the principle in which she is interested, Her Imperial Majesty finds it impossible to renounce her desire to help the Commonwealth.

Being a good neighbor and sincere friend, Her Imperial Majesty has always been and will continue to be happy for every success of the Commonwealth. It was greatly satisfying to her when she was able to help the confederated Commonwealth to regain its internal peace, to preserve its liberty, and to elect a *Piast*.

Everyone could see then the friendliness, generosity, and readiness with which Her Imperial Majesty offered the aid for which she had been asked. She was always interested in the affairs concerning her neighbor the Commonwealth in order to ensure happiness to all its citizens. She was asked to help freely elect a ruler from amongst the nation. She gave her assistance with readiness.

Although she was successful in this matter, she would consider her work imperfect if one part of the citizens was excluded from its fortunate results. She would be of the opinion that her aim was not fully accomplished as long as any difference remained in the country between the Dissidents and other citizens.

Therefore Her Imperial Majesty considers it a matter of her honor to show that the confidence, which the whole Commonwealth puts in her friendship is fully justified and not to limit the assistance which she may offer for the happiness of one part of the nation.

Her Imperial Majesty renews her application to the present Diet to put a halt to this source of unending discord and thus restore tranquillity to the Commonwealth.

She recommends this affair to the King and the entire Nation to treat it with the regard and attention it merits for its importance to the general welfare. Her Imperial Majesty looks upon it in two ways, namely, a spiritual as well as a temporal interest.

Concerning the first [the Commonwealth], without having annulled the rights of the Greeks and the Protestants, has, however, illegally multiplied the abuses to such a point that freedom of religion has been reduced to nothing or nearly so.

The undersigned demands in the name of Her Imperial Majesty, his Sovereign, that these abuses be redressed and that in the future, neither these nor any new abuses be introduced. This can be attained when the present Diet resolves the following:

1. Churches lawfully belonging to the Dissidents which were unlawfully taken from them are to be given back. No obstacle is to be made to the renovation or reconstruction of such as were damaged by time or fire. No opposition is to be made to baptisms, marriages, services for the dead, preaching of God's word in the churches or to the sick. The ecclesiastics, both for the Greeks and Protestants, are to have permission to accomplish the above-mentioned acts, and . . . all that belongs to the administration of the Sacraments and the divine services of every respective religion without any opposition. Together, these constitute entire liberty of the Divine Service.

2. For the establishment of this lasting and general religious freedom in the entire State, the present Diet will resolve that in all cities, towns, and villages in which the Greeks or Protestants have neither churches nor chapels it will be permitted to members of those religions who wish to settle there, to have churches, cemeteries, priests and pastors, and [complete freedom in the] administration of the Sacraments to the people of their religions.

3. Freedom of religion is a divine right which concerns everyone. Therefore, it is the obligation of every well-governed State to permit this advantage to all its inhabitants and not to subordinate one religion. It is evident, according to this principle, that the tribute exacted by the Catholic clergy from the Dissidents for burials, marriages, and baptisms is illegal. The variations as to its proportions in different provinces would suffice to show it has no legal title. Abuses of so pernicious a nature cannot be made lawful by any particular constitution if those interested have not established it by their free votes. It appears, therefore, most just to reform this abuse. Yet if all the Estates agree that some distinction should preserve the dominant religion in a free State, it would be necessary to establish a measure of payment which would be considered honorary rather than a tribute.

4. The Greek Seminary in Mohilev will not be disturbed in any fashion, and will, in freedom and tranquillity, give education to youths of the Greek persuasion without any hindrance from anyone.

5. The Bishop and Bishoprics of Belorussia with all their depend-

encies will be, for all time, preserved for the Greek religion as well as the churches belonging to the Greek and Protestant communities.

6. No priest or pastor of the Greeks or Protestants is to be cited under any pretext before an ecclesiastical court. They belong exclusively to the secular jurisdiction.

7. Marriages between persons of different religions are to be permitted, and children are to follow the religion of either parent, depending on the child's sex.

In a word, the Greeks and the Protestants are to enjoy the exercise of their religion and the protection that equity and reason owe to every inhabitant: This is no more than a strict right.

Justice demands the reestablishment of the Greeks and Protestants to their temporal prerogatives which Her Imperial Majesty, impelled by the friendship she feels as a neighboring power as well as by obligations of her Crown, insists can alone secure the happiness and good order of the Kingdom of Poland.

The equality of nobility is the foundation of Polish liberty and the most positive guarantee of her Constitution. All laws which have intended, from time to time, to divest the Greek and the Protestant *szlachta* from their prerogatives, were the unfortunate source of troubles and disunion. One part of the State, thinking to reap great advantages by elevating themselves at the expense of another part of the Nation, destroyed the real and only tie which cemented a national union.

In time of peace and general harmony, in which everything conspires to the establishment of a complete and lasting happiness, when the laws regain their former force by the zeal and unanimity of patriots, and promise to render the Commonwealth more flourishing than ever, all the Estates ought to comprehend that no durable prosperity and happiness can be anticipated if they are not perfectly united. To maintain one part of the Nation in the exclusive possession of the charges and dignities against the ancient laws of the Commonwealth which grants to every religion an equal right in the government of the land, would be to sacrifice the national greatness to a particular interest.

This principle of the public law of Poland which, in times of trouble and discord, was almost demolished by a succession of civil Constitutions made by one part of the State, is precisely that on which Her Imperial Majety founds her request for negotiation with those subjects of the Commonwealth who differ only by their religion in order to determine their share in the administration of the State and connection with the Crown. Until a perfect understanding on this point is established, and the solicitations of the divers Estates in the Commonwealth are satisfied, Her Imperial Majesty will feel her obligations to be unfulfilled. The aid which she accorded to the whole Nation for the public welfare cannot be refused to a part of the Nation so considerable as the Greek and Protestant communities. The heart of Her Imperial Majesty could not be satisfied if she had only procured an apparent tranquillity for the Commonwealth; if she had preserved her from the violence which had menaced her laws, her liberties, and her institutions only to abandon one part of the Nation to the persecutions of the other; if she had contributed to put into execution certain laws only to augment and perpetuate the power of abuses. Her Imperial Majesty could not be satisfied even if one part of the Nation had received her assistance, gladly and with benefit, while another part, even more considerable, with equal claim to her solicitude, also having invoked her support and contributed to render it efficacious, still continued to groan under persecution.

Religion, obligation, amicable and good neighborly relations, the engagement of treaties, the honor attached to their execution, the desire to answer the hopes of the whole Nation, enjoin Her Imperial Majesty the absolute necessity of continuing these efforts in order to bring about the reestablishment of the Greeks and Protestants in the enjoyment of the rights, both spiritual and secular, which are their due as members of a free Nation.

Her Imperial Majesty is persuaded that the good offices of a friendly and neighboring power will suffice to render general the feelings which the most sensible and patriotic of the Nation now entertain. Those who still oppose these sentiments ought to be looked upon only as enemies to themselves and to the country. No private consideration will deter Her Imperial Majesty from the end she has in view. She considers it her obligation to employ against [her opponents] every means likely to effect the restoration of the general tranquillity, and she believes she could not employ herself more worthily.

[signed by Prince Repnin][1]

[1] *ACz.*/1693/VII-XIV; and *Sb.*/LXVII/1392/84-94.

BIBLIOGRAPHY

ARCHIVES

The spellings of the archival manuscript titles are as they appeared in the original.

Kraków, Poland

ARCHIWUM CZARTORYSKICH (THE ARCHIVE OF THE CZARTORYSKIS)

Cat. no.

597 Dyaryusz seymu od 1740 do 1762 [The Diary of the Diet from 1740 to 1762]

599 Dyaryusz seymu ordynaryinego Warszawskiego w roku 1762 [The Diary of the Ordinary Diet of Warsaw in the Year 1762]

653 Protokoll konferencyi J.K.M. cum ministerio et senatu a 24 dec: 1765 ad. 18 jul: 1768 [The Protocol of Conferences of H.R.M. with the Ministry and Senate from December 24, 1765, to July 18, 1768]

754 Zbior roznych pism służących do interessu sporow między Grekami Unitami y nie Unitami tudziesz y do sprawy między wieleb: Koniskim y Wołodkowiczem [Collection of the Various Works Concerning the Quarrels Between the Uniats and the Greeks as well as the Affair Between the Venerable: Koniski and Wołodkowicz]

820 Senatus consilia ab anno 1733 ad. annum 1773 [Senate Councils from the Year 1733 to the Year 1773]

825 Dyaryusz dwa seymow. Jeyden lat 1767 y 1768. Drugi lat 1773, 1774 y 1775 [The Diaries of Two Diets. The First from the Years 1767 and 1768. The Second from the Years 1773, 1774, and 1775]

830 Pisma w początku panowania Stanisława Augusta [Works at the Beginning of the Reign of Stanilas Augustus]

831 Akta konfederacyi Barskiey [Acts of the Confederation of Bar]

867 Senatus consilia od 1676 do 1773. roku [Senate Councils from 1676 to 1773]

869 Akt elekcyi roku 1764 27. Sierpnia [The Act of Election of August 27, 1764]

871 Akta konfederacyi Radomskiej [Acts of the Confederation of Radom]

872 Oryginały do rũ 1764 i 1765 [Originals of the Years 1764 and 1765]

873 Oryginały do 1767 i 1768 rũ [Originals of 1767 and 1768]
874 Plenipotencia n: Stanisława Augusta nad delegacią 23 Pazdziernika 1767 . . . oryginały [Plenipotentiary of His Highness Stanislas Augustus for the Delegation of October 23, 1767 . . . Originals]
875 Diariusz kommissii traktatowey w 1768 roku i czynności konfederacii Barskiey [The Diary of the Treaty Commission of 1768 and the Activities of the Confederation of Bar]
878 Senatu rady . . . [Senate Councils . . .]
944 Papiery wszgłędem konfederacyi Barskiey od 1764 do 1777 [Papers Relating to the Confederation of Bar from 1764 to 1777]
945 Akta konfederacji Barskiej [Acts of the Confederation of Bar]
962 Kopie historyczne . . . [Historical Copies . . .]
966 Pisma różne za Stanisława Augusta [Various Works of the Reign of Stanislas Augustus]
1684 Zbiór aktów, listów, mów, pism i druków 1683-1794 . . . [Collection of Acts, Letters, Speeches, Works and Printed Matter 1683-1794 . . .]
1691 Dyaryusz seymu ordynaryinego . . . 1766 . . . [The Diary of the Ordinary Diet . . . 1766 . . .]
1692 Dyaryusz seymu . . . 1766 . . . [The Diary of the Diet . . . 1766 . . .]
1693 Kopie aktów, listów . . . [Copies of Acts, Letters . . .]
1694 Kopie aktów, diariuszów . . . [Copies of Acts, Diaries . . .]
1696 Za panowania Jana III, Augustów, i Stanisława Augusta, senatus consilia [Senate Councils in the Reign of Jan III, Augustus(s) and Stanislas Augustus]
1699 Akta 1766-1768 [Acts 1766-68]
1701 Akta 1769-1776 [Acts 1769-76]
1983 Odpisy z archiwów obcych Londyn Public Record Office. Tom I [Copies from Foreign Archives London Public Record Office. Volume I]
1984 Odpisy z archiwów obcych Londyn Public Record Office. Tom II [Copies from Foreign Archives London Public Record Office. Volume II]
1986 Registry z Public Record Office [Registry from the Public Record Office]
2191 Akta historyczne 1746-1769 [Historical Acts 1746-69]
2251 Polska akta 1764-1785 [Poland: Acts 1764-85]
2289 Listy Michała Ks. Czartoryskiego do Michała Oginskiego. 1764/5 [The Letters of Prince Michał Czartoryski to Michał Oginski. 1764-65]
2375 Listy Fleminga . . . [The Letters of Fleming . . .]
2471 Mowa najiasniejszego króla imci Polskiego Stanisława Augusta . . . [Speech of His Royal Highness of Poland Stanislas Augustus . . .]
2618 Silva rerum w XVIII [Various Materials in XVIII]
3081 Dzieje krolestwa Polskiego [History of the Kingdom of Poland]

BIBLIOTEKA POLSKIEJ AKADEMII NAUK (THE LIBRARY OF THE POLISH ACADEMY OF SCIENCES)

304 Rzeczy Kurlandzkie . . . [The Affairs of Kurland . . .]
314 Miscellaneci papierow publiczynch annorum 1765 et 1766 [Miscellaneous Public Papers for the Years 1765 and 1766]
315 Przydatek do zbioru pism roku 1768 [Supplement to the Collection of Works for the Year 1768]
316 Pisma do historyi Polskiey z roku 1769 [Works of Polish History from the Year 1769]
317 Różne pisma [Various Works]
318 Pisma do historyi Polskiey z roku 1771 [Works of Polish History from the Year 1771]
319 Pisma różne z roku 1772 [Various Works from the Year 1772]
320 Pisma różne z roku 1773 [Various Works from the Year 1773]
323 Delegacya traktatowey z ministrami Wid. Peters. y Berlinskie 1773. 2 [The Treaty Delegation with the Ministers of Vienna, Petersburg, and Berlin 1773. 2]
647 Zbiór dokumentów rekopismiennych i drukowanych do spraw Kurlandyi 1616-1766 [Collection of Manuscript and Printed Documents for Kurland Affairs 1616-1766]
649 Różne pisma [Various Works]
654 Materiały do historyi Różnowierców w Polsce [Materials to the History of the Dissidents in Poland]
670 Drukow i manuskryptow zebranych w roku 1768, 1769, 1770, 1771, 1773. Ksiega V [Printed Matter and Manuscripts Collected in the Years 1768, 1769, 1770, 1771, 1773. Volume V]
1082 Dyaryusz seymu convocationis . . . [The Diary of the Convocation Diet . . .]
1136 Listy oryginalne z Mitawy w roku 1763 . . . [Original Letters from Mittau in the Year 1763 . . .]
1137 Dokumenty rękopiśmienne i druki, dotyczące spraw Kurlandzkich 1763-1766 [Documents, Manuscripts, and Printed Matter, Concerning the Affairs of Kurland 1763-66]
1139 Dyariusz seymu extraordynaryinego Warszawskiego w roku 1767 [The Diary of the Extraordinary Diet of Warsaw in the Year 1767]
1141 Manuskrypt 1766-1774 [Manuscript(s) 1766-74]
1144 Listy oryginalne do Jerzego Mniszcha [Original Letters to Jerzy Mniszech]
1145 Zbior wszelkich pism y aktow tyczących konfederacyą Barską y czynnośći ich zaczęte od konfederacyi Radomskiey a Febr: 1768 ad 19 9br: 1769 [Collection of All the Various Works and Acts Concerning the Confederation of Bar and Its Activities Beginning from the Confederation of Radom from February 1768 to November 19, 1769]

1146 Spis rzeczy naleznych do konfederacyi Barskiey z rękopisow zbioru Ossolinskiego we Lwowie z dodatkiem niektorych innych [List of Things Belonging to the Confederation of Bar from Manuscripts of the Ossolinski Collection in Lwów with Some Other Additions]

1147 Odpisy dokumentów, dotyczących konfederacyi Barskiej [Copies of Documents Concerning the Confederation of Bar]

1149 Zbior wszelkich pism y aktow tyczących czynności konfederacyi Barskiey. 1 Jan: 1770 ad 26 9br. 1773 [Collection of All the Various Works and Acts Concerning the Activities of the Confederation of Bar. January 1, 1770, to November 26, 1773]

1154 Delegacya traktatowe z ministra Wid. Peter. y Berlinsk. 1773. I [The Treaty Delegation with the Ministers of Vienna, Petersburg, and Berlin. 1773. I]

1155 Dyaryusz seymu 1773 manuscript [The Diary of the Diet of 1773 Manuscript]

1646 Dziennik sejmowy z 1767 [The Diary of the Diet of 1767]

BIBLIOTEKA JAGIELLOŃSKA (JAGIELLONIAN LIBRARY)

73 Miscellanea treści [Miscellaneous Contents]

101 Zbior pism, T. VII, VIII [Collection of Works, Volumes VII, VIII]

111 Różne manuskripta od 1752 do 1782 [Various Manuscripts from 1752 to 1782]

1053 Zbior pism [Collection of Works]

5117 Widok osobliwy dziejow najciekawszych krolestwa Polskiego w r 1764. Tom I [Particular View of the Most Interesting History of the Polish Kingdom in the Year 1764. Volume I]

London, England

PUBLIC RECORD OFFICE: STATE PAPERS, FOREIGN

88 Poland (including Saxony)
Volumes 85-98, 100, 102, 104, 106-7, 118
(Papers Relating to the City of Dantzig)

90 Prussia
Volumes 90-94

91 Russia
Volumes 74-94

97 Turkey
Volumes 42, 44

BRITISH MUSEUM: ADDITIONAL MANUSCRIPTS

6809 Mitchell Papers. Vol. VI. Letters of Sir A. Mitchell. Nov. 1761–Dec. 1763.

6810 Mitchell Papers. Vol. VII. Letters of Sir A. Mitchell. 1764-1770.

6826 Mitchell Papers. Vol. XXIII. Letters from Moscow and St. Petersburg to Sir A. Mitchell. 1763-1770.

6828 Mitchell Papers. Vol. XXV. Letters from Lord Stormont, etc. 1759-1770.

6830 Mitchell Papers. Vol. XXVII. Letters from British Ministers Abroad. 1756-1770.

35485 Hardwicke Papers. Vol. CXXXVII. Correspondence of R. Keith, May 1762—1774.

35500 Hardwicke Papers. Vol. CLII. Diplomatic Letter-Book of Lord Stormont. Vol. I. 12 Nov. 1763—1 Oct. 1771.

35501 Hardwicke Papers. Vol. CLIII. Diplomatic Letter-Book of Lord Stormont. Vol. II. 21 Oct. 1771—7 Dec. 1772.

35502 Hardwicke Papers. Vol. CLIV. Diplomatic Letter-Book of R. Gunning. 1772-1775.

35504 Hardwicke Papers. Vol. CLVI. Correspondence of R. M. Keith. Oct. 1772—Jan. 1773.

35506 Hardwicke Papers. Vol. CLVIII. Correspondence of R. M. Keith. July 1773—Feb. 1774.

35572 Hardwicke Papers. Vol. CCXXIV. Diplomatic Letter-Book of R. M. Keith. 17 Nov. 1772—19 July 1774.

37054 Letter-Book of H. Shirley, Chargé d'Affairs at Moscow. 1767-1768.

BRITISH MUSEUM: EGERTON COLLECTION

2701 Gunning Papers. Vol. VI. Correspondence 1772.

2702 Gunning Papers. Vol. VII. Correspondence 1773—April 1774.

Vienna, Austria

ÖSTERREICHISCHES STAATSARCHIV HAUS-, HOF-UND STAATSARCHIV

Staatskanzlei

Polen III, Erste Teilung Polens Akten
Preussen, Berichte, Weisungen 1768-72
Russland II, Berichte 1771-72
Russland II, Weisungen 1771-72
Vorträge, 1768-72

PRIMARY SOURCES

D'Angeberg, Comte [pseudonym of J. L. Chodźko] (ed.). Recueil des traités, conventions et actes diplomatiques concernant la Pologne 1762-1862. Paris, 1862.

Arkhiv gosudarstvennago soveta [The Archive of the State Council]. St. Petersburg, 1869. Vol. I.

Arneth, Alfred Ritter von (ed.). Maria Thérèsia und Joseph II. Ihre Correspondenz. Vienna, 1867. Vols. I, II.

——— Briefe der Kaiserin Maria Theresia an Ihre Kinder und Freunde. Vienna, 1881. Vol. I.

Arneth, Alfred Ritter von, and Jules Flammermont (eds.). Correspondance secrète du Comte de Mercy-Argenteau avec l'Empereur Joseph II et le Prince de Kaunitz. Paris, 1891. Vol. II.

Arneth, Alfred Ritter von, and M. A. Geffroy (eds.). Marie-Antoinette correspondance secrète entre Marie-Thérèse et le Cte de Mercy-Argenteau. Paris, 1874. Vol. I.

Bartenev, P. J. (ed.). Arkhiv Kniazia Vorontsova [The Archives of Prince Vorontsov]. Vols. V, VII, VIII, XVI, XXI, XXV, XXVI, XXVIII, XXIX, XXX, XXXI, XXXII, XXXIV, XL. Moscow, 1870-1895.

Beer, Adolf (ed.). Die erste Theilung Polens. 2 vols. Vienna, 1873.

Boutaric, M. E. (ed.). Correspondance secrète inédite de Louis XV. 2 vols. Paris, 1866.

Broglie, Duc de (ed.). The King's Secret: Being the Secret Correspondence of of Louis XV with His Diplomatic Agents from 1752 to 1774. 2 vols. London, 1879.

Collyer, Adelaide d'Arcy (ed.). The Despatches and Correspondence of John, Second Earl of Buckinghamshire, Ambassador to the Court of Catherine II of Russia 1762-1765. 2 vols. London, 1900.

Czasy Stanisława Augusta Poniatowskiego przez jednego z posłów wielkiego sejm napisane [The Times of Stanislas Augustus Poniatowski Written by One of the Deputies of the Great Diet]. Poznań, 1865. Vol. VII of Pamiętniki z ośmnastego wieku [Memoirs from the Eighteenth Century].

Dumouriez, M. Wojna w Polsce 1770 i 1771 r. z pamiętników generała Dumourieza [The War in Poland 1770 and 1771 from the Memoirs of General Dumouriez]. Poznań, 1865. Vol. VI of Pamiętniki z ośmnastego wieku [Memoirs from the Eighteenth Century].

Z dziejów Hajdamaczyzny [From the History of the Hajdamaks]. Warsaw, 1905. Vols. V and VI of Dzieje porozbiorowe narodu Polskiego w żywem słowie [The History of the Post-Partition Polish Nation in Living Words].

Frederick II. Oeuvres de Frédéric le Grand. Berlin, 1847-57. Vols. VI, XXIV, XXVI.

——— Politische Correspondenz Friedrichs des Grossen. Berlin, 1879-1939. Vols. XXI-XXXIII.

——— Die politischen Testamente Friedrichs des Grossen. Ed. by G. B. Volz. Berlin, 1920.

Grabowski, Zbigniew (ed.). English and Polish Comments on the Partition of Poland. Glasgow, 1944.

Hertzberg, Ewald Friedrich, Graf von. Recueil des déductions, manifestes, déclaration traités et autres actes et écrits publics, qui ont été rédigés et publies pour la cour de Prusse par le ministre d'état Comte de Hertzberg depuis l'année 1756 jusqu à l'année 1790. 3 vols. Berlin, 1790-95.

Hordt, Comte Johann Ludwig de. Mémoires du Comte de Hordt. 2 vols. Berlin, 1789.

Kitowicz, A. Pamiętniki ks. A. Kitowicza do panowania Augusta III. i Stanisława Augusta [Memoirs of Father A. Kitowicz during the Reign of Augustus III and Stanislas Augustus]. New Edition. Lwów, 1882. Vols. I, II.

Krauel, R. (ed.). Briefwechsel zwischen Heinrich Prinz von Preussen und Katharina II von Russland. Berlin, 1903. Vol. VIII of Quellen und Untersuchungen zur Geschichte des Hauses Hohenzollern.

Kreczetników, Piotr. Dziennik wojennych działan jeneral-majora Kreczetnikowa [The Journal of Military Operations of Major-General Kreczetnikow]. Poznań, 1874. Vol. XIII of Pamiętniki z ośmnastego wieku [Memoirs from the Eighteenth Century].

Legg, L. G. Wickham (ed.). British Diplomatic Instructions: 1689-1789. Vol. VII, Part iv. London, 1934.

Lind, John. Letters Concerning the Present State of Poland. London, 1773.

Lutostański, Karol (ed.). Les Partages de la Pologne et la lutte pour l'indépendance. Lausanne, 1918.

Malmesbury, Third Earl of (ed.). Diaries and Correspondence of James Harris, First Earl of Malmesbury. London, 1844. Vol. I.

Maroger, Dominique (ed.). Memoirs of Catherine the Great. London, 1955.

Martens, F. de (ed.). Recueil de traités et conventions, conclus par la Russie avec les puissances étrangères. St. Petersburg, 1880-83. Vols. II, V, VI.

Martens, Geo. Fred. de (ed.). Recueil de traités de puissances et états de l'Europe. 2d ed. Göttingen, 1817. Vol. I.

Morawski, S. (ed.). Materiały do konfederacyi barskiej r. 1767-1768 [Materials to the Confederation of Bar 1767-68]. Lwów, 1851.

Mottaz, Eugene (ed.). Stanislas Poniatowski et Maurice Glayre correspondance relative aux partages de la Pologne. Paris, 1897.

Mouy, Charles de (ed.). Correspondance inédite du Roi Stanislas Auguste Poniatowski et de Madame Geoffrin (1764-1777). Paris, 1875.

Radziwiłł, Karol. Listy księcia Karola Stanisława Radziwiłła "Panie Kochanku" (1751-1790) [The Letters of Prince Karol Stanisław Radziwiłł "My Dear Sir" (1751-90)]. Warsaw, 1906.

——— Korrespondencya księcia Karola Stanisława Radziwiłła wojewody Wileńskiego. "Panie Kochanku" 1744-1790 [Correspondence of Prince Karol Stanisław Radziwiłł Governor of Wilno. "My Dear Sir" 1744-90]. Kraków, 1898.

Recueil des instructions données aux ambassadeurs et ministres de France depuis les traités de Westphalie jusqu'à la révolution française. Paris, 1888. Vol. V.

Saint-Priest, Comte de. Mémoires sur l'ambassador de France en Turque. Paris, 1877.

Sbornik imperatorskago russkago istoricheskago obschestva [The Collection of the Imperial Russian Historical Society]. St. Petersburg, 1867-1916. Vols. XII, XX, XXII, XXXVII, XLVI, XLVIII, LI, LVII, LXVII, LXXXVII, XCVII.

Schmitt, Henryk (ed.). Dzieje panowania Stanisława Augusta Poniatowskiego:

Dokumenta [The History of the Reign of Stanislas Augustus Poniatowski: Documents]. Lwów, 1868-69.
Smith, William James (ed.). The Grenville Papers. London, 1852. Vol. IV.
Smitt, Frédéric. Frédéric II, Catherine, et la partage de la Pologne. Paris, 1861.
Smyth, Mrs. Gillespie (ed.). The Romance of Diplomacy. 2d ed. London, 1861. Vol. I.
Spencer, Frank (ed.). The Fourth Earl of Sandwich: Diplomatic Correspondence, 1763-1765. Manchester, 1961.
Stanislas Augustus. Mémoires de Stanislas Auguste Poniatowski Roi de Pologne et sa correspondance avec l'Impératrice Catherine II. Posen, 1862.
——— Pamiętniki Stanisława Augusta Poniatowskiego [Memoirs of Stanislas Augustus Poniatowski]. Warsaw, 1903.
——— Die Memoiren des letzten Königs von Polen Stanislaw August Poniatowski. München, 192?. Vol. I.
——— Mémoires du roi Stanislas-Auguste Poniatowski. 2 vols. St. Petersburg, 1914-24.
Taylor, William, and John Pringle (eds.). Correspondence of William Pitt, Earl of Chatham. London, 1839. Vol. III.
Vioménil, Baron de. The Private Letters of Baron de Vioménil on Polish Affairs. Jersey City, New Jersey, 1935.
Volumina Legum przedruk zbioru praw [Volume of Laws Reprinted from the Collection of Laws]. St. Petersburg, 1860. Vols. VII, VIII.
Wybicki, Józef. Archiwum Wybickiego [The Archive of Wybicki]. Gdańsk, 1948. Vol. I.

SELECTED SECONDARY WORKS

Anderson, M. S. "Great Britain and the Russo-Turkish War of 1768-74," *The English Historical Review,* LXIX (1954), 39-58.
Arneth, Alfred Ritter von. Geschichte Maria Theresia. Vienna, 1877. Vols. VII, VIII.
Askenazy, Szymon. Die letzte polnische Königswahl. Göttingen, 1894.
——— Dantzig and Poland. London, 1921.
Bain, R. Nisbet. The Last King of Poland and His Contemporaries. London, 1909.
Beer, Adolf. Die erste Theilung Polens. 2 vols. Vienna, 1873.
Bilbassoff, B. Geschichte Katharina II. 2 vols. Berlin, 1893.
Bobrzyński, Michał. Dzieje Polski w zarysie [The History of Poland in Outline]. 3d ed. Kraków, 1890. Vol. II.
Boroviczeny, Aladàr von. Graf von Brühl. Der Medici, Richelieu und Rothschild seiner Zeit. Vienna, 1930.
Böttiger, C. W. Geschichte des Kurstaates und Königreiches Sachsen. Hamburg, 1831. Vol. II.
Brandt, Otto. Caspar von Saldern. Erlangen, 1932.

Chechulin, N. D. Vneshniaia politika Rossii v nachale tsarstvovaniia Ekateriny II [Foreign Policy of Russia in the Beginning of the Reign of Catherine II]. St. Petersburg, 1896.
Coxe, William. Travels into Poland, Russia, Sweden, and Denmark. 4th ed. London, 1792. Vol. I.
Dorn, Walter L. "Frederick the Great and Lord Bute," *Journal of Modern History,* I (1929), 529-60.
Duncker, Max. Aus der Zeit Friedrichs des Grossen und Friedrich Wilhelms III. Leipzig, 1876.
Easum, Chester V. Prince Henry of Prussia, Brother of Frederick the Great. Madison, Wis., 1942.
Eversley, George. The Partitions of Poland. London, 1915.
Fabre, Jean. Stanislas-Auguste Poniatowski et l'Europe de Lumières. Paris, 1952.
Ferrand, A. Histoire des trois démembremens de al Pologne. 3 vols. Paris, 1820.
Finkel, L. Bibliografia historyi Polskiej [The Bibliography of Polish History]. Kraków, 1891-1906.
Forst-Battaglia, Otto. Stanisław August Poniatowski und der Ausgang des alten Polenstaates. Berlin, 1927.
Gerhard, Dietrich. England und der Aufstieg Russlands. Munich, 1933.
Gloger, Zygmunt. Encyklopedia staropolska ilustrowana [Illustrated Encyclopedia of Old Poland]. 4 vols. Warsaw, 1958.
Halecki, Oscar. A History of Poland. New York, 1943.
Hanisch, Erdmann. Geschichte Polens. Bonn, 1923.
Herrmann, Ernst. Geschichte des russischen Staats. Hamburg, 1853. Vol. V.
Horn, David Bayne. British Public Opinion and the First Partition of Poland. Edinburgh, 1945.
Hubert, Stanisław. Rozbiory i ordrodzenie Rzeczypospolitej: Zagadnienie prawa międzynarodowego [The Partition and Revival of the Commonwealth: A Problem of International Law]. Lwów, 1937.
Il'enko, A. K. Nachalo kontsa Pol'shi [The Beginning of the End of Poland]. St. Petersburg, 1898.
Iorga, Nicolae. Geschichte des osmanischen Reiches. Gotha, 1908-13. Vol. IV.
Jacobsohn, Ljubow. Russland und Frankreich in der ersten Regierungsjahren der Kaiserin Katharina II 1762-1772. Berlin, 1929.
Jauffret, E. Catherine II et son règne. 2 vols. Paris, 1860.
Kareev, N. Upadek Polski w literaturze historycznej [The Fall of Poland in Historical Literature]. Kraków, 1891.
Konopczyński, Władysław. Polska w dobie wojny siedmioletniej [Poland during the Seven Years War]. 2 vols. Kraków, 1909-11.
——— Politika i ustroj generalności konfederacji barskiej [The Politics and Organization of the Generalcy of the Confederation of Bar]. Kraków, 1928.
——— Liberum Veto—Étude sur le development du principe majoritaire. Paris, 1930.

——— Dzieje Polski nowożytnej [History of Modern Poland]. Warsaw, 1936. Vol. II.

——— Konfederacja barska [The Confederation of Bar]. 2 vols. Warsaw, 1936-38.

——— "Anglia a Polska w XVIII wieku" [England and Poland in the XVIII Century], *Pamiętnik Biblioteki Kórnickiej* [Memoir of the Library of Kórnik]. Vol. 4 (Kórnik, 1947), pp. 93-129.

——— Fryderyk wielki a Polsak [Frederick the Great and Poland]. Poznań, 1947.

——— "Chronologia sejmów Polskich 1493-1793" [The Chronology of the Polish Diets 1493-1793], *Polska Akademia Umiejętnosci, Archiwum Komisji Historycznej* [The Polish Academy of Sciences, Historical Archival Commission], Ser. 2, IV (Kraków, 1948), No. 3.

——— "England and the First Partition of Poland," *Journal of Central European Affairs,* VIII (April 1948), 1-23.

Korzon, Tadeusz. Wewnętrzne dzieje Polski za Stanisława Augusta (1764-1794) [The Domestic History of Poland in the Reign of Stanislas Augustus (1764-1794)]. 2d ed. Kraków, 1897. Vols. I-IV.

Krasicka, Jadwiga. Kraków, ziemia krakowska wobec konfederacji barskiej [Kraków, the Land of Kraków toward the Confederation of Bar]. Kraków, 1929.

Krasiński, Adam. Geschichtliche Darstellung der Bauern-verhältnisse in Polen im ersten Decennium der Regierung Stanislas Augustus (1764-1774). 2 vols. Krakau, 1898.

Kraszewski, J. I. Polska w czasie trzech rozbiorów: 1772-1799 [Poland in the Time of the Three Partitions: 1772-99]. Warsaw, 1902. Vol. I.

Kraushar, Alexandr. Książe Repnin i Polska w pierwszym czteroleciu panowania Stanisława Augusta (1764-1768) [Prince Repnin and Poland in the First Four Years of the Reign of Stanislas Augustus (1764-1768)]. 2 vols. Warsaw, 1900.

Kutrzeba, Stanisław. Sejm walny dawney Rzeczypospolitej Polskiej [The Great Diet in the Old Polish-Lithuanian Commonwealth]. Warsaw, n.d.

Lambert, Francis X. "The Foreign Policy of the Duke de Choiseul, 1763-1770." Ph.D. dissertation, Harvard University, 1952, pp. 556.

Lehtonen, U. L. Der Untergang Polens in seinem wichtigsten Ursachen Dargestellt. Helsinfors, 1904.

——— Die polnischen Provinzen Russlands unter Katharina II in den Jahren 1772-1782. Berlin, 1907.

Lelewel, Joachim. Geschichte Polens unter Stanislas August. Braunschweig, 1831.

Lewitter, L. R. "Peter the Great and the Polish Dissenters," *The Slavonic and East European Review,* XXXIII (December 1954), No. 80, 75-101.

——— "Peter the Great and the Polish Election of 1697," *Cambridge Historical Journal,* XII (1956), No. 2.

——— "Poland under the Saxon Kings," The New Cambridge Modern History. VII (1957), 365-90.

Lord, Robert Howard. The Second Partition of Poland. Cambridge, Mass., 1915.

Łubieńska, M. C. Sprawa dysydencka 1764-1766 [The Dissident Question 1764-1766]. Vol. XIII of Mongrafie w zakresie dziejów nowożytnych [Monographs in the Period of Modern History]. Kraków, 1911.

Mackintosh, Sir J. "Partitions," *The Edinburgh Review,* XXXVII (June-November 1822), 462-527.

Mediger, W. Moskaus Weg nach Europa. Brunswick, 1952.

Meinert, Gustaw. "Wyniesienie na tron Stanisława Augusta" [The Accession of Stanislas Augustus], *Przewodnik Naukowy i Literacki* [Literary and Scientific Guide], XIII (Lwów, 1885), 32-54, 702-11.

Mejbaum, Wacław. O tron Stanisława Augusta [For the Throne of Stanislas Augustus]. Lwów, 1918.

Michael, Wolfgang. Englands Stellung zur ersten Teilung Polens. Hamburg, 1890.

Michalski, Jerzy. "Plan Czartoryskich naprawy Rzeczpospolitej" [The Plan of the Czartoryskis to Reform the Polish-Lithuanian Commonwealth] *Kwartalnik Historyczny* [Historical Quarterly] LXIII (Warsaw, 1956), Nos. 4-5, pp. 29-43.

——— "Propaganda konserwatywna w walce z reformą w początkach panowania Stanisława Augusta" [Conservative Propaganda in the Struggle Against Reform in the Beginning of the Reign of Stanislas Augustus], *Przegląd Historyczny* [Historical Review], XLVI (Warsaw, 1952), 536-62.

——— "Sprawa dysydencka a zagadnienia gospodarcze w opinii publicznej w pierwszych latach panowania Stanisława Augusta" [The Dissident Question and the Economic Problem in Public Opinion in the First Years of the Reign of Stanislas Augustus], *Przegląd Historyczny* [Historical Review], XL (Warsaw, 1950), 156-63.

Morawski, Teodor. Dzieje narodu Polskiego [The History of the Polish Nation]. 2d ed. Poznań, 1877. Vols. IV, V.

Mościcki, Henryk. Rządy Fryderyka II na ziemiach Polskich [The Rule of Frederick II in Polish Lands]. Warsaw, 1920.

Moszczeński, Adam. Pamiętniki do historyi Polskiej w ostatnich latach panowania Augusta III, i pierwszych Stanisława Poniatowskiego [Sources for Polish History in the Last Years of the Reign of Augustus III, and of the First Years of Stanislas Poniatowski]. Warsaw, 1905.

Padover, Saul K. "Prince Kaunitz and the First Partition of Poland." Ph.D. dissertation, Department of History, University of Chicago, 1932, pp. 140.

Pawłowski, Bronisław. Zajęcie Lwowa przez Austrye 1772 [The Occupation of Lwów by Austria 1772]. Vol. XIV of Biblioteka Lwowska [The Library of Lwów]. Lwów, 1911.

Ramsey, John Fraser. "Anglo-French Relations, 1763-1770: A Study of

Choiseul's Foreign Policy," *University of California Publications in History*, XVII (Berkeley, Cal., 1939), No. 3.

Reddaway, W. F. "Macartney in Russia, 1765-1767," *The Cambridge Historical Journal*, III (1931), No. 3, 260-94.

——— "Great Britain and Poland, 1762-72," *The Cambridge Historical Journal*, IV (1934), No. 3, 223-62.

Reddaway, W. F., *et al.* The Cambridge History of Poland. 2 vols. Cambridge, 1941-50.

Reflections of the Affairs of the Dissidents in Poland. London, 1767.

Reiman, E. Neuere Geschichte des preussischen Staates. Gotha, 1882. Vol. I.

Roepell, Richard. Polen unde die Mitte des 18 Jahrhunderts. Gotha, 1876.

——— "Das Interregnum. Wahl und Kronung von Stanislaw August Poniatowski. 5. Oktober 1763 bis 7. Dezember 1764," *Zeitschrift der historischen Gesellschaft für die Provinz Pozen*, VI (Posen, 1891), 255-342.

Rostworowski, Emanuel. "Na drodze do pierwszego rozbioru: Fryderyk II wobec rozkładu przymierza francusko-austriackiego w latach 1769-1772" [On the Road to the First Partition: Frederick II in View of the Decomposition of the Franco-Austrian Alliance in the Years 1769-1772], *Roczniki Historyczne* [Historical Annals], XVIII (Poznań, 1949), 181-204.

——— "La Pologne pendant da seconde moitié du XVIIIe siècle. Bilan de recherches 1945-1956," *Annales* (Economies-Sociétiés-Civilisations), XIII (Paris, 1958), No. 1.

Rudnicki, Kazimierz. Biskup Kajetan Sołtyk, 1715-1788 [Bishop Kajetan Sołtyk, 1715-1788]. Vol. V of Mongrafie w zakresie dziejów nowożytnych [Monographs in the Period of Modern History]. Kraków, 1906.

Rulhière, Claude de. Histoire de l'anarchie de Pologne. Paris, 1819. Vols. I, II.

Rutkowski, Jan. "Les bases économique des partages de l'ancienne Pologne," *Revue d'histoire moderne* (Paris, 1932), 363-89.

——— Historia gospodarcza Polski do 1864 [Economic History of Poland to 1864]. Warsaw, 1953.

Rybarski, Roman. Skarbowość Polski w dobie rozbiorów [Polish Finances during the Partitions]. Kraków, 1937.

Saint-Priest, M. Alexis d. Etudes diplomatiques et littéraires. Paris, n.d. Vol. I.

Schlözer, Kurd von. Friedrich der Grosse und Katharine die Zweite. Berlin, 1859.

Schmidt, Otto Edward. Minister Graf Brühl und Karl Heinrich von Heinecken: Briefe und Akten, Charakteristiken und Darstellungen zur Sachsischen Geschichte (1733-1763). Berlin, 1921.

Schmitt, Henryk. Dzieje panowania Stanisława Augusta Poniatowskiego [History of the Reign of Stanislas Augustus Poniatowski]. 3 vols. Lwów, 1868-69.

Seraphim, Ernst. Geschichte Liv-, Est-und Kurlands. Reval, 1896. Vol. II.

Smoleński, Władysław. Dzieje narodu Polskiego [History of the Polish Nation]. 5th ed. Warsaw, 1919.

——— Przyczyny upadku państwa Polskiego [Causes of the Fall of the Polish State]. Warsaw, 1921.

Solov'ëv, Sergei Mikhailovich. Istoriia Rossii s drevneishikh vremën [History of Russia from the Oldest Times] 2d ed. St. Petersburg, 1851-79. Vols. XXV-XXVIII.

——— Istoriia padeniia Pol'shi [History of the Fall of Poland]. Moscow, 1863.

——— Geschichte des Falles von Polen. Gotha, 1865.

Sorel, Albert. The Eastern Question in the Eighteenth Century. London, 1898.

Śreniowski, Stanisław. "Rzeczypospolita i Galicja w latach 1772-1795 [The Polish-Lithuanian Commonwealth and Galicia in the Years 1772-1795], *Przegląd Historyczny* [Historical Review], XLIII (Warsaw, 1952), 83-104.

Sybel, H. von. "The First Partition of Poland," *The Fortnightly Review,* XVI, New Series (August 1, 1874), 149-70.

Szujski, Józef. Historyi Polskiéj treściwie opowiedianéj ksiąg dwanaście [Concise History of Poland Narrated in Twelve Books]. Warsaw, 1880.

Tomkiewicz, W. "Cerkiew dyzunicka w dawnej Rzeczypospolitej Polskiej 1635-1795" [Greek Orthodox Churches in the Old Polish-Lithuanian Commonwealth 1635-1795], *Przegląd Powszechny* [Universal Review], CCI (Kraków, 1934), 196-220.

Tooke, William. The Life of Catherine II, Empress of Russia. 4th ed. London, 1800. Vols. I, II.

Volz, G. B. "Prinz Heinrich von Preussen und die preussische Politik vor der ersten Teilung Polens," *Forschungen zur brandenburgischen und preussischen Geschichte,* XVIII (Leipzig, 1905), 151-201.

——— "Friedrich der Grosse und die erste Teilung Polens," *Forschungen zur brandenburgischen und preussischen Geschichte,* XXIII (Leipzig, 1910), 71-143, 225-26.

——— "Prinz Heinrich und die Vorgeschichte der ersten Teilung Polens," *Forschungen zur brandenburgischen und preussischen Geschichte,* XXXV (Munich, 1923), 193-211.

——— "Prinz Heinrich als Kritiker Friedrichs des Grossen," *Historische Vierteljahrshrift,* XXVII (Dresden, 1932), 390-400.

White, John Albert. "The Occupation of West Prussia after the First Partition of Poland." Master's thesis, Faculty of Political Science, Columbia University, 1940, pp. 113.

Woliński, Janusz. Polska i kościoł prawosławny [Poland and the Greek Orthodox Church]. Lwów, 1936.

Zinkeisen, Johann Wilhelm. Geschichte des osmanischen Reiches in Europa. Hamburg, 1840-63. Vol. V.

INDEX